P9-EDF-977

Tahiti
& French Polynesia
a travel survival kit

Robert F Kay

Tahiti – a travel survival kit
2nd edition

Published by
Lonely Planet Publications
Head Office: PO Box 88, South Yarra, Victoria 3141, Australia
US Office: PO Box 2001A, Berkeley, CA 94702, USA

Printed by
Colorcraft, Hong Kong

Photographs by
Rob Kay (RK)
Giles Hucault (GH) (facing page 145)
Tahiti Tourist Board (TTB)
Front cover: Tetiaroa (RK)
Back cover: A Marquesan girl (GH)

First published
October 1985

This Edition
September 1988

Although the author and publisher have tried to make the information as accurate
as possible, they accept no responsibility for any loss, injury or inconvenience
sustained by any person using this book.

National Library of Australia Cataloguing in Publication Data

Kay, Robert F., 1953-
Tahiti & French Polynesia, a travel survival kit.

2nd ed.
Includes index.
ISBN 0 86442 049 8.

1. Polynesia – Description and travel – Guide-books.
2. Tahiti – Description and travel – Guide-books.
I. Title.

919.6'204

© Rob Kay 1988

Rob Kay

Rob Kay is a 35-year-old Californian whose travel experiences are culled from having lived and worked in the destinations he writes about. He feels that only by rubbing shoulders with the local population can a travel writer even begin to transmit the true 'spirit of place'. Rob has worked as a freelance journalist in Tahiti and Fiji, a bartender and publicist in San Francisco, and a radio newsman in California's San Joaquin Valley. Rob contributes regularly to newspapers and magazines in the United States and resides in San Francisco. He is fond of balmy climates, trout fishing, and cold, dark beer.

From the Author

My first interest in French Polynesia resulted from a six month stay in 1977. During that period I had the opportunity to travel throughout the beautiful islands of French Polynesia and meet a variety of people. In a few instances, some of these acquaintances became friends for life. I have returned to the islands on subsequent occasions and most recently to update this book.

For their aid and assistance I would particularly like to thank Bengt and Marie-Therese Danielsson who were unfailingly kind to someone they knew only as a vagabond; and I will always be in awe of and grateful for their pioneering work in Tahiti. Thanks to Marie Ateni and Tiare Sanford of the Tahiti Tourist Board, and Al Prince of Tahiti Sun Press, for assistance in preparing this second edition. Thanks to Mr Gilles Hucault for his photographs of the Marquesas and the Tuamotus.

To be quite accurate the title of this book need only be *French Polynesia – a travel survival kit*. But who knows where that is? It's Tahiti which is the name with the magic, so that's the name that goes on the cover. Tahiti is just one of the many islands – with

evocative names like Bora Bora, Huahine, Rangiroa or Fatu Hiva – which are representative of the five main island groups of French Polynesia.

Lonely Planet Credits

Editor	Susan Mitra
Maps & design	Graham Imeson
Cover design & illustrations	Vicki Beale

Thanks also to the LP editors who helped with proof-reading - Jon Murray, Peter Turner, Debbie Lustig and Katie Codie; and to LP designer Vicki Beale for map corrections.

From the Publisher

This edition is the first Lonely Planet book to have been laid out and designed using desktop publishing technology. All our books are written, updated and edited using word processors but this time the floppy disks containing the edited files were given to a designer instead of going to our typesetter. Jim Hart and Graham Imeson spent

---

Dedication To Philippe Guesdon, a loyal friend.

many hours working out programs and methods to convert the existing typesetting commands to those accepted by Ventura. Using the Ventura Publisher program, Graham laid out the text for each chapter on the screen and then printed it with a laser printer; maps and illustrations were added and the completed pages then went to the printer.

At Lonely Planet we are always trying to find new ways to get the information into print as fast as possible. In 1983 we installed a computerised phototypesetter which interfaced with our word processors. A few years later we had a lot more books going though so it was time to upgrade to faster editing and typesetting equipment.

Electronic layout is the latest step. It is much faster and more versatile than the traditional cut-and-paste methods, and we expect to be doing more books this way.

Acknowledgments

Thanks must go to the travellers who used the first edition of this book and wrote to Lonely Planet with information, comments and suggestions.

Kaye Bailey (Aus), Delores Burke (USA), Francis A Byrne (USA), Sally Champe (USA), P Coman (Aus), Doug de Selles (USA), Nancy Fowler (USA), Palle Frese (Dk), Sally Goodsell (UK), James Green (USA), Gregg (Tah), Ralph Haack (D), David Harcombe (Aus), Mary Lou Ingram (USA), Keith John (USA), Bill Johnstone (USA), Naomi Kashiwabara (USA), Wolfgang Kasper (A), Steve & Joann Lynch (USA), Marian Martinez (Aus), A Mason (UK), Shirin Moayyad (Aus), Youssef Pauline (Tah), Pat Pautu (Tah), Wombat Tahanga (Aus), Denis & Fariua Tehiva, and Philip Wofstenholme (USA).

A – Austria, Aus – Australia, D – West Germany, Dk – Denmark, Tah – Tahiti, UK – UK, USA – USA

A Warning & A Request

Things change – prices go up, schedules change, good places go bad and bad places go bankrupt – nothing stays the same. So if you find things better or worse, recently opened or long since closed, please write and tell us and help make the next edition better! All information is greatly appreciated and the best letters will receive a free copy of the next edition, or any other Lonely Planet book of your choice.

Extracts from the best letters are also included in the *Lonely Planet Update*. The *Update* helps us make useful information available to you as soon as possible – it's like reading an up-to-date noticeboard or postcards from a friend. Each edition contains hundreds of useful tips, and advice from the best possible source of information – other travellers. The *Lonely Planet Update* is published quarterly in paperback and is available from bookshops and by subscription. Turn to the back pages of this book for more details.

Contents

Introduction

To this day, Tahiti, the best known of French Polynesia's 130 islands, is synonymous with the modern world's romantic vision of the South Seas. This vision is a blend of fact and fiction born from glowing reports of its earliest visitors. On his arrival in 1768, the French explorer Bougainville thought he had been transported into the Garden of Eden. He promptly named the island New Cytheria, after the birthplace of Aphrodite, the Greek goddess of love. The inhabitants' kindness was summed up in the first report of the London Missionary Society:

Their manners are affable and engaging; their step easy and firm, and graceful; their behaviour free and unguarded; always boundless in generosity towards each other, and to strangers; their tempers mild, gentle and unaffected; slow to take offence, easily pacified, and seldom retaining resentment or revenge, whatever the provocation they may have received.

Captain Wallis, the first European to set foot on Tahiti (in 1767) noted that 'the women in general are very handsome, some really great beauties ....' They were also very accessible, and tales of a newfound Garden of Eden filtered back to Europe.

The myth of Tahiti as an unspoiled paradise was further fuelled by the 18th-century philosophy of Jean-Jacques Rousseau. The reports of a nonviolent Tahitian society bound by free love coincided neatly with Rousseau's social theory that natural man was an innately good animal whose problems originated with the introduction of private property, agriculture and industry. Rousseau's adherents were elated to hear that the noble savage was alive and well in Tahiti, which proved what they had been saying all along.

Unfortunately, the tales of paradise that followed Tahiti's discovery did not match the subsequent realities of influenza, tuberculosis, venereal disease and other maladies which decimated the vulnerable population, and the accompanying breakdown of the fabric of native society that marked the initial

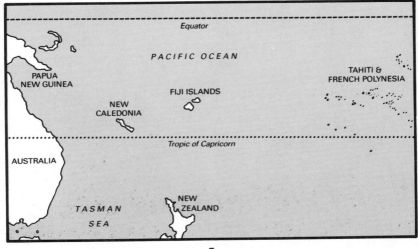

stages of the island's colonisation. This was evident to the famous painter Paul Gauguin, who arrived in Tahiti in 1891 and was sorely disappointed by what he saw. Little was left of Tahitian culture; Tahiti had been replaced by a narrow-minded provincial French colony. Despite these changes, Gauguin immortalised the languid grace and unquenchable spirit of the Tahitian people, qualities they still possess today.

Both the advent of jet travel accompanied by tourism and the bureaucracy created by nuclear testing have accelerated change in the islands. New buildings have gone up, new jobs have been created and the cost of living has soared. Like all South Pacific island nations, French Polynesia will continue to experience the impact of 20th-century values and technology on traditional ways of life. Among the islands, Tahiti is influenced most by the west because it is a centre of tourism and trade. Meanwhile, the outer islands evolve more slowly. In Papeete, French Polynesia's capital city, residents suffer from traffic congestion and young men and women dance to the disco beat, while dwellers on some of the outer islands still kindle lanterns at night to keep ghosts away. Although tourism has changed the face of Tahiti, many of the outer islands remain relatively untouched by large-scale commercialism and the inhabitants continue to enjoy the novelty of entertaining visitors.

Facts about the Country

HISTORY

The most widely accepted theory of the origin of the Polynesian race is that it is a blend of peoples originating in various parts of Asia. Indications are that this amalgamation took place in the area extending from the Malay Peninsula through the islands of Indonesia. After an indeterminable period of time in this region the people made their way across the Pacific, possibly between 3000 and 1000 BC.

Perhaps the most famous alternative theory, expounded by Thor Heyerdahl, is that Polynesians may also have migrated from South America. His theory was given at least some credence by the successful crossing of the *Kon Tiki* expedition (from Peru to French Polynesia) in 1947.

Archaeologists tell us that the ancient history of Tahiti and its neighbouring islands goes back about 2000 years when the Marquesas Islands were first settled by migrations of Polynesians from the Samoa and Tonga region. From this point of dispersal Hawaii, New Zealand, Easter Island and the Society Islands (of which Tahiti is part) were settled by ancient Polynesian mariners in huge double-hulled canoes.

The Polynesians were among the finest sailors in the world. They used the sun, stars, currents, wave motion and flight patterns of birds to navigate the vast reaches of the Pacific. When for some reason – whether tribal warfare or over population – Polynesians had to settle elsewhere, they put their families, worldly goods, plant cuttings, animals and several months' supplies of food into their canoes and set sail to find new homes.

Through radiocarbon dating techniques and comparative studies of artefacts, scientists pinpoint the settlement of Tahiti and its neighbouring islands at around 850 AD. The most intensive research in this area is currently being undertaken by Dr Y H Sinoto of the Bishop Museum in Honolulu. In 1973 Sinoto began excavation of the Vaito'otia/Fa'ahia site (on the grounds of the Bali Hai Hotel) on Huahine and found it to be the oldest settlement yet discovered in the Society Islands. Implements excavated closely match those found in the Marquesas Islands, strengthening the theory that the islands were settled by Polynesians migrating from the Marquesas.

The most visible (but certainly not the earliest) traces of precontact Tahitian culture are the stone remains of open-air temples called *marae*. Marae are found on all the Society Islands but nowhere are they more abundant than on Huahine. The most important marae (a national monument) is Taputapuatea on Raiatea, which was the most prominent political and religious centre in the Society Islands.

First European Contact

In 1767 the English navigator Captain Samuel Wallis, commander of the HMS *Dolphin*, became the first European to set foot on Tahiti and claimed it in the name of King George III. It was pure chance that no Europeans had arrived in Tahiti earlier than Wallis. Close to 250 years had passed since Magellan sailed to the East Indies and about 20 explorers had sailed the Pacific since then. But islands were few and far between on this vast ocean and navigational aids were often inaccurate, leaving explorers with no idea where they were. Thus even if they discovered a new island, it might be difficult to ever find it again.

The initial contact between the crew of the HMS *Dolphin* and the Tahitians was of a mixed nature. The crew bartered beads, looking glasses and knives for food and eventually for sex. Nails quickly became the most sought-after item by the Tahitians, who used them to make fish-hooks. To the horror of those responsible for the seaworthiness of

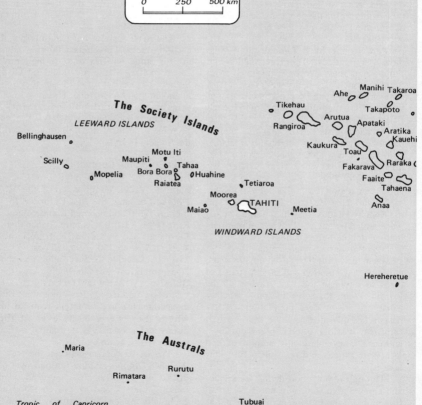

French
Polynesia

0   250   500 km

Ahe   Manihi Takaroa
Tikehau   Takapoto
The Society Islands   Arutua   Apataki
LEEWARD ISLANDS   Rangiroa   Aratika
                                            Kauehi
Bellinghausen   Kaukura   Toau
                                        Fakarava   Raraka
Scilly   Maupiti Motu Iti   Faaite
        Mopelia Bora Bora Tahaa   Tahaena
                Raiatea Huahine
                    Tetiaroa   Anaa
                Moorea
        Maiao   TAHITI   Meetia

                WINDWARD ISLANDS

                                    Hereheretue

        The Australs

    Maria
            Rurutu
        Rimatara
Tropic   of   Capricorn   Tubuai
                                Raivavae

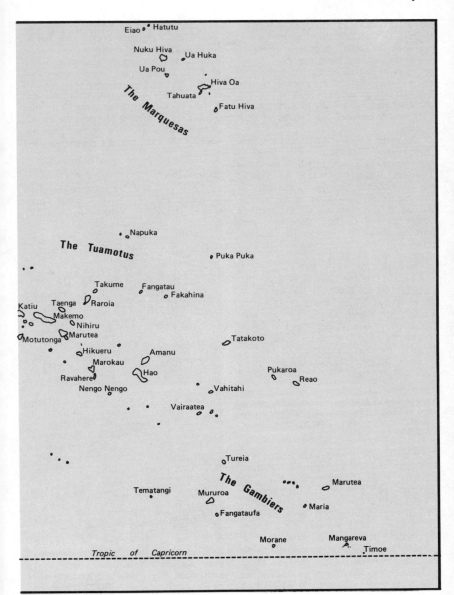

the vessel, nails rapidly disappeared from the *Dolphin* and became the chief medium of exchange for sexual encounters. However, not all the meetings were amicable. On one occasion the English were pelted with stones and in savage reprisal the *Dolphin* opened fire with cannon and muskets. The Tahitians set about making amends by giving lavish gifts, which included the favours of their women.

Although Captain Wallis and his crew 'discovered' Tahiti, the first English explorers really learned very little about the Tahitians. Wallis, who was ill for most of the time, never had the opportunity to investigate the new land as he should. Although the crew found the natives hospitable and carefree, they discovered nothing about the island's government, religion or laws. These remained for later explorers to understand.

In April 1768, while Wallis was on his way back to England, Louis de Bougainville, commanding the *Boudeuse* and the *Etoile*, found his way to Tahiti and (not realising the English had beaten him to the task) took possession of it for France. The Frenchman was met by a flotilla of canoes bearing green boughs, bananas, coconuts and fowl as presents. Bougainville in return gave them nails and earrings. Bougainville described the scene:

They pressed us to choose a woman and come on shore with her; and their gestures, which were not ambiguous, denoted in what manner we should form an acquaintance with her.

Once ashore the French were treated with kindness and quickly learned the most obvious qualities about their guests – the Tahitians were friendly, generous, sexually uninhibited and they stole. To their credit the French were philosophical about the latter characteristic, realising that the islanders simply did not have the same sense of private property Europeans did. In contrast to the experience with the English, the French visit produced only one report of violence which was fairly easily mitigated. Bougainville's

stay was cut short by anchorage problems among the dangerous coral heads but in retrospect the French visit was more fruitful than the English one. Bougainville, unlike his English counterpart, was a distinguished scholar and perhaps a better observer, and because of his good health during the visit had the opportunity to mix more freely with the Tahitians. In just a few days the French captain had acquired a skeletal working knowledge of the island's government and customs.

Captain Cook

In 1769 perhaps the greatest English navigator who ever lived, Captain James Cook, arrived in Tahiti on the HMS *Endeavour*. However, the purpose of his visit had relatively little to do with Tahiti or its residents. Cook came to study the transit of Venus with the sun, which would enable scientists to precisely measure the distance between the sun and the earth. The determination of this would be an invaluable navigational aid. For the voyage, an impressive group of scientists, scholars and artists was assembled to study Tahiti as well as the transit. However, their 18th-century instruments weren't accurate enough to gather needed data, and from the aspect of observing the transit the voyage was a failure.

Cook's three-month Tahitian sojourn did provide a wealth of information about the island and its people. His experience was generally a good one but there were problems. Cook was a tolerant man but simply could not deal with one aspect of the Tahitian character – thievery. Tahitians found it amusing to confound their visitors by devising ways of relieving them of their property. For the natives it was a game to outwit the English and usually they gave back what was taken. For Cook the matter was deadly serious. At one point he impounded Tahitian canoes in order to get equipment back. In another instance, he unfairly imprisoned five chiefs and held them for ransom until two of his sailors, who had deserted with their Tahitian 'wives', were returned to his custody.

Cook cared desperately about his and his crew's behaviour towards the Tahitians and was bothered by a shooting incident that left a Tahitian dead. He was also concerned about the spread of venereal disease (which the English later blamed on the French), and about the internment of the chiefs. Two days before the *Endeavour* lifted anchor he wrote, 'We are likely to leave these people in disgust at our behaviour'. Perhaps Cook was too sensitive. One of the Tahitians' greatest qualities is their forgiving nature and when Cook left the Tahitians genuinely wept. He was to return to Tahiti two more times before his death in Hawaii.

Bligh & the Bounty

The year 1788 marked the arrival of the HMS *Bounty*, a name that will forever be associated with legendary Tahiti. It also marked the end of the era of exploration and the beginning of exploitation.

The *Bounty's* mission was to retrieve breadfruit plants needed as a cheap source of food for the numerous slaves working in West Indies plantations. The voyage was led by Captain Bligh, a former sailing master who accompanied Cook on a previous visit to Tahiti. Bligh, who may have been unfairly maligned in the annals of history because of his reputation as a ruthless taskmaster, stayed six months in Tahiti supervising his crew's transplanting of the valuable plants onto a makeshift greenhouse aboard the ship. The crew made the most of their time, befriending the very fun-loving Tahitians and living like sultans, so that some of the crew did not really wish to depart. Three weeks after leaving Tahiti a mutinous band of men led by Fletcher Christian coldly turned Bligh and 18 other crew members adrift in a 23-foot cutter with a minimal amount of provisions.

Bligh and his followers faced what seemed like certain death through uncharted waters, tempestuous weather and islands teeming with savage cannibals, but they miraculously travelled 5822 km (3618 miles) and 41 days in an open craft to the Dutch-held island of Timor in Indonesia. Meanwhile, the *Bounty* returned to Tahiti searching for a safe haven. Fearing retribution, Christian left 16 doubtful mutineers on Tahiti. The remaining crew took Tahitian wives and servants on board and made several attempts to start communities on various islands, only to be chased out by angry natives. The *Bounty's* final destination was lonely Pitcairn Island, where Fletcher Christian and his men soon quarrelled. Only one survived the butchering that ensued during the following months. Christian's beloved Tahitian wife died shortly after the *Bounty* arrived on Pitcairn, and the grief-stricken Christian was shot by a Tahitian after taking up with the man's wife. The mutinous crew's descendants still live on Pitcairn Island today.

Bligh returned to Tahiti for his breadfruit – this time with a contingent of 19 marines aboard. He was not one to take chances on another uprising. The survivors of the crew that Christian had stranded on Tahiti were rounded up by another British ship, put in shackles and taken back to England to stand trial.

Still a matter of debate is the cause of the celebrated mutiny. Historians write that the real cause of the uprising may have been the sailors' longing to return to their Tahitian girlfriends rather than Captain Bligh's cruelty. Still, subsequent novels and films (the exception being the 1983 production *Return of the Bounty* by De Laurentiis) have portrayed Bligh as a monster, when in fact the real villain may have been the unstable and perhaps emotionally disturbed Fletcher Christian. In his book *Pitcairn: Children of Mutiny*, Australian journalist Ian M Ball tells us that if anything, Bligh, a former officer under the legendary Captain Cook, was a tolerant man who treated his men better than did the average English captain of his day. After the *Bounty* affair Bligh was promoted to admiral and eventually became governor of New South Wales in Australia.

The Missionaries

As always, in the wake of explorers came the men of the cloth. In 1797, 30 members of the London Missionary Society came to Tahiti. While previous visitors had been appalled by customs such as human sacrifice, the Society seemed more distraught at the overt sexual proclivities of Tahitians. They attempted to dissuade the population from this 'immoral' behaviour by first converting the king to Christianity. Anthropologist Bengt Danielsson writes that they also persuaded the natives to drink tea, eat with a knife and fork, wear bonnets and coats, sleep in beds, sit on chairs and live in stone houses, in short, to emulate the English lower-middle-class manner of Society members. Within a few years, the missionaries succeeded in converting the entire population and managed to rid them of customs such as infanticide and human sacrifice. However, they never quite convinced the natives to give up their 'hedonistic' ways. As example of this, even after his conversion to Christianity Tahitian King Pomare II continued his relationship with two sisters (only one of whom he was married to) and died from the effects of alcoholism.

The French

In 1836 a French naval vessel under Admiral du Petit-Thours arrived in Papeete and demanded indemnity for a previous expulsion of Catholic missionaries from Tahiti. Queen Pomare, the current ruler, paid the money under threat of naval bombardment and later was forced to sign an agreement that would allow French missionaries to spread Catholicism. Admiral du Petit-Thours returned to Polynesia in 1842 and annexed the Marquesas Islands with the idea of turning them into a penal colony. In the process of procuring land, he decided to annexe Tahiti as well. This move outraged the London Missionary Society and almost whipped up enough anti-French sentiment in England to send the two nations to war. The French returned to Tahiti with three ships in 1843 to take formal possession of the island.

This marked the beginning of European colonisation in the South Pacific.

After the Tahitians realised the French were there to stay, they took up arms (bush knives and a few muzzle-loaders) and waged a guerrilla war on French garrisons, settlements and missionary stations that lasted three years. In the end, the Tahitians were crushed and Queen Pomare came out of hiding to become a rubber stamp monarch. Likewise, the Missionary Society, seeing the futility of resisting French influence, ceded their holdings to a French Protestant group and headed for greener pastures.

The Islands in the 20th Century

French Polynesia remained a backwater colony until the 1960s, when three events triggered drastic changes in the islands. These were the building of an international airport in Tahiti, the beginning of nuclear weapons testing in the nearby Tuamotu Islands and the making of the MGM film *Mutiny on the Bounty* starring Marlon Brando and Trevor Howard. As tourists – lured no doubt by Hollywood's version of the islands – and military personnel flooded Tahiti in increasing numbers, the character of the once sleepy island changed dramatically. Money was pumped into the economy, new businesses sprang up to accommodate the influx of arrivals, and thousands of Polynesians left their far-flung island homes to look for work in Papeete. Suddenly, Tahiti was very much in the 20th century. The topics of the day were dissent over nuclear testing, brawls between soldiers and Tahitians, inflation and a shift from a subsistence economy to one completely based on money.

The increased French presence was not without its positive effects, such as new roads, schools, hospitals, agriculture and aquaculture projects, many new airstrips and eventually the highest standard of living in the South Pacific. Accompanying economic growth was a greater political awareness and a demand by Polynesians for more voice in the government, which was controlled more or less by France. In 1977 French Polynesia was finally granted a much greater degree of autonomy under the auspices of a new constitution. The new arrangement provided Polynesians with a larger voice in internal affairs, which included managing their own budget.

In 1984, a statute passed by the French Parliament in Paris created yet another incarnation of the French Polynesian constitution, giving Tahiti even greater self-government. For the first time the legislative body was allowed to elect the Territorial Government's own president. Previously the highest position a Tahitian could hold was vice president of the Territorial Government Council. Thus, instead of sharing power with the Paris-appointed High Commissioner, which as vice president he had to do, the president is able to run his Council of Ministers alone.

The 1984 statute has not created complete autonomy for Tahiti's local government but it has increased its self-governing role tremendously. In areas that remain apart from local government control, such as defence or foreign affairs, Tahitian government has been granted the right to participate in far more negotiations regarding matters that may have a bearing on French Polynesia's future.

GEOGRAPHY

French Polynesia lies in the South Pacific halfway between Australia and California, and approximately halfway between Tokyo and Santiago. Although French Polynesia is spread over an expanse of water the size of Western Europe, the total land mass of its 130 islands adds up to only 4000 square km. The islands are divided into five archipelagos, all culturally, ethnically and climatically distinct. They include the Marquesas, the Tuamotus, the Society Islands, the Australs and the Gambiers.

Geologically, the islands are divided into two categories: atolls (or low islands) and high islands. An atoll is what Daniel Defoe had in mind when he wrote *Robinson Crusoe* – a flat island with little more than scrub growth and coconut palms. An atoll is actually a ring of coral that once surrounded a volcano. The volcano sank so all that is left is the coral, which now surrounds a lagoon. The colours of an atoll are so brilliant they assault the retina. The ocean laps at a blindingly white coral shore. The sun shines with dazzling intensity on a lagoon made up of many primitive blues and greens – lapis lazuli, cobalt and turquoise.

High islands can either be volcanic in origin or the result of an upheaval from the ocean floor, as is the phosphate island of Makatea. Their terrain can be smooth, rocky and barren or incredibly precipitous and covered with a lush rainforest. Unlike atolls, where drinking water must be collected in cisterns and limited types of crops can be grown, high islands often have an abundance of water and have the soil to support a variety of fruits and vegetables.

CLIMATE

French Polynesia has a climate ranging from subtropical in the southern archipelagos near the Tropic of Capricorn (Gambier and Austral) to steamy and equatorial in the Marquesas to the north. The Society and Tuamotu groups have a mild tropical climate that ranges between the two extremes. There are basically two seasons: the warm and humid period between November and April when rains can fall intermittently, and the dry season between May and October. The average annual temperature in the Society Islands is 25°C with variations from 21°C to 34°C. As a result of vegetation and wind factors, high islands are generally more humid than atolls, where you can enjoy the cooling influence of the trade winds.

FORCES OF NATURE

Although many of French Polynesia's high islands are volcanic in origin, strong earthquakes are rare. Cyclones are also infrequent, but when they strike the results can be devastating. Until 1983 the Society Islands had been spared this type of natural disaster for 76 years. As a result of the warming caused by the now infamous 'El Nino', Tahiti and neighbouring islands were battered by five consecutive cyclones in 1983 which cost one life and destroyed millions of dollars' worth of property.

If you're interested in reading about the destruction wrought by cyclones and hurricanes, find a copy of *Islands of Desire* by Robert Dean Frisbie. The author describes in nearly unbelievable terms how, during a storm that inundated his tiny island home, he saved his family by tying them to trees.

FLORA & FAUNA

When the original settlers of French Polynesia, the Polynesians, arrived in the 7th or 8th century the variety of vegetation was limited to the seeds and spores borne by wind, sea and bird life that happened to find their way to the islands. To provide food and materials for shelter the Polynesians brought taro, yams, coconuts, bananas and breadfruit. To the bafflement of scientists they also cultivated the American sweet potato – a plant that does not exist in Asia. Later the missionaries introduced corn, cotton, sugar cane, citrus fruits, tamarinds, pineapples, guavas, figs, coffee and other vegetables. Tahiti also owes quite a bit to Edouard Raoul, a pharmacist-botanist who in 1887 brought a cargo of 1500 varieties of plants to the islands. He experimented with the cultivation of hundreds of types of fruit trees. Other tree species included kauri (from New Zealand), red cedar, eucalyptus, rubber, gum and jack. A decade after his arrival Raoul's gardens were donating about 150 species of plants to farmers to improve their stock.

In 1919 Harrison Smith, an American university professor turned botanist, purchased 340 acres in Papaeri and settled down to cultivate hundreds of plant varieties he imported from tropical regions throughout the world. Like Raoul, he too helped local farmers by giving them seeds and cuttings to better their crops. For more information on Smith see the information on the Botanical Gardens in the Around the Island section in the Tahiti chapter.

Tahitians take pride in their gardens, which are richly ornamented with flowers and shrubs, including frangipani and a variety of camellias. Fruits are usually abundant on every home site; during the harvest season they provide an important staple. They include a species of huge avocado, mangoes, papayas, custard apples, bananas, pomplemousse, oranges and pineapples.

Like the flora, most of the fauna found in Tahiti was introduced by humans. Pigs, dogs, chickens, lizards and even rats were brought by the Polynesians. Later, Captain Cook imported cattle and cats. The only 'wild' animals are pigs, the descendants of those that escaped domestication and now live in the bush.

GOVERNMENT

French Polynesia is governed by a 34-member Territorial Assembly which is elected by popular vote every five years. The members select 10 among them to form a Council of Ministers (Conseil de Ministres), the most powerful ruling body. The assembly also elects the president.

French Polynesia's official status is 'Overseas Territory of France', which roughly means it is a semiautonomous colony, much like the United States' territories of Puerto Rico and Guam. However, unlike people in the US territories, French Polynesians are permitted to vote in national elections and elect representatives (two deputies and a senator) to the metropolitan French National Assembly and Senate in Paris.

The metropolitan French government runs French Polynesia's foreign affairs, defence, police, justice system and secondary education. In addition to local rule a French high commissioner is charged with administrative duties, especially in regards to the observance of French law.

The first French Polynesian President, Gaston Flosse, was elected in 1984. In 1986 Flosse became Secretaire d'etat charge du Pacifique Sur (Under Minister for South

Pacific Problems) a subministerial position with the metropolitan French government while still holding on to his presidency of French Polynesia. He was forced to resign the presidency in 1987 at the request of Jacky Teuira, a political adversary.

Jacky Teuira, of Flosse's consevative (Gaullist) Tahoeraa Huiraatira Party, was subsequently elected president by the Territorial Assembly.

Teuira's Presidency was to be short lived. On 7 December 1987 (nine months after Teuira's election as president) he resigned when it became obvious that his former Minister of Economics, Alexander Leontieff, had formed a majority coalition which ultimately would have unseated him. On 9 December 1987 Leontieff was installed by the new majority coalition as Tahiti's third territorial president.

The catalyst for Tahiti's political upheaval came on 'Black Friday', 23 October, or as one local newspaper perhaps over-dramatically called it – 'The Night of Living Hell in Paradise'. On this evening French security forces were sent to Papeete's docks in order to break up a picket line set up by local longshoremen. The result was pandemonium. American journalist Al Prince described it this way:

... strikers, curious onlookers, juvenile delinquents and just plain ordinary citizens suddenly turned into a human wave of destruction that descended on downtown Papeete as night fell. It took French security forces and local firemen three hours to bring everything under control after the worst violence and social unrest the city of more than 23,000 had ever witnessed.

More than 100 stores and businesses were damaged or destroyed by the rioting, looting, burning and general mayhem. Damage was estimated at around US$70 million. The riot made people acutely aware of the social and economic problems that had too long been buried under the rug. In November 1987 the then minister Leontieff released a sensational report on the state of the economy in French Polynesia. It spelled out in no uncertain terms that Tahiti faced dire economic

problems and needed a forceful recovery programme. President Teuira proposed an austere provisional budget for 1988 which was criticised both by party stalwarts and opposition leaders. Meanwhile, on 1 December, Leontieff and two other ministers resigned from the Teuira government. By the end of the month Leontieff was the new president.

ECONOMY

Although French Polynesians cling to traditional values, the face of Tahiti has changed drastically in the past 25 years. The influx of money from both tourism and the large military presence has transformed the region's economy from an agriculturally based subsistence level to a modern consumer society. Money, not essential to an islander years ago, is now necessary for buying outboard motors, stereos, colour televisions, video decks, cars, motorcycles, gasoline and – when one can afford them – the latest fashions. The younger generation has become enamoured with the things money can buy and their ability to consume is tempered only by the high price of imported goods.

The main source of hard currency for French Polynesia is the tourism industry and moneys generated by bureaucracies of the metropolitan French government. The bulk of French Polynesians make their living working at jobs associated with tourism, retail business or government.

Agriculture, the second main source of revenue, plays an important role in supporting the rural population. The leading product is copra (dried coconut), produced by drying coconut meat in the sun, after which it is processed into oil for copra cakes (cattle feed), soap, cosmetics, margarine and other items. Processed coconut oil known as *monoi* is scented with flower blossoms and used locally for skin care. It makes a fine, inexpensive souvenir. Copra is a vital source of income to families on the outer islands who have difficulty eking out a living on remote islands because of poor resources and/or accessibility of distant markets. The government buys the dried coconut at higher prices to subsidise French Polynesians caught in this situation. Other aquacultural and agricultural products include cultured black pearls, pearl shell, vanilla, coffee, fruit, fish, shrimp and oysters.

Lured by the promise of a better life, French Polynesians from the outer islands have moved to Tahiti in ever greater numbers. Life in Papeete, however, is often not easy for those who have left their distant homes. In the capital the cost of living is high, and assimilation for the new inhabitants is fraught with basic problems such as finding housing and employment. In Papeete it is simply not possible to fish for an evening meal or gather fruits and vegetables from the land. Thus for those who have migrated, traditional life has been exchanged for an urban existence and all its woes. To counter this trend, the Tahitian government promotes economic development of the outer islands. Through aquaculture, tourism and commercial pearl ventures, the authorities hope to encourage the rural population to stay put.

Black Pearl Industry

Prior to the commercial exploitation of pearl shell in French Polynesia early in the 19th century, locals had utilised it for religious and decorative ornamentation as well as for implements such as fish-hooks and lures. Harvesting oysters for pearls gained importance in the Tuamotu Islands during the 1850s but it wasn't until the early 1960s that scientists began cultivation experiments with the indigenous black pearl oyster *Pinctada margaritifera*. Today the pearls are cultivated in the Gambier and Tuamotu islands.

Over the last several years pearl cultivation has become an increasingly important source of income for French Polynesia, particularly as consumers become more aware of the black pearl in the international marketplace. The Tahiti Perles Center & Museum, on Boulevard Pomare next to the Pizzeria, was opened in May 1984 by a Tahitian entrepreneur with precisely this 'PR' factor in mind – to educate the public about the black pearl. Although the 'museum' is privately owned and is more a shop-cum-exhibition, it does a remarkably thorough job – through placards, display cases and videotapes – of illustrating the history of the pearl in civilisation with particular emphasis on the black pearl.

The process of 'making pearls' is briefly as follows: three to five-year-old oysters are collected by divers and selected for pearl cultivation. A nucleus, or tiny mother-of-pearl sphere fashioned from the shell of a Mississippi River mussel, is then attached to a graft of tissue from the oyster and placed inside the animal's gonad (sex organ). If all goes well the tiny graft grows around the nucleus, an irritant which causes the slow formation of layer upon layer of black pearl. After a donor nucleus has been added to each oyster, they are placed inside protective cages to keep them from predators. Under ideal growing conditions they are left to recuperate from the operation for 18 months to three years before they are ready for harvesting. Meanwhile the shells are repeatedly inspected and hauled to the surface for cleaning. Water conditions are scrupulously checked for salinity, temperature and possible pollutants.

Only 20% of the oysters implanted with the nucleus will ever bear saleable pearls, and only 5% of the crop harvested will bear 'perfect' pearls – specimens that adhere to the exacting industry standards. Value is determined by size, lustre, sheen, colour and lack of defects such as bumps, dents or scratches. The price for a perfect pearl is about 100,000 CFP (US$1000) but prices may range from 5000 CFP to 250,000 CFP (US$50 to US$2500) for an individual pearl. The museum is open from 8 am to noon and 2 to 5 pm from Monday to Friday, and Saturday 8 am to noon.

POPULATION

The population of French Polynesia is an amalgam composed roughly of 75%

Polynesians, 10% Chinese and 15% Europeans. Among these racial categories exists every conceivable mixture. It would not be unusual for a Tahitian named Pierre Jamison to have ancestors of Chinese, American, Polynesian and French ancestry. Racial intermarriage, which is not frowned upon, accounts for the genetic strength and physical beauty of the inhabitants.

The current population of French Polynesia numbers around 170,000, half of whom are under 20 years of age. Approximately 75% of the population lives on the island of Tahiti.

Tahitian Society

The social structure of French Polynesia is a complicated study in politics, economics and intermarriage. Economically, the Chinese are the most powerful group while the 'demis' (half-castes) control the political sphere. The demis, those of Polynesian and Caucasian blood, make up a class of Europeanised Tahitians. The demi population maintains an interesting mixture of Tahitian and European values. While some have adopted French culture and eschew speaking Tahitian, others identify with both cultures and find no shame in their Tahitian heritage. The majority of the population, those whose ancestry is mostly Polynesian, are known as *kaina* (rhymes with myna), and are at the lowest rung of the socio-economic ladder.

The Chinese first came to Tahiti as plantation workers during the time of the American Civil War. They were the labour force in a scheme hatched by two Scottish businessmen to produce cotton, then unavailable in the northern United States. When the Civil War ended, the venture went bankrupt and the Chinese indentured workers remained. Through the years, Chinese have continued to migrate to Tahiti while keeping their culture. Many have married Polynesians or Europeans. Due to their wealth, they are sometimes the objects of resentment and jealousy from Polynesians but without the Chinese to run the shops and

businesses, the French Polynesian economy would be in serious trouble.

Sex & the Tahitian Myth

A visitor who is romantically inclined should be handsome and have money, preferably lots of money.
    John W McDermott, travel writer

When discussing Tahiti, it is only a matter of time before the subject of sex arises. Since the time of Wallis and Cook, the myth of Tahiti as the 'Isle of Love' has flourished and is still used as a major selling point by the travel industry. As a result of books like *The Marriage of Loti* and movies such as *Mutiny on the Bounty*, countless men have travelled to Tahiti's shores in search of its beguilements.

From early accounts we learn that Tahitian women genuinely relished lovemaking. According to the accounts, sailors arrived in the islands to be greeted by boatloads of willing maidens. For Tahitians the arrival of a ship was like a circus visiting a small town. Days and nights were filled with wild abandon, rum drinking and the comic sight of pale white men in strange costume. Amorous flings had the benefit of material rewards as well, usually a trinket of some sort. In Cook's day nails were often given as gifts. This sometimes reached a hazardous stage as eager sailors began to wrench nails from the very ships themselves.

Today things are quite a bit different. Tahitians have by no means lost their gay abandon, but the male visitor is very mistaken if he thinks Tahitian women share his amorous notions. The overseas tourist is advised not to adopt the attitude that he is God's gift to Tahitian women. More often than not, he will feel that he is on the outside, looking into a totally different world.

And what a different world it is. It may appear that Tahitians are promiscuous by western standards but their behaviour shouldn't be judged according to European or American morality. The customs and traditions that rule their conduct were in existence long before white visitors appeared on the scene and are foreign to the Judeo-

Christian ethic. Perhaps the biggest problem in understanding Tahitian sexuality arises from our own prurient perceptions. However, it is equally wrong to assume Tahitians are totally uninhibited and free from neuroses. As with people everywhere, they have their share of hang-ups and sexual problems.

A final word on this subject: for those of us lucky in love, Tahiti will be just like anywhere else, only warmer.

Tahiti's Third Sex

Homosexuality has been a culturally accepted life style in Polynesia for centuries. When the Europeans came they were shocked and puzzled at the behaviour of male transvestites who did striptease acts for the crews and unabashedly had sexual relations with other men. Commenting on this behaviour, Captain Bligh said:

It is strange that in so prolific a country as this men should be led into such sensual and beastly acts of gratification, but perhaps no place in the world are they so common or extraordinary as in this island.

In the years that followed, the brethren from the London Missionary Society did their best to convert the Tahitians into becoming upright Protestants, but with little success. The cultural heritage of the *mahu* (transvestite) lives on and they still continues to play an important role in Polynesian culture. According to Bengt Danielsson, the mahu is 'a popular and honoured member of every village throughout the Society Islands'.

Anthropologist Robert I Levy writes that one becomes a mahu by choice, by being coaxed into the role, or both, at an early age. The individual associates primarily with females and learns to perform the traditionally feminine household tasks. After puberty, the mahu may assume a woman's role by cooking, cleaning, looking after children and wearing feminine clothing. He may dance what are normally the women's parts during festivals, often with greater skill than the women around him. In the villages he may work as a maid, and in Papeete can often find employment as a waiter, professional dancer or bartender.

Although Tahitians may poke fun at mahus there is none of the deep-seated hostility which exists towards homosexuals in the west. Young adolescents may seek out mahus for sexual favours, but generally only if there are no girls available. If a young man does have sex with a mahu, there is little stigma attached to the act. Mahus are accepted as human beings, not aberrations. In Papeete there are several nightclubs which feature male striptease acts and cater to a varied sexual spectrum.

Anthropologist Danielsson fears that the mahu tradition is in danger of disappearing because of what he calls the 'brutal modernisation process'. He has already noticed the trend of mahus turning to western-style homosexual prostitution as a way of making a living in a modern society incompatible with the traditional mahu way of life.

ART & CULTURE

Upper-class Tahitians have adopted western pop culture to a 'T'. French Polynesians wear the 'chicest' fashions, the tightest jeans, listen to the latest pop music and, if they can afford it, drive the newest American cars and Japanese motorcycles. Yet they still have their own language and customs that despite 200 years of foreign influence have not completely disappeared.

As in all cultures, modern Tahitian music and dance owe quite a bit to outside influence. The music is an admixture of popular American songs, French chansons and hymns borrowed from the missionaries. Tahitian bands equipped with the most modern Fender guitars and Yamaha amplifiers crank out endless songs about love, romance and betrayal just like any other band in the world. Traditional percussionists, who always accompany dance troupes, are one of the purest expressions of Polynesian music and are as much a part of the music scene today as electric guitarists. To hear the thunder of their drumming for the first time is a stirring experience.

Perhaps the most popularised aspect of Tahitian culture is expressed in dance, in particular the hip-shaking and often very erotic *tamure*, a step that every Tahitian is taught at an early age. The tamure resembles the Hawaiian hula from the waist down, but is more forceful, suggestive and sometimes more violent than the Hawaiian dance. Tahitian dancers have amazingly flexible and controlled hip movements – an art that has to be seen to be appreciated. The modern tamure is descended from traditional dance forms presented by troupes acting out a legend or event depicting warriors, kings, fisherfolk, heroes, priests and the like – a far cry from today's slick, often showbiz-style productions.

Cultural Renaissance

As with other Third World peoples, Tahitians experienced a cultural blossoming and reawakening in the 1970s, manifested through the 'Maohi' or 'Neo-Polynesian' artistic movement. Artists explored traditional Polynesian motifs while writers and playwrights went digging into their own mythology for themes. According to Bobby Holcomb, a respected Hawaiian-American artist who resides in Tahiti, Neo-Polynesian painters like himself utilise the Polynesian colour scale (earthy browns, reds, yellows) as well as traditional Polynesian historical and mythical themes. Neo-Polynesian art is often more abstract than traditional Pacific art and may exhibit heightened eroticism, sensuality, local flora and fauna, and classic Polynesian geometric patterns as displayed in tattoos and tapa cloth. Politically the movement produced nationalist stirrings, calling for greater autonomy or even independence from France.

Today the maelstrom has died down but the 'back to the roots' sentiment has taken hold over a greater portion of society. Teaching the Tahitian language in schools, once against the law, is now part of the curriculum. Politicians of every stripe espouse traditional Tahitian culture, and painters and artists enjoy the support of the state instead of fighting against it. In the last several years the French Polynesian government has nurtured the talents of young artists by displaying their works in exhibitions and providing cash prizes. Displays of Tahitian art and a re-enactment of ancient ceremonies – such as the crowning of a king – can be readily seen during Tiurai, the Bastille Day celebrations.

On the popular front, singers and musicians (whose profession is Tahiti's national pastime) continue to compose music for the masses on subjects they have always written about – love and the sea – while enriching their songs with reggae and Latin rhythms. Throughout the country, women's groups are reviving dying art forms such as hat making, mat weaving, quilting and the fashioning of floral crowns.

One of the most novel groups to appear on the cultural scene is 'Pupu Arioi', a small but dedicated organisation that specialises in teaching children awareness of their Polynesian heritage. Named after an ancient Polynesian society that allowed members to criticise their leaders and rise in an otherwise rigid world, Pupu Arioi began its existence in 1977 as a theatre troupe. Later the group's emphasis shifted from theatre to education. Members now go from school to school, teaching teachers and pupils relaxation techniques which calm sometimes unruly children and put them into a more receptive state so as to introduce them to theatre, dance, music and costume. Children are not pushed, but nudged into thinking about their culture and traditions. Pupu Arioi members may also discuss Polynesian mythology and philosophy with the idea of educating children in the oral traditions which were once the backbone of Tahitian culture. Perhaps they will be successful in reinfusing values in a society that for many reasons has lost its old traditions.

EDUCATION

Compulsory education is mandatory in Tahiti for every child to the age of 14. Primary education begins at age five, and continues to the age of 12, when children begin secondary education.

There are several technical and vocational schools in Tahiti, and a large adult education programme. Vocational training includes hotel, restaurant, nursing and teaching programmes.

RELIGION & THE SUPERNATURAL

The majority of French Polynesians are Protestants who comprise about 55% of the population, followed by Roman Catholics (30%), Mormons (6%), Seventh Day Adventists (2%) and a number of Buddhists and Confucianists among the Chinese colony (2%). The church is an important institution throughout the Pacific Island nations and French Polynesia is no exception. On the outer islands the local priest or minister often wields a powerful hand in community affairs. In most areas church attendance is high.

Although Christianity has spread throughout the islands, there is still a strong belief in vestiges of the pre-Christian religion. In the outlying areas especially, myths of gods, giants and supernatural creatures are spoken of as fact and it is not unusual for a person to have had encounters with *tupa'pau* (ghosts).

One man in Maupiti matter-of-factly described to me the occasion on which he had seen a dozen ghosts floating down a moonlit road outside his village. 'These ghosts', he said, 'were the spirits of passengers who had perished in a shipwreck several weeks earlier'. The spirits were native Maupitans returning home as the dead always do.

Accepting the locals' belief that the supernatural is a normal part of life often makes westerners question their own beliefs. In the Tuamotus, I met a young Frenchman by the name of Patrick who had spent several years living on the atoll of Ahe. He said that one evening he and an old villager were fishing in a skiff inside the atoll's lagoon. The Frenchman spotted an object resembling a ball of fire which rose from a spit of land on the lagoon's far edge and floated in the direction of the village. Awe-struck by the sight, he pointed it out to the old man who sat contentedly fishing. The Tahitian glanced at the luminous ball and nonchalantly remarked that it was only the spirits returning to the village and really nothing to get excited about.

USEFUL CONCEPTS

Those who have spent any time in the Islands are sure to run into catch phrases that are important concepts in trying to understand the Tahitian character:

Fiu

This expression encompasses varying shades of boredom, despair, hopelessness and frustration. Put yourself in the place of a person who has spent his or her life on a small island, perhaps only a bit of coral in the the midst of a blue expanse of ocean. The only stimuli are the ceaseless trade winds, the sound of the waves crashing on the reef, the sight of the sun bleaching the coral white and the sweltering heat. You can always go fishing or turn on Radio Tahiti, but this can get boring after a while. Life can be an endless monotone, and when someone mutters, 'I'm fiu' with husband or with job, very little explanation is necessary. The essence of 'fiu' is in the languorous tropical air.

Aita P'ape'a'

Another often-used expression, aita p'ape'a' translates literally as 'no problem'. It means take things the way they are and don't worry about them. It is basically the Tahitian equivalent of 'manana'. At best it implies a fatalistic and easy-going acceptance of the here and now. At worst, it is a kind of intellectual lethargy and lack of concern.

HOLIDAYS & FESTIVALS

New Year's Day
　　Celebrated on 1 January, friends and families gather for merrymaking.
Chinese New Year
　　Celebrated during January/February with dances and fireworks.

Miss Bora Bora Contest
  Held in April.
Maire Day
  Fern exhibition held in May in Papeete followed by a ball.
Miss Moorea Contest
  Held in June
Miss Tahiti & Miss Tiurai Contest
  Miss Tahiti is chosen in July to represent the country in international beauty pageants. Miss Tiurai reigns over the Bastille Day celebrations.
Bastille Day
  France's Independence Day and the biggest holiday of the year. It is celebrated on 14 July and is known as *La Fete* by the French and *Tiurai* by the Polynesians, the carnival actually begins 29 June and lasts about three weeks.
Night of the Guitar & Ute
  In August local musicians compete in performing *ute*, satirical improvisational songs.
Te Vahine e te Tiare (The Woman & the Flower)
  Tahitian women dress up for floral theme ball in September.
All Saints Day
  On 1 November families visit cemeteries and illuminate graves with candles.
Thousand Flowers Contest & Pareu Day
  In November there are exhibitions of flowers followed by (you guessed it) another ball. Attendees wear pareu dresses.
Tiare Tahiti (National Flower Day)
  In December flowers are distributed throughout Papeete – on the streets, in hotels and on departing planes. Yet another ball.

Bastille Day

The Bastille Day celebration, or *Tiurai* as it is called in French Polynesia, is a month-long orgy of dance, food and drink. It is the islands' most important holiday, a combination of Mardi Gras, 4th of July and Walpurgis Night rolled into one. During this period, which starts from the end of June until the third week of July, business grinds to a halt and is replaced by serious partying. Many island communities put on their own fête consisting of traditional dance competitions, rock 'n' roll bands, foot and canoe races, javelin throwing, spearfishing and other sports activities. The largest celebration occurs in Papeete, which assumes a carnival air. There the waterfront is turned into a fairground crowded with hastily constructed booths, makeshift bars and restaurants, a

ferris wheel and a grandstand for viewing the dance competition.

The event opens with a parade featuring beauty contestants, sports association members, folkloric and tamure (dance) groups, and flower-studded floats. On the first day of the celebrations there is usually a historic reinactment at Arahurahu Marae. In times past this has been the 'crowning of the king' ceremony. On Bastille Day (14 July) there is a military parade which begins with a salvo of canons, followed by a sea of uniforms, brass bands playing military marches, and baton twirling troupes of majorettes. The grand finale in the evening is the 'Ball' held at the mayor's residence.

The three weeks are crowded with numerous activities such as horse races, speedboat races, bicycle races, parachuting displays, motorcycle competition, an international golf tournament and water-skiing. There is even room for the more traditional Polynesian sports of fruit carrying races, archery contests, as well as displays of tattooing, basket weaving, tapa cloth manufacture, copra cutting, and displays of Polynesian arts and crafts.

During this period tourists from all over the world and French Polynesians from throughout the islands converge on Tahiti to watch the dancing and partake in the good times. It is not unusual for Tahitians to stay up all night and frolic, sleep through the day, start chug-a-lugging Hinano beer and begin the cycle again. When it comes to dissipation, Tahitians are indefatigable; their capacity to enjoy themselves is superhuman. Tiurai is above all a time to socialise, forget your troubles, spend a good deal of money on liquor and perhaps mend fences with a neighbour.

One criticism longtime residents of Papeete have about Tiurai in their town is that it has become too commercialised. During the holiday, prices shoot up and merchants realise windfall profits. Commercialised or not, Tiurai in Papeete is packed with shoulder-to-shoulder throngs of people shoving their way along the carnival row. In one section, a crowd gathers in front of madly gesticulating Chinese shills, who spin the wheels of fortune in their gambling booths and attempt to outbark each other on bullhorns. Meanwhile, locals try their luck at the shooting galleries, vendors hawk kewpie dolls and cowboy hats, and young children tug their parents' arms in the direction of the merry-go-round. The temporary outdoor cafes selling beer, barbecued chicken and steak swell with inebriated tourists and Tahitians.

Outside the grandstand entrance, the scene is a mob of performers and gawkers. Troupes of tasselled, straw-skirted dancers mill around on the grass awaiting their turn to go on stage. They are the créme de la créme of all French Polynesian dancers. The troupe directors hype up the youngsters like football coaches before a big game. The air is thick with nervous energy and the scent of Tiare Tahiti blossoms. Nearly everyone has a crown of flowers on his or her head, or a single blossom behind the ear.

Tiurai offers more than a carnival atmosphere. For local entrepreneurs of the smaller island communities, the festival is economically important. Not only is it a big affair for the established merchants, but ordinary families can cash in on the holiday spirit by setting up small concessions selling food and liquor. The Tiurai festivities are in part subsidised by the French Polynesian government and the individual communities, which share the cost of maintenance and cash prizes for the various sports and competitions. The celebration also performs an important educational function. It provides French Polynesian youth with an outlet for traditional cultural expression which is more and more in danger of being lost with the encroaching influence of western culture.

LANGUAGE

The official languages of French Polynesia are Tahitian and French but other tongues spoken are Paumotu (the language of the Tuamotu Islands), Mangarevan (spoken in the Gambiers) and Marquesan (the language of the Marquesas Islands). These languages belong to the great Austronesian or Malayo-European language family. This widely scattered family includes the languages of Micronesia and Melanesia as well as Bahasa Malay (the language of Malaysia and Indonesia), Malagasy (the language of Madagascar) and the original languages of Taiwan. Thus the origins of Tahitian date back 5000 years to ancient languages of Indonesia which later spread to Fiji and then to Samoa and Tonga.

The first explorers to set foot on Tahiti thought the Tahitian language childishly simple. Cook recorded 157 words and Bougainville estimated the entire vocabulary to be only about 500 words. Tahiti was chosen as a fertile ground for evangelical groups such as the London Missionary Society partly because Tahitian seemed a simple language to learn. As the missionaries were to discover, their assumption was certainly wrong. As each day passed they encountered subtleties that were baffling, idioms that were foreign and sounds that were confusing. The slightest change in pronunciation, barely discernible to the untrained ear, could give a very different meaning. Although there were no words to express western ideas about the arts, sciences or business there were words describing the natural environment such as the weather, the ocean, the stars, animal behaviour and the like that the Europeans could not even begin to understand – their powers of observation were not attuned to see what Tahitians took for granted.

At least one of the reasons Tahitian was so difficult for early visitors to grasp was because it was a language of oral record. People were expected to know their genealogies and could recite them seemingly forever back into time. Thus they knew intimately the details of their forebears' lives and sometimes the origins of property claims. When no written language existed, memory was relied upon exclusively.

Once exclusively the language of Tahiti and its neighbours, Tahitian is now spoken on about 100 islands of French Polynesia. The language gained prominence because Tahiti was the most populous island and the chief one chosen for missionary work. As the written word and Christianity spread through native pastors, the printed Tahitian word more or less superseded other local dialects and languages.

Like all languages, Tahitian was influenced by foreigners, mostly early missionaries and seafarers who mingled with the local population. Many languages, including Hebrew, Greek, Latin, English and French, contributed words that have become part of modern-day Tahitian. The translation of the Bible into Tahitian necessarily introduced words like *Sabati* (Sabbath); but the English connection provided many loan words such as baby, butter, money, tea, pineapple and frying pan, which became *pepe, pata, moni, ti, painapo* and *faraipani* in Tahitian.

Pronunciation

There are five vowels in Tahitian:

a   as in 'but'
e   as in 'day'
i   as in 'machine'
o   as in 'gold'
u   as in 'flute'

There are eight consonant sounds in Tahitian:

f   as in 'fried'
h   as in 'house'; pronounced 'sh' as in 'shark' when preceded by 'i' and followed by 'o', as in *iho* (only, just)
m   as in 'man'
n   as in 'noted'
p   as in 'spark' – shorter than the 'p' of 'pan'
r   as in 'run' – sometimes trilled like a Scottish 'r'
t   as in 'stark' – softer than the 't' of 'tar'
v   as in 'victory'

Aside from the eight consonants a glottal stop is used in many words. For example, the word for 'pig' is *pua'a*; man is *ta'ata*; and coconut is *ha'ari*. An American English equivalent, as D T Tryon points out in his excellent Tahitian primer *Say it in Tahitian*, is 'co'n' for 'cotton'.

Although English is spoken by many shopkeepers, hotel personnel and students, it would help to have some command of French. If you really want to talk with the people and acquire knowledge of the culture, learn Tahitian.

Place Names

Papeete	Pa-pee-ay-tay
Raiatea	Rye-ah-tay-ah
Tahaa	Tah-ha-ah
Maupiti	Mau-pee-tee
Rangiroa	Rang-ghee-row-ah
Manihi	Mahn-nee-hee
Ahe	Ah-hay
Mangareva	Mahng-ah-rave-ah
Tubuai	Toop-oo-eye
Nuku Hiva	New-kew-hee-vah
Faaa	Fah-ah-ah
Tuamotu	Too-ah-mow-too
Huahine	Who-ah-hee-nay
Gambier	Tahm-bee-aye

Some Useful Words & Phrases

good morning; good day
    ia ora na
    your-rah-nah
goodbye
    nana
    nah-nah
thank you
    maruru
    mah-rhu-rhu
good
    maita'i
    my-tye
very good
    maita'i roa
    my-tye-row-ah
no
    aita
    eye-tah

no good
aita maita' i
eye-tah-my-tye
no problem; don't worry
aita pe' ape' a
eye-tah-pay-ah-pay-ah
woman
vahine
vah-hee-nay
man
tane
tah-nay
friend
e hoa
ay-oh-ah
American
marite
mah-ree-tay
finish, finished
oti
woh-tee

Cheers! Down the hatch.
manuia!
mahn-wee-ah
I'm bored; disgusted
fiu
phew
ancient temple
marae
mah-rye
traditional dance
tamure
tah-mu-ray
house
fare
fah-ray
crazy
taravana
tar-ah-vah-nah
pretty, beautiful
nehenehe
nay-he-nay-he

Facts for the Visitor

VISAS

Visitors need passports and onward tickets, but visas are not required for citizens of EEC countries. Citizens of the US, Canada and Japan are required to have passports and visa, but the visa may be acquired easily upon arrival at the airport in Tahiti. Thus for these three countries it is *not* necessary to visit the French consulate beforehand and obtain your visa. Australian and New Zealand citizens must have a visa before going to French Polynesia otherwise they may not be granted permission to enter. This is what happened to one Australian who arrived in Papeete in December 1987.

I arrived in Papeete ... and was told that it was now necessary for Australian citizens to have a visa before entering French Polynesia. I was forced to sign a document in French stating that I had arrived in Papeete without a visa. ... I was denied entry, told that it was useless trying to contact the Australian Consulate on a Sunday and then escorted back to the plane to Sydney.

Visitors from Sweden, Norway, Finland and a host of other nations from South America, Africa and Asia are obligated to apply for their visa before entering French Polynesia, but do not need the approval of the local French High Commissioner. Visitors from Eastern Europe and the remaining nations need the approval of the French High Commissioner before visiting the country.

In most cases visitors will be automatically granted visas of up to three months without the High Commissioner's approval. Upon expiration, tourist visas may be extended for another three months, with a possibility of renewal for an additional six-month period. No foreigner can stay for more than a year with a tourist visa.

Entry Formalities for Yachts

Captain and crew must have valid passports and previously secured tourist visas. A five-day transit visa is also desirable. If coming from a country that does not have a French consulate, the visitor must after five days secure a valid visa from the Immigration Service – good for three months for all of French Polynesia, counting the first day of arrival.

Along with the visa each crew member must have a deposit in a special account at a local bank or at the Tresorerie Generale equal to the return fare from Tahiti back to the country of origin. During the yacht's stay in French Polynesia the crew list must correspond with the list of passengers made at the time of arrival. Any changes must be accounted for with the Chief of Immigration. Crew changes can only be made in harbours or anchorages where there are gendarmes. Debarkation of crew members can only be authorised if the person in question has an airline ticket with a confirmed reservation. Yachts may not stay longer than one year. There is a branch of the Immigration Office adjacent to the Fare Manihini (Visitors' Bureau) directly on the waterfront.

WORK PERMITS

To live and work in Tahiti is not easy for non-residents. A work permit is necessarily tied with a residence permit and is issued two months following the request for a work contract. The permit is issued in care of the employer, who is responsible for the employee's return to his or her homeland. A local is always given first priority regarding jobs so the person seeking work in Tahiti has to be able to provide a specialty not found on the island. To sum it up, landing a job in Tahiti is extremely difficult. US citizens skilled in the hotel/restaurant business may have the best chance as some of the hotels in Tahiti are owned or operated by Americans.

MONEY

The currency used in French Polynesia is the French Pacific Franc or CFP. Notes come in denominations of 100, 500, 1000, 5000 and 10,000. Coins are in francs of 1, 2, 5, 10, 20, 50 and 100. Visa credit cards are accepted (banks will give you a cash advance), as is American Express and in some places, Master Charge. Travellers' cheques are easily cashed.

US$1	=	105 CFP
A$1	=	85 CFP
UK£	=	191 CFP
C$1	=	86 CFP
NZ$1	=	73 CFP
DM1	=	61 CFP

Regular banking hours are 7.45 am to 3.30 pm and some banks, ie the Bank of Tahiti, are open 7.45 to 11.30 am on Saturday mornings. If you need to get to a bank on Saturday get your hotel to find out the nearest one open. Note that banks charge a standard 300 CFP commission on every travellers' cheque transaction.

TIPPING

Tipping is discouraged by the tourism office but Tahitians have been introduced to this practice and are not adverse to it.

TOURIST INFORMATION
Tourist Office

The main information office (OPATTI) is on the quay nearly opposite the Vaima Shopping Center, in a cluster of brown buildings constructed to resemble traditional Tahitian dwellings known as *fares*. It is known as the Fare Manihini, which translates as 'guest house'. Inside you will likely find several 'demi' (half-caste) Tahitian women who will be more than happy to give you information in perfect English. The address of the Tahiti office is Fare Manihini, (tel 42-96-26), Boulevard Pomare, BP 65 Papeete, Tahiti, French Polynesia.

Overseas Offices

Overseas addresses of the Tahiti Tourist Board are:

Australia
    BNP Building, 12 Castlereagh St, Sydney, NSW 2000 (tel (02) 221-5811, 235-0703)
Belgium
    Office du Tourisme de Tahiti et ses Iles, Metsijsdreef 3-B-1900 Overijse, Brussels (tel 687-92-00)
Chile
    Delegacion General de Tahiti, Santiago Centro Edificio, Suite 709, Box 14002 STG 021 Santiago (tel 562 696-10-08, 005 262-76-10-08)
France
    Office du Tourisme de Tahiti et ses Iles, 52 Champs-Elysees – 75008 Paris, (tel (43) 590-242)
Hong Kong
    Tahiti Tourist Promotion Board – c/o Pacific Leisure Group, Tung Ming Building, 10th floor, Des Voeux Rd, Central Hong Kong, (tel (5) 241-361)
Japan
    New Tahiti Promotion, 6F Roppongi Kowa Building, 3-1-1 Roppongi, Minato-Ku, Tokyo (tel (03) 586-6599)
USA
    12233 West Olympic Boulevard, Suite 110, Los Angeles, California 90064 (tel (213) 207-1919)

In the USA the airline UTA has a toll free number (1-800-2-Tahiti) to call for free information on Tahiti. 1 800-553-3477

Foreign Consulates

Austria
    BP 4560, Papeete; Honorary Consul Paul Maetz (tel 43-91-14 office or 43-21-22 home)
Belgium
    BP 1602, Papeete; Honorary Consul Pierre Soufflet (tel 42-53-89 office or 53-27-20 home)
Chile
    BP 952, Papeete, Immeuble Norman Hall, Rue du General de Gaulle; Honorary Consul Roger Divin (tel 43-89-19 office or 43-25-67 home)
Finland
    BP 2870, Papeete; Honorary Consul Janine Laguesse (tel 42-97-39 home)
West Germany
    BP 452, Papeete, Rue Le Bihan-Fautaua; Honorary Consul Claude Eliane Weinmann (tel 42-99-94 office or 42-56-30 home)
Italy
    BP 420, Papeete, c/o Tikichimic, Fare Ute, Papeete; Honorary Consul Augusto Confalonieri (tel 58-20-29 office or 43-91-70 home)
Korea
    BP 2061, Papeete; Honorary Consul Bernard Baudry (tel 43-04-47 office or 42-58-96 home)

Monaco
> BP 33 Papeete; Honorary Consul Paul Emile Victor (tel 42-53-29)

Norway
> BP 306, Papeete, c/o Services Mobil, Fare Ute Papeete; Honorary Consul Victor Siu (tel 42-97-21 office or 42-05-62 home)

Netherlands
> BP 2804, Papeete, c/o Immeuble Wong Liao, Building d'Alsace, Papeete; Honorary Consul Jan Den Freejen Engelbertus (tel 42-49-37 office or 43-58-74 home)

Sweden
> BP 2, Papeete, c/o Ets Soari, Passage Cardella; Honorary Consul Michel Solari (tel 42-53-59 office or 42-47-60 home)

GENERAL INFORMATION

Post

The French Polynesian postal system is generally efficient. Due to the numerous flights in and out of Papeete, delivery time from the islands to the US, Australia and Europe is usually no longer than a week. The main post office in Papeete is a gleaming 20th-century wonder. Stamps from Polynesie Française are gorgeous and sought after by collectors. Sets are available in special philatelic windows.

Foreigners wishing to receive mail may do so by asking at the poste restante (general delivery) window. Holders of American Express cards and/or travellers' cheques may receive mail at the American Express office at Tahiti Tours, Rue Jeanne d'Arc. Telegrams, telexes and a new 'FAX' service are also available from the post office.

Telephone

The phone service in Tahiti is quite good. There are a few public phones scattered here and there but more often than not in an emergency you may have to ask a shopkeeper's permission to make a call. A local phone call costs 50 CFP to 100 CFP. Long-distance or overseas calls can be made at post offices and from hotels.

Electricity

The current is 220 volts AC in the more modern hotels and 110 in the older facilities. Don't plug in a thing before you check with the hotel. If in doubt check the voltage on the light. Many hotels have converters as well for your appliances.

Time

French Polynesia is 10 hours behind GMT, two hours behind US Pacific Standard time and 21 hours behind Australian Eastern Standard time. Thus, when it is noon Sunday in Tahiti, it is 2 pm Sunday in Los Angeles and 9 am Monday in Sydney. Once in French Polynesia you will realise that locals have their own standard of time, usually one to two hours behind what you had planned.

Business Hours

Most businesses open their doors between 8 and 10 am and close at 5 pm. Some larger stores stay open until 7 pm; smaller family

corner stores may not close until 10 pm. Banking hours are 7.45 am to 3.30 pm Monday through Friday, and some banks, ie the Bank of Tahiti, are open on Saturdays 7.45 to 11.30 am. Exchange counters are available at Faaa International Airport.

Security

Papeete is very safe by American big-city standards but there are still occasional reports of robberies. Some Tahitians are very poor and occasionally the youth may resort to crime. Even though this is rare, visitors are urged to keep an eye on valuables as you would anywhere else in the world. Depositing jewellery and the like in a hotel safe is a good idea. Outside Papeete and on the outer islands there are relatively few problems.

MEDIA

The local radio station, France Region 3, also known as Radio Tahiti, broadcasts in French and Tahitian. Along with local news and international news from the national French network, it features a pop music format with selections by French, American and Tahitian artists. The one television channel, which broadcasts in colour, carries drama, quiz shows, highbrow French programming, interviews, locally produced news and footage from international correspondents. The station also broadcasts in Tahitian and French. A new development in Tahiti broadcasting is the privately owned radio stations. These include Radio Tiare – which broadcasts in French and has mostly a pop music format – as well as two smaller district stations in Papara and Papenoo.

Newspapers & Magazines

Scattered throughout Papeete are kiosks and book stores selling the *International Herald Tribune* (flown in regularly from Paris) and the Pacific edition of *Time* and *Newsweek*, as well as French, German and other European publications. The kiosk at the Vaima Center on the waterfront is a convenient place to browse.

French Polynesia is served by two daily French-language newspapers – *Les Nouvelles* and *Le Depeche de Tahiti* – and an English-language weekly, *Tahiti Sun Press*, published by American expat Al Prince. Prince covers the local scene extensively (often better than the French press) and has excellent travel trade reportage regarding hotels, airlines and tourism in general. The tabloid-style weekly is given away free at most hotels in French Polynesia.

A local French-language, general-interest magazine is *Tahitirama* which has the TV scheduling. Three English-language magazines circulating throughout the Pacific are *Pacific Islands Monthly (PIM)*, *Pacific*, and *Islands Business*. *PIM*, published in Sydney, is an excellent regional publication and a venerable institution in the Pacific oriented mostly toward the old Anglo colonies. *Pacific*, (formerly *New Pacific*), published in Honolulu, is a younger upstart that also covers the Pacific basin but has better reportage of former US Trust Territories and current US dependencies than its rival. *Islands Business* is a Fiji-based monthly magazine which attempts to cover business and political developments in the Pacific. With the recent coup in Fiji its advertising has been seriously reduced and no doubt its objectivity vis-à-vis the political situation in Fiji has been compromised.

HEALTH

Tahiti is malaria-free and inoculations are not required except for those arriving from an area infected with smallpox, cholera or yellow fever, which exempts 99.9% of visitors. Water is generally safe and plentiful in most areas but for the skitterish there is always bottled water, Coca-Cola or Hinano beer. To date, I have never had problems with the drinking water anywhere in French Polynesia but I have had reports of visitors having come down with water-borne parasites in the outer islands. It might be prudent to drink bottled water when in doubt. In some areas mosquitoes are pesky and numerous, ergo it is suggested that you bring a good insect repellent. In the less expensive hotels and pensions it might even be a good idea to utilise a mosquito net.

In addition to modern clinics and hospitals in Tahiti many of the outer islands also have hospitals. These include: Moorea, Huahine, Raiatea, Bora Bora, Maupiti, Rangiroa, Tubuai, Hiva Oa, Ua Huka, and Nuku Hiva. If there is no hospital on an island there will at least be a clinic.

Listed are guidelines and suggestions gleaned from professional medical sources regarding several major concerns in the South Pacific. When in doubt excellent medical care is available in Tahiti and the visitor should not hesitate to see a doctor.

Sunshine
No matter how hot it feels on a given day in the tropics the sun is less filtered by the atmosphere than in other climes and is much more potent. Damage can be done to skin and eyes so take heed. To avoid horrendous sunburn use sunscreen. Tanning can still occur with sunscreen so don't be discouraged if you are not bronzed overnight. You will only peel that much sooner if you burn. A bad burn can ruin a vacation and a severe burn will require medical attention. A minor burn can be treated with a cool shower or compresses, soothing cream or steroids. An aspirin two or three times a day will also ease the pain. Some people are allergic to ultraviolet light which results in redness, itching and pinpoint-sized blisters. For these unfortunates, clothing is the only answer. Fair-skinned people beware in the tropics!

Humidity
Humidity not only means discomfort but also the possibility of rashes caused by yeasts and fungi which thrive in the warm, moist environment. The problem is compounded by tight-fitting clothing and moist, hot skin rubbing against the same. You don't have to be a doctor to deal with these difficulties. Keeping as cool and dry as possible is step number one. Loose-fitting clothing (cotton is best) is also a good idea, as are open-toed sandals. To reduce chafing, talcum powder or corn starch can be applied to body creases (under arms, on necks, under breasts, etc). If all else fails, medications are available to combat fungal and yeast rashes.

Bacterial Infections
Besides fostering the growth of fungi and other microorganisms, the tropics are a prime breeding ground for staph bacteria. A common bacteria found on the skin, these little devils can multiply enormously under the right tropical conditions, especially if there is a cut, blister or insect bite on the skin releasing the fluids they thrive on. Infection can spread if you are not careful. To prevent this, wash the injury, no matter how insignificant, with soap and then treat it with antibiotic ointment and cover with a clean dressing.

Gastrointestinal Problems
Perhaps the most common complaint of visitors anywhere is the 'travellers' trots', which can stem from any number of causes. There are several things you can do to guard against this, one is to make sure all meals are cooked properly. Virtually all organisms that thrive at body temperature are killed in the cooking process. As mentioned earlier, water in French Polynesia is potable but if you have the slightest fears drink bottled water or soft drinks. Peel or thoroughly wash any fruit or vegetables purchased in a market. Peeling fruit yourself is always a good idea. Finally, avoid swimming, walking barefoot or collecting seafood from beaches or lagoons directly in front of settlements. Raw sewage is often dumped or piped into the nearest convenient grounds: the beach that forms the villagers' front yard.

For those who have never been in the South Seas, the extreme changes in humidity, food and other conditions may tax the system. The best advice is to take it easy for the first few days until you are acclimatised. Like good scouts you would do well to be prepared and bring sunscreen, Band-Aids, ice bag, baby powder/corn starch, Ace bandage, antacid, laxative, aspirin, cold tablets, cough syrup, antibiotic ointment and antihistamine.

FILM & PHOTOGRAPHY

Photographers are permitted to take 10 rolls of film when they leave the islands. Should you need them, film and photographic accessories are readily available in Papeete's modern shops but they are much more expensive than you will be accustomed to. Colour prints can be developed from Kodacolor in one hour at QSS in Papeete's Vaima Center. Agfachrome, Ektachrome 50 and Fujichrome R100 processing are also available at other places.

Keep in mind that daylight is very intense in the tropics so if in doubt when shooting film, underexpose. That is, if you really want that photo, shoot according to what your normal meter reading dictates and then shoot another at a third to one full stop under. It's always best, of course, to take photos at dawn or dusk for best lighting conditions.

Always keep film dry and cool, and have your camera cleaned if exposed excessively to the elements – the humidity and salt air can ruin sensitive photo equipment in no time. If you plan to go through customs at airports frequently, it's advisable to buy a laminated lead pouch for film, available in any photo shop.

When taking photos of the locals, smile and ask permission first. Most of the time people will be happy to let you photograph them but on other occasions some Tahitians may not want to be part of your future slide show.

ACCOMMODATION

An important step in reducing hotel food costs was implemented by the local government which reduced import tariffs on booze and encouraged hoteliers to lower prices on food. This has reduced prices dramatically on MAP and AP programmes at various hotels as well as tabs at hotel bars. Though it varies from hotel to hotel the new law has resulted in a 15% to 40% reduction in food bills. For example, one hotel in Moorea

formerly charged 8000 CFP per day for three meals on its American Plan. It now charges 4500 CFP. Tipplers will be happy to know that instead of paying US$8 or US$9 for a shot of whiskey, they will only pay US$5 or US$6.

That's the good news.

The bad news is that the falling US dollar is nibbling away at the discounts that the French Polynesian government has tried so hard to implement. Unfortunately, room prices for hotels in Papeete and in French Polynesia still fall into two general categories – expensive and very expensive. Aside from air-conditioning, beach frontage, discos, restaurants and bars, upscale resorts may provide tennis courts, swimming pools, bicycles and free snorkelling gear. Prices for this type of hotel range from US$100 to US$250 for a single.

On the lower end of the scale is accommodation for the budget-minded traveller. These are either older hotels that lost their lustre when the more modern resorts opened up, smaller family-operated pensions, or boarding arrangements with families. These do not afford all the luxuries but nevertheless are quite adequate for many people.

The smaller hotels may have air-conditioning, pools and lovely gardens but not much else in the way of extras. Prices range from US$40 to US$75 for a single.

Hotel prices do not include 7% 'room tax' and – like all things in this world – are subject to change.

For campers, the news is getting better all the time. There are now excellent facilities on Tahiti, Moorea and Bora Bora.

FOOD

Although the government has made a valiant attempt to bring prices down by slashing import duties on booze, these reduced prices apply only to special 'tourist menus' featured at hotels and some restaurants which have volunteered to go along with the new pricing scheme. Most à la carte items retain their normal (usually expensive) price. The FP government is encouraging all restaurants to

provide discounts in the future and this has occurred in many of the hotel restaurants.

There are four excellent varieties of food available in Tahiti: French, Vietnamese, Chinese and Tahitian. Tahitian fare is more or less the same as in the rest of Polynesia – fish, shellfish, breadfruit, taro, cassava (manioc), pork, chicken, yams, rice and coconut. Beef, very popular in Tahiti, is rare on most of the outer islands. Vegetables such as tomatoes and onions are grown on Tahiti and some of the outer islands, but are non-existent on atolls. On most of the high islands, tubers such as manioc and taro are staples for the locals. Visitors soon find them bland and heavy. In the Tuamotus, where taro and manioc cannot be grown, rice, breadfruit and white bread are the main starches.

The dish most likely to be found on a French Polynesian meal table is *poisson cru*. It consists of chunks of raw fish marinated in lime juice or vinegar and salt and is usually topped with coconut cream, onions and oil.

Chevrettes, found on most high islands, are freshwater shrimp. *Salade Russe* is a potato salad with tiny pieces of beet. Taro and manioc are usually boiled and eaten as the main starch. Taro, which is served in large slices, contains significant quantities of fluoride and keeps teeth healthy. Young taro leaves, boiled and topped with coconut cream, resemble and taste like spinach. Finally, *poi* is a heavy, sweet pudding usually made with taro, bananas or papayas. It is served warm and topped with coconut milk.

The Polynesians who originally settled the islands brought with them bananas, breadfruit, taro, yams and, strangely enough, the American sweet potato. How the Polynesians got this last item is a mystery, but Dr Y H Sinoto of the Bishop Museum conjectures that Polynesian mariners made it to South America, perhaps traded with the locals and made their way back to Polynesia with the sweet potato. The missionaries later introduced sugar cane, cotton, corn, limes, oranges, guavas, pineapple, coffee and numerous other fruits and vegetables. Most Tahitians have adopted some eating habits from the French, including coffee, French bread, butter and canned goods. Unfortunately, it is a sign of the times to see them opening cans of Japanese tuna instead of fishing for the real thing.

BOOKS & BOOKSHOPS
A formidable number of books have been written about French Polynesia, some of them only readily available in the islands themselves. There are also a number of good bookshops in French Polynesia.

Bookshops
Hachette Pacifique on Avenue Bruat is the largest book distributor in French Polynesia and has several bookstores (known as *librairies*) in Papeete. They stock a limited number of English titles as well as American magazines. The stores are at the following locales: Latin Quartier branch, Rue Gauguin; and Vaima Shopping Center (upstairs branch).

Other bookstores include Libraire Klima, Place Notre Dame; Ping Pong, next to the Moana Iti restaurant on Boulevard Pomare (sell and trade books); Le Kioske, Vaima Shopping Center (street level); and Bookstore, across the side street from the main post office in Papeete.

Exploration & History
The classic edition of Cook's logbooks is *The Voyages of the Endeavor, 1768-1771* by Captain James Cook, edited by J C Beaglehole, four volumes (1955).

Tahiti a Paradise Lost by David Howarth (1984) is the best book I've encountered on the experience of the early explorers of French Polynesia – Wallis, Cook, Bougainville and company. It's fascinating and reads almost like a novel. A must for South Pacific addicts.

The Fatal Impact by Alan Moorehead is, along with Howarth's book, the best available historical account of early Tahiti. It

centres mainly around the three voyages of Captain Cook, portraying him as a humane commander but with the premise that contact with white civilisation in general was to have horrible repercussions. Moorehead points out that within 80 years of Cook's visit to Tahiti the population decreased from 40,000 to 9000 and the culture deteriorated because of disuse; by the end of the 19th century Australia's coastal aborigines had been decimated; and 50 years after Cook's exploration of the Antarctic icepack the once plentiful whales and seals had been virtually wiped out.

Modern Accounts
Kon-Tiki by Thor Heyerdahl is a contemporary nonfiction classic describing the 1948 voyage of a crew of Europeans aboard a Polynesian-style raft sailing from the coast of South America to French Polynesia. The purpose of the voyage was to 'prove' Heyerdahl's theory that Polynesians may have migrated from the South American continent instead of Asia. Whether or not you subscribe to Heyerdahl's ideas, the book is a great adventure story.

In *Moruroa Mon Amour – the French Nuclear Tests in the Pacific* by Bengt & Marie-Therese Danielsson (1977), the Danielssons trace the history of the bomb in French Polynesia and the socio-economic effects the programme has had in Tahiti. Danielsson, who originally came to French Polynesia aboard the *Kon-Tiki*, has been the leading spokesperson against the nuclear testing programme and at times a lonely voice of conscience.

Tin Roofs & Palm Trees by Robert Trumbull (1977) is a serious socio-economic/political overview of the South Pacific nations with a particular emphasis on their emergence into the 20th century. Trumbull is a former *New York Times* correspondent and writes with authority on the subject. This is a good primer on the background of modern-day South Pacific.

Tahiti; Island of Love by Robert Langdon is, as one of my esteemed colleagues says, one of the more 'popular' accounts of Tahiti's history. Though most likely out of print, it's worth looking for.

A Writer's Notebook by W Somerset Maugham (1984) is a collection of notes, journals and character sketches some of which Maugham later used in his short stories and novels. Though the collection covers the period 1892 to 1944, 40 pages are devoted to his travels in the Pacific and include Tahiti, Samoa, Fiji and Hawaii. For Maugham lovers, the reading is fascinating.

Guidebooks

How to Get Lost & Found in Tahiti by John McDermott (Waikiki Publishing, Honolulu, 1979). McDermott is a retired ad man who likes to get 'lost and found' in the Pacific. His books are rambling, chatty accounts of his wanderings with his wife (the 'lady navigator'), and contain some interesting tidbits of information if you don't mind wading through a lot of verbiage.

Tahiti Circle Island Tour Guide by Bengt Danielsson (Les Editions du Pacifique, Papeete, 1981) is the most complete historical tour guide available on Tahiti or perhaps any South Pacific island for that matter. Exhaustively researched and sardonic in tone, it is available only in Tahiti.

Moorea by Claude Robineau, photos by Erwin Christian (Les Editions du Pacifique, Papeete, 1983). Same format as the Marquesas book by the same publisher. Again, very good background information and great shots by Christian. It is only available in bookstores in Tahiti.

Moorea – A Complete Guide by James Siers (Millwood Press, Wellington, 1982). Another background book on Moorea. Whereas the previous book is more concerned with history and culture, this guide reads more like a slick brochure or a travel edition of *Vogue*. Lots of practical information about shopping, where to eat, where to stay and what to do. Very nice photography, but very commercial.

Bora Bora E by Milas Hinshaw (Milas Hinshaw Productions, Hollywood, 1984). A useful guidebook and map to Bora Bora. Information on all the restaurants, historical sites, hotels, etc. Gossipy and entertaining, especially Hinshaw's unnerving experiences with *tupa'pau* (spirits). Hinshaw's most memorable quote is 'E tai oe i teie puta ia ite oe i te parau mau' (Read this book and know the truth). Decide for yourself.

The Marquesas by Greg Denning, photos by Erwin Christian (Les Editions du Pacifique, Papeete, 1982). Comprehensive overview of the Marquesas with great photos by renowned Tahitian photographer, Erwin Christian. About the best book available on the Marquesas. This book is sold only in Tahiti.

Island Tales

The Blue of Capricorn by Eugene Burdick (1977) is a delightful collection of short stories and nonfiction essays about the South Pacific. Burdick, a master of the craft and coauthor of *The Ugly American*, explores in particular the whites' fascination with the tropics. One of the best collections of the South Pacific genre available.

South Seas Tales by Jack London is not London's most famous work but includes a few good tales including 'The House of Mapuhi', the slanderous 'story' of an avaricious pearl buyer. Based on a real-life character with whom London had an axe to grind. The real-life person sued London and collected a handsome settlement.

Typee; a Real Romance of the South Seas and *Omoo: a Narrative of Adventures in the South Seas; a Sequel to Typee*; or the *Marquesas Islands* by Herman Melville are based on Melville's experiences in the islands.

Art & Culture

The Art of Tahiti by Terence Barrow, (Thames & Hudson, 1979) gives an overview of Polynesian art before European contact, with an emphasis on Tahiti.

Noa Noa by Paul Gauguin is an autobiographical account of Paul Gauguin in Tahiti.

Tahitians – Mind & Experience in the Society Islands by Robert I Levy (1973) is a tome-like work written by an anthropologist for anthropologist types. A bit unwieldy but packed with all kinds of cultural information. A good reference book.

TAHITI LITERATI

Ever since its depiction as a Garden of Eden by 19th-century romantics, Tahiti has attracted not only missionaries and vagabonds but artists and writers as well. The writers who have sojourned in French Polynesia read like a Who's Who of world literature. Here is a summary of their varied but always piquant experiences.

Herman Melville

In June 1842 the *Acushnet*, a Yankee whaler, dropped anchor off Nuku Hiva in the Marquesas. Aboard the vessel, 22-year-old Herman Melville couldn't wait to step ashore. He had already faced 1½ years of deprivation at sea and knew he wouldn't be returning home until all the whale oil barrels were filled, perhaps two, three or even four years later. He and a friend named Toby stuffed a few biscuits beneath their clothing and jumped ship. They hid in the deep, forested recesses of the island's interior, safe from the ship's crew that would surely come looking for them. They hiked for days on end with little food and no shelter. The fact that Melville's leg was burning with infection made the trek even more excruciating. The two young men found their way to the Typee Valley, home of a tribe known for its ferocity.

Toby disappeared looking for medical aid for his friend and Melville was to spend the next four months with the Typees, an experience that would be the basis for his first book, *Typee*. He was treated well by the Marquesans, who gave him a servant and royal attention from Mehevi, the chief. However, Melville was never sure of the natives' intentions. Was he being treated as a distinguished visitor or simply being fattened for the kill? After all, these people were cannibals.

Fortunately for world literature, Melville survived his sojourn with the Typee, during which he was held in a sort of protective custody. He dwelt with the Marquesans neither in bliss nor in terror. He observed closely and made some startling revelations. 'There were', said Melville, 'none of the thousand sources of irritation that the ingenuity of civilized man has created to mar his own felicity'. He noted that there were no debtors, no orphans, no destitute, no lovesick maidens, no grumpy bachelors, no melancholy youth, no spoiled brats and none of the root of all evil – money.

Melville adapted well, enjoying the company of a vahine named Fayaway and the companionship of the men. His foot, however, was still inflamed and spiritually he was isolated. He needed medical care but the Typees were unwilling to let him go. His situation was well known on the island and with the help of sympathetic natives and a captain who was hard up for crew members, he escaped by joining up with the Sydney whaler the *Lucy Ann*, which sailed to Tahiti.

Apparently the conditions on this vessel – inedible food, cockroach and rat infestation and rotten rigging – were so god-awful that upon reaching Tahiti Melville decided to join the crew members in a mutiny rather than continue. His fellow travellers – with such romantic names as 'Doctor Long Ghost' (the ship's surgeon!), 'Bembo' (a tattooed Maori harpooner), 'Jingling Joe', 'Long Jim', 'Black Dan', 'Bungs', 'Blunt Bill' and 'Flash Jack' – didn't need much persuading. When they refused to sail and complained to British Consul Charles Wilson in Papeete, Wilson decided against the mutineers and with the support of the French Admiral Dupetit Thouars, had them locked up. Melville was imprisoned in the Calabooza Beretanee, the local jail. After his release six weeks later, he went to the remote village of Tamai on Moorea (now near the airport) and talked the chief into allowing the women to dance the 'Lory-Lory' (the precursor of the Tamure), an erotic, passionate performance that the missionaries had naturally forbidden.

Four years later Melville labouriously put together *Typee: a Peep at Polynesian Life*, which received immediate attention in America and Europe. Some critics hailed it, some doubted its authenticity, and others called it 'racy'. The missionaries (who weren't treated too kindly in the book) found it appalling. Both *Typee* and *Omoo* were outspoken tirades against the ruination of the Pacific by 'civilisation'. Why, Melville asked, should the natives be forced to participate in an alien church, to kowtow to a foreign government, and to adopt strange and harmful ways of living? In *The Fatal Impact*, Alan Moorehead writes that although Melville was 'possibly libellous and certainly scandalous in much that he wrote', his account of the 'sleaziness and inertia that had overtaken life' in Papeete in 1842 is remarkably vivid. Perhaps Melville was remarkably accurate as well. Moorehead says that many of the Tahitians – by this time caught between the missionaries, the whalers and finally the French – had 'lost the will to survive – the effort to adjust to the outside world had been too much'.

Pierre Loti

Midshipman Louis Marie Julien Viaud, who later became known to the world as Pierre Loti, first came to Tahiti in the 1880s aboard a French naval vessel. His largely autobiographical book, *The Marriage of Loti*, brought him fame and is credited with influencing Paul Gauguin to come to Tahiti. In the book he describes his friendship with Queen Pomare IV and his all-consuming love affair with Rarahu, a young girl from Bora Bora.

Loti's book tells how he came upon Rarahu bathing in a pool (which still can be visited today) in the Fautaua Valley near Papeete. There he witnessed the girl accepting a length of red ribbon from an elderly Chinese as payment for a kiss. Rarahu was poor and this type of behaviour was not unusual for a girl of little means. Nevertheless, as a result of what the incensed Frenchman saw, the Chinese in Tahiti suffered for years following the 1881 publication of *The Marriage of Loti*. Despite Loti's virulently anti-Chinese propaganda, the book did give an accurate account of life in Tahiti during the late 19th century.

Robert Louis Stevenson

Robert Louis Stevenson arrived in the Marquesas with his wife and mother in 1888, which marked the first leg of his six-year voyage to the South Seas aboard the *Casco*. The South Pacific held him spellbound and in the Marquesas the health of the nearly always frail writer improved dramatically. He spent his days wading in the lagoon, searching for shells, or on horseback. The Stevenson clan was impressed by the generosity and kindness of the locals so much that even Stevenson's mother, a staunch supporter of the missionaries, began to question whether such activities were actually beneficial to the natives.

From the Marquesas the *Casco* set sail for the Tuamotu atoll of Fakareva where the Stevensons spent the balmy evenings trading tales with Donat Rimareau, the half-caste French governor of the island. The author's *The Isle of Voices* utilised Rimareau's tales to a great degree.

Tahiti was the next stop on the *Casco's* itinerary. The travellers found Papeete to have a 'half and halfness' between western and Tahitian culture which they disliked and soon set sail for the other side of the island. There the Stevensons befriended a Tahitian princess (whom Pierre Loti had much admired) and a chief, both of whom helped them considerably. By this time Stevenson had become very ill, the family was short of money and the *Casco* needed extensive repair. The generous Tahitians, who offered the wayfarers food, shelter and moral support, were a godsend. The long stopover allowed Stevenson time to work and recuperate. Stevenson's wife wrote that the clan sailed from Tahiti for Honolulu on Christmas Day of 1888 'in a very thankful frame of mind'.

Jack London

Perhaps the most controversial American writer of his day, Jack London came to French Polynesia in 1906 on the ill-fated voyage of the *Snark*. He first arrived in the Marquesas after nearly dying of thirst at sea when one of the crew members inadvertently left the water tap open during a storm. The Londons stayed on Nuku Hiva for several weeks, renting the house used by Robert Louis Stevenson. They also visited the Typee Valley, immortalised in Melville's *Typee*, one of London's favourite childhood books. London was, however, disappointed by what he saw. Melville's vision of 19th-century French Polynesia no longer existed and London referred to the natives as 'half-breeds', blaming the whites for the corrupting influence that decimated the Marquesan race physically and spiritually. He spent his days feasting on tropical fruits, relaxing in the sun, collecting curios and trying to ward off huge wasps and *no-nos*, vicious flies that inflict a nasty bite.

Next stop was Tahiti, where London was greeted by the news that his cheques had bounced back home. To make matters worse, he did not get along with some of the French officials, and thieves stole many items from his boat. Perhaps this is why the writer did not speak of Tahiti in more flattering terms. In *The Cruise of the Snark* he wrote that: 'Tahiti is one of the most beautiful spots in the world', but that it was for the most part inhabited by 'human vermin'. He also took a dislike to a well-known pearl buyer, Emile Levy, and in *South Sea Tales* unfairly depicted the Frenchman as an avaricious businessman who cheated a native out of a huge pearl and then met a horrible death. London did not bother to change Levy's name or physical description in the story, and the pearl buyer was furious. Even the other residents of Tahiti, who were not terribly fond of the hard-driving businessman, thought London had gone too far. In the end, Levy successfully sued London, who had long since returned to the United States but paid dearly for his outpouring of venom.

Rupert Brooke

In 1915, on a hospital ship off Skyros, the great soldier/poet of the Edwardian age, Rupert Brooke, died of food poisoning at the tender age of 28.

While visiting the west coast of the United States in 1913, Brooke had suddenly decided to tour the South Seas. He came to Tahiti in January 1914 where he lingered until April, nursing an injury caused by grazing against coral. During this time he fell in love with a beautiful Tahitian, Taata (who he called 'Mamua') and composed perhaps his three best poems, 'The Great Lover', 'Retrospect' and 'Tiare Tahiti'. According to biographer John Lehman, it was with Mamua that Brooke most likely had the only 'perfect and surely consummated love-affair of his life'. Wrote Brooke in 'Tiare Tahiti':

Mamua when our laughter ends,
And hearts and bodies, brown as white,
Are dust about the doors of friends,
Or scent a-blowing down the night,
Then, oh! then the wise agree,
Comes our immortality...

On returning to San Francisco Brooke's thoughts returned to Tahiti and his lover continued to haunt him. Months later, on his deathbed in the Aegean, he wrote in his last letter of instructions to a friend: 'Try to inform Taata of my death. Mlle Taata, Hotel Tiare, Papeete, Tahiti. It might find her. Give her my love'. Several years later, when Somerset Maugham came to Tahiti to research a book on Gauguin, Brooke's old friends still wept uncontrollably at the mention of his native name, 'Purpure', the only name they knew him by.

Somerset Maugham

Among the works of the English writer Somerset Maugham is *The Moon & Sixpence*, a novel based on the life of Paul Gauguin. During WW I, when according to Maugham 'the old South Seas characters were by necessity confined to the islands', he visited Tahiti to research the book. There he not only culled reminiscences of the painter from people who knew him but also learned more of writers like Loti, Brooke, Robert Louis Stevenson and Jack London. Like those writers before him, Maugham was entranced by the magic of the South Seas and spent his time interviewing everyone who knew Gauguin, including businessmen, a sea captain, a hotel proprietress and others. In Maugham's words, he wanted to make the protagonist of his novel as 'credible as possible'.

Despite Maugham's enchantment with Tahiti, most of his short stories about the South Pacific – including 'Rain', which immortalised the prostitute Sadie Thompson – took place in Samoa. Of this the author commented, 'The really significant fiction of the world today involves a husband and wife relationship, the problems that lovers encounter and overcome, a cuckolded man, a jilted woman, an unrequited or pretended love for the other. From sexual conflicts we have our revenge and homicidal motives'. However, Maugham observed that in a place like Tahiti, 'where there are sexual licenses, excesses, the condoning attitude on infidelity, a tolerance of promiscuity, and an absence of sexual possessiveness, there does not exist the emotional tension that precipitates human drama ....' In addition, Maugham asserted 'that Tahiti is a French possession, and the French with their *laissez faire* and *ménage-à-trois* tolerance of sexual philanderings and indulgences don't really provide believable fictional protagonists for any human-triangle, story or play unless you want to make a comedy or farce out of the situation'.

Paul Gauguin's case, however, falls into a different category. When the artist came to Tahiti, 'the languor of this island, the Polynesian playfulness, the castrative sexuality that abounded there, could not save him from his ultimate and wretched fate. That of course was Gauguin's predetermined course of tragedy', Maugham said.

Nordhoff & Hall

James Norman Hall and Charles Nordhoff

first met in the military service at the end of WW I when they were commissioned to write a history of the Lafayette Flying Corps. They were vastly different in temperament. Hall was shy, optimistic, romantic and a native of Iowa. Nordhoff, outwardly more confident, was pessimistic, skeptical and had been raised in California. They distrusted each other at first, but their opposite natures were complementary and they eventually became the best of friends. Nordhoff convinced Hall that Tahiti was the place to go and write. When the *Atlantic* assigned them a piece on Tahiti and gave them an advance, they were on their way to the South Seas.

Years later, Tahiti had become their home and an outpouring of articles and books by the two ensued. They wrote some works separately but continued to work well as a team, and after their collaboration on a boy's adventure Nordhoff proposed doing another book in the same vein. Hall refused but instead suggested an idea that was to become the most famous seagoing novel written in the 20th century – *Mutiny on the Bounty*.

During their initial research Nordhoff and Hall could scarcely believe that the most recent book on the *Bounty* incident had been published in 1831! No one had ever ventured to write a fictionalised account of the event even though it was the kind of story that begs to be transformed into literature. Based at the Aina Pare' hotel in Papeete, the two writers plunged into their work. From the British Museum they procured accounts of the voyage, the mutiny, Bligh's open-sea voyage and the bloody Pitcairn experience, along with copies of the court martial proceedings and the Admiralty blueprints of the *Bounty*. Both immersed themselves in 19th-century prose, which helped to set a common style. The resulting narrative was divided into three sections: the *Mutiny On the Bounty*, *Men Against the Sea* (Bligh's open-sea voyage) and *Pitcairn Island* (the adventures of Fletcher Christian, his mutineer cohorts and the Tahitians who accompanied them). The trilogy was completed in 1934, after five years of work. Fifty years and three cinematic versions later, the story still hasn't lost its charm and fascination.

Hall is buried facing Matavai Bay where the *Bounty* dropped anchor and where he and Nordhoff used to sit discussing their work. A bronze plaque on the grave is inscribed with a poem he wrote as a young boy:

Look to the Northward, stranger
Just over the hillside, there
Have you in your travels seen

ENTERTAINMENT
Cinemas
There are seven movie houses in Papeete and a number scattered in the larger rural areas. As you would expect, most films are French, or American dubbed in French. Admission is about 500 CFP – approximately US$5.

Sports & Games
It is no understatement to call the Tahitians sports fanatics. On Tahiti there are facilities for golf, bicycle racing, tennis, basketball, track and field, soccer and swimming. French Polynesia also participates in the annual South Pacific Games, a regional Olympics-like event featuring only South Pacific athletes.

The closest thing to a national sport is *pirogue* (outrigger canoe) racing, which is highlighted during the Bastille Day celebrations of Tiurai. Tahitians take great pride in the Polynesian tradition of canoeing and were shocked in 1981 when for the first time the visiting American club, 'Imua', trounced the leading Tahitian team in a major race.

Atimaono Golf Course
Atimaono, Tahiti's only golf course, is a 6352-metre (6950-yard) par 72. It is in the Papara district. The course area was formerly a cotton plantation established during the American Civil War to provide Europe with the fibre then in short supply. It is a 45-minute drive from Papeete and is open daily from 8 am to 5 pm year-round. The course has recently undergone a 100 million franc renovation which includes a new clubhouse,

restaurant, pro shop, pool, tennis courts and driving range. The resident pro is Exalt Hopu. Green fees are 1300 CFP for adults and 500 CFP per day. Clubs can be rented for 1500 CFP per day.

THINGS TO BUY
Import duties imposed by the government are an important source of Tahiti's income. Despite these tariffs, Tahiti's duty-free shops offer good discounts on liquor, tobacco and perfume. For the fashion-conscious there are a number of boutiques with island-style and French clothing. Crafts, seashells and handmade shell leis sold in the market, at outdoor booths or at fairs make good mementoes. If you have money to spend, black coral and the indigenous black pearl make even nicer acquisitions. Philatelists should stop at the special booth at the post office – French Polynesia issues beautiful stamps. And if you stay long enough in the islands you will undoubtedly adopt the local article of clothing called a *pareu*. This practical item is a brightly coloured wraparound cotton cloth worn by men and women and is sold in every store.

Shoppers in Papeete can purchase items from around French Polynesia: tie-dyed pareus from Moorea, black pearls from Manihi, wood carvings from Ua Huka, shell hatbands from Rangiroa, fine woven hats from Tubuai and tapa cloth from Fatu Hiva.

Shopping hours are usually 7.30 am to 5 pm on weekdays and shops close at 11 am on Saturdays. There is always a very long lunch hour, usually 12 noon to 2 pm, but banks are open during this time.

CLOTHING
The national costume for men and women is the pareu (par-ay-you), a rectangular piece of cloth about two-metres long. It can be tied a number of ways but is usually wrapped skirt-like around the waist and worn with a T-shirt. Although western men might at first cringe at the idea of wearing a skirt, they soon find that in Tahiti's often sweltering climate it is a practical item of clothing to wear around the

house. Get hooked and you will find yourself bringing a few pareus back home. They come in a variety of colours and patterns and in several grades of quality.

Although flowers are ornaments rather than clothing, you will never see a race of people so enamoured with putting them in their hair. Fresh *tiare* or hibiscus blossoms are always worn behind the ear or braided with palm fronds and other greenery into floral crowns. Tradition has it that if a woman or man tucks the flower behind the left ear she or he is taken; a flower placed behind the right ear means the person is available. Tahitians joke that if someone waves a flower behind his or her head it means 'follow me'. I have never witnessed this but will report the outcome of such an invitation if fortunate enough to experience it.

WHAT TO BRING

Dress in Tahiti is almost always casual and, because of the warm climate, it is easy to subscribe to the adage 'travel light'. Unless you are planning to travel to the outer fringes of French Polynesia, say the Austral Islands, you can be certain it will always be warm, even at night. Therefore, clothing should be light. Bathing suit and shorts (both for men and women) are always practical and fashionable. Cotton shirts and dresses are also necessary, as are sandals, a light plastic raincoat or a windbreaker for the odd tropical downpour, a light sweater, a hat to shield you from the intense rays, sunscreen, insect repellent, first-aid kit and perhaps small souvenirs or toys for Tahitian children.

SCUBA DIVING, SNORKELLING & OTHER WATER SPORTS

Most of the islands of French Polynesia are bounded by reefs where tropical fish of every colour and description thrive. Snorkelling, easily learned, is safe and fascinating. Mask and fins are readily available and reasonably priced – one of the few reasonably priced items in the entire country. Fish watching is adequate on Tahiti and Moorea but better snorkelling is found on the outer islands where marine resources have been less affected by humans.

For the serious diver there are several dive shops and outfitters who will take you out. All scuba divers must have a certificate from a doctor indicating that the individual is in good health. A medical exam can be taken in Tahiti if the diver lacks the proper papers. Divers also need a certificate indicating the depth specifications allowed. A lead diver must have an international or a French licence allowing the person full responsibility to lead divers to designated depths.

Average water temperature in lagoons is 28 to 29°C. Outside the reef, temperatures range from 26 to 28°C.

For above the surface activities speed boats for water-skiing can be hired as well as charter boats for sport fishing. Boats do not come cheap but if you are concerned about price, you should not be in Tahiti in the first place. Game fish includes marlin, sailfish, barracuda and other pelagics. Some of the resorts (such as the Beachcomber and Maeva Beach Hotels) have glass-bottomed boats for viewing undersea life out of harm's way.

Dive Specialists

Tahiti Aquatique, (tel 42-80-42), BP 6008, Faaa, Tahiti, is run by an American, Dick Johnson. Adjacent to the Maeva Beach Hotel, this shop operates a variety of nautical activities including glass-bottom boat trips, cruises and sailboat rentals. Johnson's guided scuba tours range from 5000 CFP (one to six people) to 2500 CFP (seven to 20 people). Underwater photography lessons are also available.

Tahiti Plongee, (tel 43-62-51), BP 3506, Papeete is nine km from Papeete at the Marina Lotus and is headed by Henri Pouliquen. It is open seven days a week to divers of all levels. 'First dive' instruction and night diving available; the prices start at 2500 CFP per dive.

Yacht Club de Tahiti, (tel 42-23-55, 42-78-03, 42-78-95), BP 1456, Papeete, calls itself Tahiti's 'first diving school' and has all equipment available, two dive boats, and a decompression chamber only three minutes by car from the premises. They offer instruction, night diving and diving outside the reef. Prices begin at 4500 CFP per dive and 5500 CFP per lesson.

Hotel Beachcomber, (tel 43-79-88), BP 6014 Faaa, Tahiti, is a small dive operation equipped with a Boston Whaler. The cost is 4000 CFP per dive. MUST Plongee, (tel 56-17-32, 56-15-83), BP 13, Paopao, is equipped to take out groups of up to 15 divers on Zodiac rafts. The cost is 4500 CFP per dive.

Club de Plongee Moorea, (tel 56-15-35), BP 205 Tamae, Moorea, offers diving in lagoon, passes, outside lagoon as well as night dives and instruction. Dive transportation is via Boston Whaler and the cost is 4000 CFP per dive. Hotel la Bouteille a la Mer, (tel 43-99-90, ext 334), BP 17 Avatoru, Rangiroa, offers resort dives, teaching and diving in lagoon, passes and outside the reef at a cost of 3500 CFP per dive. Hotel Kia Ora Rangiroa, BP 706, Rangiroa, provides diving in lagoon, passes and outside the reef as well as resort dives. The cost is 3500 CFP per dive, 5500 CFP for exploratory dives and 2500 CFP for resort dives. Hotel Kaina Village Manihi, (tel 42-75-53), BP 2460, Papeete, lead dives in the lagoon, the passes and outside the reef. Equipment includes a speedboat.

Club de Plongee Uturoa, (tel 66-37-10), BP 272, Uturoa, Raiatea, Michele Philippe is Raiatea's only dive operator. He transports divers in a large, motorised outrigger and will pick up divers from yachts or hotels anywhere within the Raiatea-Tahaa area. He teaches as well as leads divers to any spot in the lagoon or the passes. According to Michele, Raiatea is 'virgin' territory for divers and there are a number of excellent sites near to shore, within five to 10 minutes of his pension. The cost ranges from 2000 CFP to 3500 CFP per dive and 4000 CFP for a resort dive.

Moana Adventure Tours – Hotel Bora Bora, (tel 67-70-33), BP 5, Bora Bora. Erwin Christian, the well known local photographer has an exclusive contract with the Bora Bora Hotel. He will take divers both to lagoon and open sea. The prices are 6000 CFP per dive inside the lagoon, 7000 CFP outside the reef and 6000 CFP for a resort dive.

Divers should note that like all other prices in this book, costs for diving are subject to change. In other words, plan on things being more expensive than you had anticipated. Best bet is to write to the dive operators you are considering and find out exactly how much it will cost. Some of the dive operators also run their own pensions (as in Raiatea or MUST in Moorea) which cater exclusively to divers. This usually means less expensive accommodation.

Getting There

AIR

Apart from those people who arrive on a cruise ship or by yacht, all visitors to French Polynesia arrive by air at the Faaa Airport near Papeete, Tahiti. Air services through Tahiti are generally operated using Tahiti as an intermediate stop between Australia or New Zealand and the USA although there are also connections between Tahiti and Chile in South America via Easter Island. There are also some connections to other Pacific islands.

Airlines that fly into Tahiti include Air New Zealand, Lan Chile, Polynesian Airlines, Qantas, South Pacific Island Airways and UTA. Needless to say, the best fares can be found by travellers who shop around travel agents and check out the newspaper ads for discounted air tickets in the travel sections.

From the USA

The main departure cities from the continental United States to Tahiti are Los Angeles and San Francisco but there are also flights from Honolulu and Dallas or Fort Worth. The carrier with the lion's share of passengers is UTA. Other airlines from the US to Tahiti include Air New Zealand, Qantas, Air France, Continental and Hawaiian Airlines. A charter carrier, Minerve, also operates regularly out of San Francisco. Round-trip excursion fares from Los Angeles or San Francisco (during low season – 25 December to 15 June) to Tahiti are US$849. The tariff for Air New Zealand's flight from Dallas or Fort Worth is US$1159 From Honolulu, round-trip fare to Papeete is US$678. Better deals are available such as the circle Pacific fares to New Zealand (US$1195) or to Australia (US$1246) which can be routed via Tahiti. Alternatively discounted round-trip tickets to Tahiti can be found for around US$600 from the US west coast if you are prepared to shop around and look at the advertisements in the Sunday newspaper travel sections in major west coast cities.

From Australia

There are no great discounts on direct flights to Tahiti from Australia despite the relatively short distance. The cheapest way is to make Tahiti a stopover en route to the USA. Shop around and remember there are three pricing seasons for flights out of Australia – low, shoulder and high. The cheapest direct flight to Tahiti (low season) is a 30-day excursion fare for A$1050 return – minimum six days, maximum 30 days, no stops. (This jumps to A$1385 in the peak season). UTA flies Sydney/Tahiti return for A$2568, A$1353, A$2696 (low, shoulder, high). UTA's one-way fare is A$1818; or one-way to Los Angeles with a stop in Tahiti is A$2142. You can fly to the US west coast or Vancouver via Papeete with Qantas for A$1446 return (low season), or one-way for A$1013. Another alternative is to fly via New Zealand.

From New Zealand

Air New Zealand flies from Auckland to Papeete return for NZ$1090 (low season, from 14 January to 30 June and 15 September to 13 December); or NZ$1281 (high season, 14 December to 13 January and 1 July to 14 September). These fares can be combined with the APEX fares from Australia, which means a return flight from Melbourne to Papeete via Auckland can be as little as A$997 or as much as A$1393. Air New Zealand fares from Melbourne to Auckland range from A$399 to A$657 return. Continental Airlines also flies to Tahiti from New Zealand.

From the UK

Few travellers are going to fly all the way to the South Pacific with a visit to Tahiti as their sole goal. Tahiti can, however, be easily visited en route to Australia or on a round-the-world ticket. Airline ticket discounters (bucket shops) in London offer round-the-world tickets which include Tahiti in their itinerary for UK£850 to UK£1000. Flying from London west-bound to Australia it is also possible to include Tahiti. A typical route is London / New York / Los Angeles / Tahiti / Sydney for UK£464. As with the flights out of Asia, UTA is likely to be the operator through Tahiti although Air New Zealand flights may also be used from London (via Los Angeles).

From Other Pacific Islands

There are surprisingly few connections between Tahiti and other Pacific nations. UTA flies between Noumea in New Caledonia and Tahiti with a one-way fare of US$432. They also have a connection from Fiji, via Noumea, to Tahiti using Air Caledonie. The one-way fare is US$612. Air New Zealand fly Rarotonga to Tahiti for US$140 one-way.

There are also various circle-Pacific fares. For example Air New Zealand has a US$1195 fare from Los Angeles to New Zealand with stopovers in Tahiti, Fiji or the Cook Islands. A similar ticket is available to Australia for US$1246.

From Asia

For several years now one of the most popular tickets out of South-East Asia to the USA has been the southern loop through the Pacific. Using UTA flights, this ticket travels Singapore / Jakarta / Sydney / Noumea / Auckland / Tahiti / Los Angeles. There are numerous ticket discounters in Singapore, Bangkok, or Penang in Malaysia, who sell tickets on this or a similar route. Typical costs are around US$800.

From South America

Lan Chile connects Tahiti with Santiago, Chile via Easter Island. Flying to Tahiti and then connecting with this flight is the most direct, though not the cheapest, way to fly to South America from Australia or New Zealand. The round-trip excursion fare from Papeete to Santiago is US$1319.

PACKAGE PLANS

Packages may not appeal to the vagabond but they are the way most visitors travel to the South Pacific. The main advantage of utilising a package is that it will undoubtedly save you money on the air fare side of the travel equation. Naturally, the agent will make money on the 'land' and excursion end of the deal. After you have decided what island you'd like to visit and for how long, consult an agency that specialises in Tahiti. The agent should be able to answer questions such as: Does the hotel have a mountain or oceanside view? Will your accommodation be over the water, on the beach or in the garden? Is the hotel a super deluxe one or more moderate? How far away is the beach? A specialist will be familiar with the tour packages available and should be able to answer these questions so that there are no unhappy surprises.

A competent agent should also be able to prepare a tailor-made itinerary for the person who has special interests such as golf, snorkelling, diving, etc. In most cases US South Pacific specialists have toll-free telephone numbers and can advise you of the current air fare bargains and seasonal discounts. They should also have fares for inter-island travel. Last but not least, a reputable agency can save you money. For US residents, I can recommend Manuia Tours (tel 800 5323000) in San Francisco. It is owned by a Tahitian family and they know their destination.

SEA

Unfortunately, the romantic days of catching a tramp steamer in the United States and working your way across the Pacific no longer exist. Unless money is no object, the prohibitive cost of taking ships long distances makes it much more feasible to fly. However, once you are in the islands it is still possible (although difficult) to take freighters from one South Seas port to another. Booking passage on a freighter entails going down to the dock and talking the vessel's skipper into giving you a berth. If there is room aboard and the captain likes your looks, you are in luck. On US-registered ships, hitching a ride is impossible unless you have seaman's papers. The schedule of cargo vessels coming into Papeete is posted at the waterfront branch of the immigration police adjacent to the tourist office. You can also island-hop by contacting private plane owners and negotiating with them for rides.

Yacht

For persons with time on their hands and adventure in their hearts, travelling to Tahiti by yacht is also feasible. To become a crew member, go to Honolulu or one of the larger ports on the western coast of the US – preferably Los Angeles, San Diego or San Francisco – which are departure points for the majority of Tahiti-bound yachts.

To find the boats headed in this direction, you must do some sleuthing down on the docks of the local yacht club. Usually notices are placed on yacht club bulletin boards by skippers needing crew members, or by potential sailors looking for a yacht. The best thing to do is ask around the docks or marine supply shops. Naturally someone who has previous sailing experience, is a gourmet chef or a doctor will have a good chance to get on as a crew member. A six-week sailing season starts during the last half of September with a secondary 'window' opening in January and continuing through March.

If you are serious about getting on a yacht, it's best to start doing research at least six months ahead of time. Get to know the people you are going to sail with and help them rig the boat. Sailing time from the US west coast to French Polynesia requires about a month, with nowhere to get off in the middle of the Pacific. Papeete is one of the major transit points for yachts in the entire South Pacific, and once you are there it is generally no problem for an experienced sailor to hitch a ride from Papeete to all points east and west.

Getting Around

Travelling to and within the islands of French Polynesia is not a difficult affair. Thanks to French largesse the transportation infrastructure is quite sophisticated. There are modern airstrips, well-paved highways, numerous boats and ferries, and a bus system that works. Visitors will find that most transportation is reasonably priced, and despite the general 'manana' attitude, things generally run on time.

Since there is only one international airport in French Polynesia (Faaa near Papeete), a trip to the surrounding islands must begin on Tahiti. The two means of transport are air and copra boat. Travelling by air is the fastest and most efficient, but not necessarily the most economical. Although the local carrier, Air Tahiti, (formerly known as Air Polynesie) flies to quite a few destinations, it does not go to all the islands.

Copra boats, on the other hand, do go to every inhabited island but take more time and overall, they are a much cheaper form of transport than planes. On shorter routes they can be a great bargain and also give you the chance to meet some of the locals who will undoubtedly be journeying with you.

A third possibility is to combine both air and sea transportation. For example, if you want to visit Ahe, which has no air service, it is possible to book a flight to Manihi and then catch a speedboat from there to Ahe.

AIR

Since French Polynesia's importance as a military base was established in the early 1960s, the government has developed an extensive air transportation system serving all the distant archipelagos. Although it would be impractical to build runways on every island, most areas can be reached by flying to an island with an airstrip and then catching an outboard motor-powered skiff or inter-island boat to the place you wish to visit. The major carrier, Air Tahiti, provides a well-run air service to every island group. For schedules go to the Air Tahiti office on Boulevard Pomare or the visitors' bureau (Fare Manihini) on the quay. Several smaller airlines also charter planes or helicopters for visitors. The chart shows the prices in CFP for one-way flights to major destinations. There are additional flights so if you want to travel to an island not detailed check one of Air Tahiti's brochures. To calculate round-trip fares just double the one-way fare.

Travellers should note that the baggage allowance on inter-island flights is only 10 kg (22 lbs). They will charge you without hesitation if your baggage is overweight.

In some cases flights to and from the outer islands are direct while in other cases they are routed via Papeete. For example one may fly directly from Huahine to Raiatea but in order to fly from Huahine to Rangiroa the traveller must pass through Faaa Airport in Papeete. The type of aircraft used on most flights are the older Fokker F27s (48-seat aircraft) or the new ATR 42s, a hi-tech, twin prop, 46 seater. Nineteen-seat Twin Otters and smaller Britten-Norman Islanders are used on shorter routes. Recently, Air Tahiti introduced a new pass which allows the purchaser several different options: Papeete / Moorea / Huahine / Raiatea / Bora Bora / Rangiroa and Manihi for 38,000 CFP; Papeete / Moorea / Huahine / Raiatea and Bora Bora for 26,000 CFP; and Papeete / Moorea / Huahine / Raiatea / Bora Bora / Rurutu and Tubuai for 42,000 CFP. The restrictions are that one is allowed one stop per island and the pass is valid for 28 days. The fare will undoubtedly be subject to change so check with Air Tahiti for details.

The newest thing going in Tahiti air travel is a helicopter service by Tahiti Helicopter (tel 43-34-26) and Pacific Helicopter Service (tel 43-28-90) to Moorea from Faaa Airport. Pacific Helicopter also provides rides form Faaa on Sundays

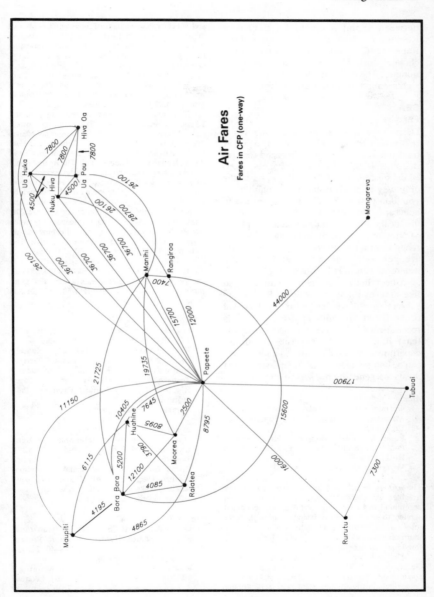

Air Fares
Fares in CFP (one-way)

between 1 and 3 pm to Le Belvedere Restaurant, 550 metres (1800 feet) above Papeete. The ride, aboard an Ecureuil chopper costs US$46, and takes about 15 minutes. The company also has five-minute sightseeing tours over Papeete for US$24.

SEA
Ferry
Despite the increase in air transportation, inter-island vessels remain a vital transportation link for travellers and cargo to the outer islands. In many instances, inter-island steamers or much smaller skiffs are the only way to reach isolated communities. If you don't mind roughing it, inter-island boats are a wonderful way to travel and meet the locals. Make sure that you allow plenty of time for this type of voyaging. Trips may range from a few hours to a few weeks and are generally inexpensive. Check the itineraries carefully before setting sail.

Boat schedules are generally reliable but like so many things in the South Pacific, are subject to change. Departure and arrival times listed are only approximate. It is recommended that one purchases tickets at least half a day before the scheduled departure date. In the outer islands tickets can be bought on the dock. Keep in mind that meals are generally not served aboard.

Aranui
> Operator: Compagnie Polynesienne de Transport Maritime, (tel 42-62-40), BP 220, Papeete (Motu Uta), Tahiti
> Route: Rangiroa / Takapoto / Hiva Oa / Ua Pou / Ua Huka / Tahuata / Fatu Hiva / Nuku Hiva / Papeete
> Voyage length: about 16 days

The *Aranui*, French Polynesia's largest inter-island freighter, was completely revamped in late 1984 to accommodate 40 passengers for regularly scheduled service to the Marquesas Islands. Although other inter-island boats are available (as well as air transportation), this is the only vessel specifically fitted for passenger traffic.

The 264-foot *Aranui* was built in Hamburg, Germany in 1967 and has three classes of air-conditioned cabins as well as deck passage. First-class cabins include private shower and toilet facilities; 2nd

and 3rd class share communal showers. The only real difference between 2nd and 3rd class accommodation is a wash basin in 2nd class cabins. Accommodation has been refurbished for tourists and is large considering the boat was never designed as a passenger vessel. Bunks and three showers are provided for deck class. 'Public' rooms consist of a small lounge with a modest library and selection of games and a bar area on the upper deck.

The itinerary consists of three days in the Tuamotu Islands (Rangiroa, Takapoto and Arutua) and a 10-day swing through the Marquesas Islands (Nuku Hiva, Ua Pou, Hiva Oa, Tahuata and Fatu Hiva). Activities include fishing, a visit to a pearl 'farm', land tours and horse riding. The *Aranui* is still a working cargo boat and offers you an opportunity to visit the islands in comfort while seeing a slice of outer-island life. The ship has a French chef and the daily food includes plenty of fresh fish, lobster and shrimp. Meals are Tahitian, French and Chinese. The length of the voyage is 16 days. Prices vary between low and high season on all classes of cabins and, all of the 'A' cabins have individual prices. First class costs from US$2330 to US$3160, 2nd class from US$2144 to US$2360, 3rd class from US$1750 to US$1920 and deck class from US$1030 to US$1130. The price includes three meals a day. For more information in the US call (415) 5410674 in San Francisco.

Ara Nui II
> Operator: Sunny & Bene Richmond, (tel 3-76-17), BP 1291, Papeete (Fare Ute), Tahiti
> Route: Kaukura / Niau / Fakarava / Kauehi / Raraka / Katiu / Faaite / Makemo / Taenga / Nihiru / Anaa / Kaukura / Motutunga / Tuanake / Tepoto / Haraiki / Tahanea / Toau / Hikuera / Takume / Raroia / Fakahina / Puka Puka / Napuka
> Voyage length: three weeks

Manava I
> Operator: Heritiers Richmond, c/o Bene Richmond, (tel 3-76-17, 2-86-53), BP 1291, Papeete (Fare Ute), Tahiti
> Route: Arutua / Kaukura / Apataki / Rangiroa / Tikehau (eventually to Ahe / Manihi / Toau / Aratika / Fakarava / Raraka / Kauehi)
> Voyage length: one week

Manava II
> Operator: STMI (Societe des Transports Maritimes des Iles), Simeon & Pierrot Richmond, (tel 2-93-66 work, 2-74-40, 2-69-80 home), BP 1816, Papeete, Tahiti
> Route: Makatea / Rangiroa / Mataiva / Tikehau / Ahe / Manihi / Takapoto / Takaroa / Aratika / Kauehi / Fakarava / Toau / Arutua /

Apataki / Kaukura
Voyage length: 15 to 17 days

Matariva

Operator: Ste Matariva, Gerant E Degage, c/o Societe des Douanes (tel 2-01-20 poste 38)
Route: Arutua / Kaukura / Apataki / Toau / Fakarava / Faaite
Voyage length: one week
Note: this ship does not take tourist passengers

Rairoa Nui

Operator: Albert Tang, (tel 2-91-69), BP 1187, Papeete (Avenue du Regent Paraita), Tahiti
Route: Tikehau
Voyage length: four days, departs Monday, returns Thursday
Note: this ship does not take tourist passengers

Tereira

Operator: Karl M M Salmon & Lucien Utahia (tel 3-75-53)
Route: Kaukura / Arutua / Apataki (eventually Fakarava / Faaite)
Voyage length: one week

Taporo II

Operator: Compagnie de Navigation Inter Marquises, Jean Charles M Tekuataoa, (tel 3-86-82), BP 2516, Papeete (Rue Colette), Tahiti
Route: Hao / Amanu / Vairaatea / Tureia / Rikitea / Marutea Sud / Reao / Tatakoto / Vahitahi / Nukutavake / Hao / Amanu / Papeete (Tematangi / Anuanuraro / Hereheretue)
Voyage length: three or four weeks

Maire II

Operator: Companie de Navigation Inter-Marquesas, (tel 43-33-29), Rue Colette, BP 2516, Papeete, Tahiti
Route: Hao / Amanu / Vairaatea / Tureia / Mangareva / Marutu Sud / Reao / Pukurua / Takakoto / Vahitahi / Nukutavake / Tamatangui Fare: Deck passage – 1700 CFP, cabin – 9625 CFP (without food). Price with food is 1700 CFP per day (deck passage) and 2200 CFP per day (cabin). Every two months the *Maire II* goes only to the Gambier Islands.
Voyage length: takes 12 days

Ruahatu

Operator: c/o Mr Henri Grand, (tel 42-44-92), Motu Uta, Papeete, Tahiti
Route: Hao / Amanu / Takakoto / Pukarua / Reao / Marueta Sud / Mangareva / Tematangi / Vanavana / Tureia / Vahitahi / Vairaatea Fare: Deck passage is 6050 CFP
Note: This vessel operates very irregularly within the Gambier Islands Group. Not the kind of boat to take if you have a schedule to maintain.

Tamarii Tuamotu

Operator: Mme Kong Tao Vonken & Cie, (tel 2-95-07), BP 2606, Papeete (Avenue du Prince Hinoi), Tahiti
Route: Fangatau / Napuka / Tepoto / Fakahina / Puka Puka / Tatakoto / Vahitahi / Aki Aki / Tureia / Nukutavake / Vairaatea / Amanu / Pukarua / Reao / Papeete
Voyage length: one month

Taporo IV

Operator: Compagnie Francaise Maritime de Tahiti, (tel 42-63-93, 43-79-72), BP 368, Papeete (Fare Ute), Tahiti

itinerary	days	departs	arrives
Papeete/Huahine	M, W, F	5 pm	2 pm next day
Huahine/Raiatea	Tu, Th, Sa	4 am	6 am
Raiatea/Bora Bora	Tu, Sa	8 am	12 noon
alternate route			
Raiatea/Tahaa	Th, Sa	8 am	9 am
Tahaa/Bora Bora	Sa	10 am	12 noon
return	days	departs	arrives
Bora Bora/Raiatea	Tu	1 pm	4 pm
Bora Bora/Tahaa	Su	9 am	11 am
Tahaa/Raiatea	Th	10 am,	11 am
	Su	12 noon	1 am
Raiatea/Huahine	Tu	5 pm	7 pm
	Su	2 pm	4 pm
Huahine/Papeete	Tu	10.30 pm	5 pm
	Th	4 pm	3 am
	Su	5 pm	3.30 am

The *Taporo IV* can carry 160 passengers, 50 in cabins and 110 on deck. Voyage times are Papeete/Huahine 11 hours, Huahine/Raiatea two hours, Raiatea/Bora Bora two hours, Bora Bora/Tahaa two hours, Tahaa/Raiatea one hour. The fares in CFP are:

from/to	deck	cabin
Papeete/Huahine	1100	1540
Papeete/Raiatea	1300	1820
Papeete/Bora Bora	1500	2100
Papeete/Tahaa	1300	1820
Huahine/Raiatea	800	1200
Huahine/Tahaa	800	1200
Huahine/Bora Bora	750	1050
Raiatea/Tahaa	500	700
Raiatea/Bora Bora	800	1200
Bora Bora/Tahaa	800	1200

Temehani II

Operator: Societe de Navigation Temehani, (tel 42-98-83), BP 9015, Papeete (Motu Uta), Tahiti

Route: first voyage – Papeete / Huahine / Raiatea / Tahaa / Bora Bora / Raiatea / Huahine / Papeete

Voyage length: first voyage – departs Monday at about 5 pm, returns Thursday at 10.30 pm, second voyage – departs Thursday at about 5 pm, returns Friday at 9.45 pm

The *Temehani II* has passenger capacity of 120 including cabin berths for 34. Voyage times are Papeete/Huahine 11 hours, Huahine/Raiatea 2½ hours, Raiatea/Bora Bora 3½ hours, Bora Bora/Tahaa 2½ hours, Tahaa/Raiatea one hour. The fares in CFP are:

from/to	deck	cabin	luxury
Papeete/Huahine	1100	2200	2000
Papeete/Raiatea	1300	2600	2400
Papeete/Bora Bora	1500	2800	2600
Papeete/Tahaa	1300	2600	2400
Huahine/Raiatea	550	1100	
Huahine/Tahaa	550	1100	
Huahine/Bora Bora	750	1500	
Raiatea/Tahaa	330	660	
Raiatea/Bora Bora	550	1100	
Bora Bora/Tahaa	550	1100	

Tuhaa Pae II

Operator: Societe Anonyme d'Economie Mixte de Navigation des Australes, (tel 2-93-67), BP 1890, Papeete (Motu Uta), Tahiti

Route: Tubuai / Rurutu / Rimatara / Raivavae / Rapa

Voyage length: about 15 days

Vaihere

Operator: Sarl Sepna, c/o Bene Richmond, (tel 3-76-17, 2-86-53), BP 1291, Papeete (Fare Ute), Tahiti

Route: Anaa / Marokau / Hao / Takume / Raroia / Nihiru / Taenga / Makemo / Katiu / Fakarava / Faaite / Niau / Amanu / Raraka / Kauehi / Toau (eventually Tauere / Rekareka)

Voyage length: three or four weeks

Raromatai Ferry

Operator: BP 9012, Papeete, Tahiti (tel 43-90-42)

Route: First voyage – Papeete / Huahine / Raiatea / Tahaa / Bora Bora / Raiatea

Return voyage – Bora Bora / Tahaa / Raiatea / Huahine / Papeete.

Voyage length: Leaves Papeete Tuesday and Saturdays at 8.30 pm, arrives in Raiatea on Thursday at 3 pm.

Return voyage: Leaves Bora Bora on Sundays at noon and arrives on Thursdays or Sundays.

Fare: A deluxe cabin with three bunks is 8000 CFP per night, 'tourist' cabin with four bunks is 5500 CFP per night, deck passage is 3600 CFP (entire trip) and inter-island (between two islands) fare is 1200 CFP. The cost of a vehicle is 6600 CFP for the entire journey and 3300 CFP for inter-island travel.

Note: The *Raromatai Ferry* transports both passengers and vehicles within the Society Islands. For those with sail/drive plans this would be the ferry to take.

Taporo I

Operator: Societe Taporo Teaotea, (tel 66-32-30, 66-30-03), BP 68, Uturoa, Raiatea

Route: Raiatea / Maupiti / Raiatea

Voyage length: one day departs Raiatea Tuesdays at midnight and arrives 6 am Wednesday at Maupiti. Leaves Wednesday afternoon at 3 pm and arrives Raiatea at 9 pm same evening.

Fare: The cost on deck is 850 CFP and 1450 CFP bunk

Note: The *Taporo I* sails every three months from Raiatea/Scilly/Bellinghausen/Mopelia/Raiatea. The cost of deck passage or bunk is 8000 CFP and the voyage takes six days.

Saint Corentin

Operator: Lucien Utahia, (tel 2-61-70, 3-75-86), Immeuble Tracqui et Fils (1er etage), Rue Leboucher, Papeete, Tahiti

Route: Papeete / Rangiroa / Papeete

Voyage length: four days

Cruises

For those who like the idea of exploring the islands by sea, and don't want to rough it, there are two passenger vessels that ply French Polynesian waters – the 152-foot *Majestic Explorer* operated by Exploration Cruises and the 440-foot motor sailor *Wind Song* managed by Windstar Sail Cruises.

Exploration Cruises, owned by the Anheiser-Busch Company, operates in the continental United States, Mexico and the Caribbean. The year-round Society Island cruises seem to be very popular with lower to mid-budget package travellers. I have never taken this cruise but have heard mixed reviews. An elderly French couple said they thought the food was mediocre, the water on board the vessel was poor, and the ship rolled badly in foul weather. On the other hand, I spoke to Americans who took the cruise and said they were perfectly satisfied with the food and the service.

Cruising the islands has a distinct advantage for the traveller who wants their needs taken care of and is willing to deal with a 'structured' tour package. The disadvantage is that limited time is spent on the islands – obviously there is no opportunity to linger on the beach with a new found friend when the boat is ready to leave.

The standard seven-day Exploration Cruise debarks from Tahiti and visits Raiatea, Bora Bora, Tahaa, Huahine, Moorea and returns to Tahiti. There are variations on this seven-day cruise which are nine and 13-day trips that include longer land tours on Papeete and Moorea. There are also two shorter (three and four day) versions of the trip. The four-day version entails cruising to Bora Bora from Tahiti (via Moorea, Huahine, Raiatea, Tahaa) and then flying back to Tahiti. The three-day version begins with a flight to Bora Bora and then returns to Tahiti via Tahaa, Raiatea and Moorea. The main difference between the two short cruises is that the four-day cruise includes a visit to Huahine and a land tour of Moorea.

The land excursions entail visits to marae, dance shows, traditional *tamara'a* (feasts), circle-island tours, a trip up the Faaroa River in Raiatea and other sightseeing. Except for the nine and 13-day trips, no more than a single day is spent on any one island. There are four classes of cabins and the fare includes three meals a day. Food is reportedly very good.

Cost for the seven-day cruise ranges from US$1999 for 'B' class stateroom and goes up the ladder to US$2139 for 'A', US$2385 for 'AA' and US$2525 for 'deluxe'. Depending on the time of the year and availability of promotional fares Exploration Cruises may have special air/sea packages which includes reduced rate or even free air fare from the US for clients that purchase the seven, nine or 13-day packages.

The US-built and registered 44-cabin ship (capacity 88) was constructed in 1982 and is operated by Explorer Cruises of Seattle, Washington. For further information (tel 1-(800) 426-0600) in the United States.

The 150-passenger *Windsong* is a four masted, luxury motor sailer catering to an upscale crowd of 30 to 40 people. Though reminiscent of an old-fashioned yacht there is nothing anachronistic about this boat. Its sails are operated by computer (thus eliminating the need for a crew) and high-tech gadgets such as VCRs and colour TVs are found in every room. The 75-cabin *Windsong* has the advantage of having a shallow draft which means it can enter small coves and secluded beaches. Inside the vessel (built in France) is exquisitely detailed and crafted, using hard woods such as teak. It's a class act, but then, you are paying for it.

Unlike the *Majestic Explorer*, the *Windsong* provides a comprehensive recreation programme for its well heeled passengers. Sports equipment and instruction is available for water-skiing using zodiac inflatable motor launches, and there is windsurfing, sailing, deep-sea fishing, scuba diving and snorkelling. A Tahitian dive master is on board to provide scuba assistance, but passengers must be certified divers to use the diving gear.

Other on-board recreational facilities include a gymnasium with five exercise machines, a sauna and a masseuse, an outdoor pool with piano bar, a casino with about 10 slot machines and two black jack tables, skylighted disco and a video cassette and book library.

All 75 cabins are basically the same with only a slight difference in bed configuration. Most cabins have either two twins or a queen-sized bed, and 20 rooms provide a third bed. Rooms are all outside cabins, each with a colour TV, VCR, three channel radio, minibar and refrigerator, safe, pull-out table, international direct dial telephone and sitting area. A far cry from the rusty bucket copra boats that were the only mode of transportation in the old days.

The seven-day Tahiti cruise sails from

Papeete after midnight and calls in Huahine at 2 pm the next day. The ship sets sail again at 5 am the next morning. This schedule is repeated at each of the next stops in Tahaa and Bora Bora, arriving at noon. When sailing conditions permit, the fourth day is spent on Maupiti or Tupai from 10 am to 5 pm. On other occasions the ship either remains at Bora Bora for that extra day or proceeds to Raiatea and Moorea one day ahead of schedule. The price for the seven-day cruise is US$2635 per person, double, including use of all sports equipment.

Beginning service in October 1988, the *Sea Venture*, a 425-foot 'deluxe' cruise vessel will be based in Tahiti and will make seven-day tours to the Society Islands. The itinerary will include Bora Bora, Raiatea, Tahaa, Huahine and Moorea. The vessel will be the lap of luxury, equipped with 180 state rooms (all with outside suites) and will have colour TV, phone, bar, sofa and large viewing windows instead of portholes.

Copra Boats

To book passage on a copra boat, walk down to where they are moored (past the naval yard in Fare Ute in Papeete) and see what boats are in port. You can obtain a list of all the copra boats and their destinations at the government tourist office. Chat with the skippers on the dock, double-check the current prices and determine where they are going and when they are departing. Often you have the options of either bringing your own food for the journey or eating the ship's fare; the difference in price can be substantial. Sometimes only deck passage is available, which means just that – sleeping, eating and drinking on deck with other islanders who have chosen the economy route. Keep in mind that a round-trip voyage may last a month or more. Also, jumping ship on an island that has no air service may turn out to be a long-term commitment – at least until another ship comes along.

A sea cruise on a copra boat can be appealing as long as things like rain, sea sickness, diesel fumes, engine noise,

claustrophobia and huge cockroaches do not get on your nerves. On the other hand, the camaraderie, adventure, salt air, drifting, dreaming, guitar playing and drinking Hinano beer by moonlight are hard to beat.

Charter Boats

Rentals Revatua Charter Launch (tel 43-28-21, 48-04-39) has tours to Tetiaroa, Moorea, Papeete Harbour and deep-sea fishing expeditions. Those interested in seeing the outer islands via motor launch might be interested in the Motor Yacht Manavaroa which begins its itinerary in Raiatea then visits Huahine, Tahaa and Bora Bora. Call 66-20-62 for details and prices.

For people with more modest needs Tac Boat has rentals of 10 to 14-foot dingys and outrigger canoes in Tahiti. They also have accessories such as fishing rods, underwater cameras, fins and mask, ice boxes, etc. Daily rental prices range from 5000 CFP to 8000 CFP – call 42-28-65 for information. The office is next to the Maeva Beach Hotel.

ROAD

Except for the island of Tahiti, most areas do not have much paved highway. However, the roads that do exist are modern and well maintained. On all the islands there is a marvellous bus system consisting of owner-operators driving jitney-like vehicles known as 'le truck' – a triumph of small-scale, entrepreneurial capitalism. Most French Polynesians cannot afford cars or motorcycles so these buses transport the majority of the population, especially on Tahiti where commuting to work in Papeete from the 'district' has become a way of life.

On the outer islands, where commuting is not so big a factor and the population density is much smaller, buses are less frequent. On these islands (such as Bora Bora, Huahine or Moorea) it definitely behooves the visitor to rent a car, motorcycle or bicycle for the day's sightseeing rather than to depend on public transportation. Taxis can be found everywhere but tend to be expensive.

The Society Islands

Introduction

The Society Islands are divided into two groups: to the east are the Windward Islands (Isles du Vent), which include Tahiti and Moorea; and to the west, the Leeward Islands (Isles sous le Vent) which comprise Raiatea, Tahaa, Huahine, Bora Bora and Maupiti.

The Society Islands were given their name by Captain James Cook, but the name originally referred only to the Leeward group. The English navigator Captain Samuel Wallis had already named Tahiti 'King George III's Island' and Moorea 'Duke of York's Island,' and Cook respected his predecessor's wishes. Later, however, both Tahiti and Moorea were included in references to the Society Islands.

But where did the name 'Society' originate? In Cook's own words, published in 1773, 'To these six islands (Raiatea, Tahaa, Huahine, Borabora, Tupai and Maupiti), as they lie contiguous to each other, I gave the names of Society Islands.' Thus the common notion that the name referred to the Royal Society or the Royal Geographical Society is false.

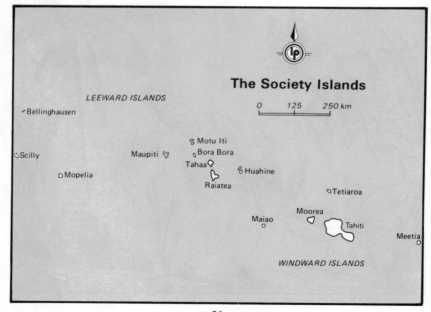

The Society Islands

LEEWARD ISLANDS

0   125   250 km

Bellinghausen

Scilly

Mopelia

Maupiti

Motu Iti
Bora Bora
Tahaa
Huahine
Raiatea

Tetiaroa

Maiao

Moorea
Tahiti

Meetia

WINDWARD ISLANDS

Tahiti

Tahiti is the largest island in French Polynesia, with an area of 1041 square km (402 square miles). Its shape can best be visualised as a figure eight on its side. The larger section of the island (Tahiti Nui) is connected to the smaller section (Tahiti Iti) by the narrow Isthmus of Taravao. The island's rugged terrain, crossed by numerous rivers and deep valleys, is marked by precipitous green peaks. The highest points are Mt Orohena at 2236 metres (7339 feet) and Mt Aorai at 2068 metres (6786 feet), both of which are eternally shrouded in wispy clouds. Because of Tahiti's mountainous interior, the vast majority of the population lives on the coastal fringes. Politically, Tahiti is divided into 20 districts, most of which were formal tribal domains.

Paul Gauguin & Tahiti

The reason why I am leaving is that I wish to live in peace and to avoid being influenced by our civilisation. I only desire to create simple art. In order to achieve this, it is necessary for me to steep myself in virgin nature, to see no one but savages, to share their life and have as my sole occupation to render, just as children would do, the images of my own brain, using exclusively the means offered by primitive art, which are the only true and valid ones.

When Paul Gauguin uttered these words five weeks before his departure from France, he firmly believed that Tahiti was still an unspoiled paradise. On April Fool's Day in 1891, he departed from Europe and 69 days later arrived in Papeete. He left behind his Danish wife, Mette, and their five children in hopes that he would remain in Tahiti long enough to paint a sufficient amount of pictures for an exhibition that would establish his name.

Thanks to a letter of introduction to the local colonial administration, Gauguin was well received in Tahiti. He was wined and dined, and soon painted his first portrait in Tahiti for a fat commission. Unfortunately,

the painting was unflatteringly accurate and it was his last commission for quite a while. At this point Gauguin decided it would be better to spend his time with the natives, and he moved into a Tahitian-style hut far from Papeete. Although disappointed at the little that remained of the native art and culture he had journeyed so far to see, Gauguin was happy to partake in village life. 'Koke', as he was known to the villagers, soon took a 13-year-old wife, Teha'amana, and spent his happiest year in Tahiti with her. The artist worked feverishly and by 1893 sailed back to France with 66 paintings and a dozen wooden sculptures for his planned exhibition. Unfortunately, nobody seemed to recognise Gauguin's genius, and his exhibition failed. To add to his troubles, Mette refused to see him again, he was assaulted and severely injured by a gang of sailors, and he contracted syphilis from a Paris dance hall prostitute. He departed for Tahiti once more and on arrival sought his Tahitian wife. She would have nothing to do with him, so he found another young girl. Despite poverty and constant suffering from the injury he had received from the sailors, Gauguin finished his masterpiece, *Where do we come from? What are we? Where are we going?*. He then swallowed an enormous dose of arsenic but vomited the poison and slowly recovered. His taste for life returned and he got a job with the public works department copying building plans, fathered a child, paid off his debts and devoted much time to writing anti-government editorials in local publications.

In 1901 Gauguin received an unexpected offer from a Paris art dealer who agreed to pay him a salary for every picture he produced. With his chronic money problems out of the way, Gauguin, still in search of paradise, decided to move to the isolated Marquesan Island of Hiva Oa. Again he was disappointed with what he saw, and wrote:

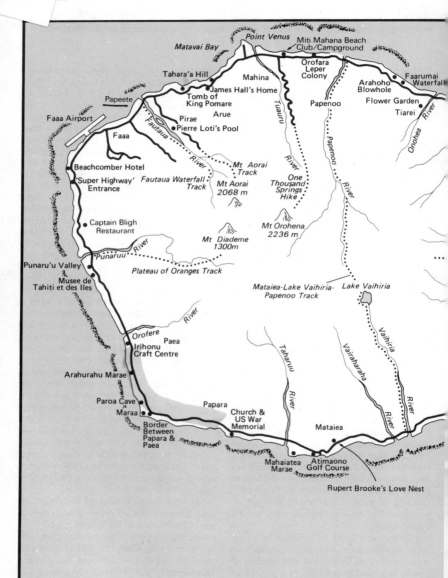

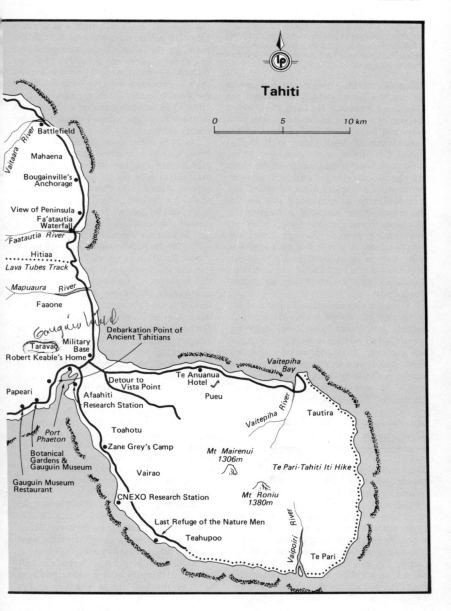

Tahiti

0   5   10 km

Vaitaara River

Battlefield

Mahaena

Bougainville's
Anchorage

View of Peninsula
Fa'atautia
Waterfall
Faatautia River

Hitiaa
Lava Tubes Track

Mapuaura River

Faaone

Gauguin Well

Debarkation Point of
Ancient Tahitians

Taravao Military
Base
Robert Keable's Home

Papeari

Detour to
Vista Point
Afaahiti
Research Station

Te Anuanua
Hotel

Pueu

Vaitepiha
Bay

Vaitepiha River

Tautira

Toahotu

Zane Grey's Camp

Mt Mairenui
1306m

Te Pari-Tahiti Iti Hike

Port
Phaeton

Botanical
Gardens &
Gauguin Museum

Vairao

Mt Roniu
1380m

Gauguin Museum
Restaurant

CNEXO Research Station

Vaipoiri River

Last Refuge of the Nature Men

Teahupoo

Te Pari

Even if one is willing to pay high prices, it is no longer possible to find any of those splendid objects of bone, turtle, shell or ironwood that the natives made in olden times. The gendarmes have stolen them all and sold them to collectors.

Gauguin soon built himself the finest home in the Marquesas, which he dubbed the 'House of Pleasure'. He lived there with a 14-year-old vahine, Marie-Rose, who until then had been a resident of the Catholic mission school. With plenty of money to spend, Gauguin became well known for his wild parties and quickly incurred the wrath of the local clergy and the police. Meanwhile, his health further declined and his suffering necessitated the use of morphine. One morning a Marquesan neighbour found the artist lying on his bed with one leg hung over the edge. The visitor was not absolutely sure that his friend was still alive so he resorted to a Marquesan tradition – a bite on the head – to determine Gauguin's state. He then sang an ancient death chant.

Gauguin's legacy to modern art lies not in having introduced exotic subjects but, according to Bengt Danielsson, in having 'destroyed all existing conventions, dogmas, and academic taboos and rules that up to this time, had confined European artists to a narrow pedantic realism'. In Gauguin's own words, he provided future generations of artists with 'the right to dare anything'.

Papeete

The translation of Papeete is 'water (from a) basket', which most likely means that it was a place where Tahitians came to fetch water. At the time of Cook and Wallis it was a marshland with a few scattered residents and didn't attract too much attention until 1818 when Reverend Crook of the London Missionary Society settled there with his family. Papeete began to grow in earnest when Queen Pomare made it her capital in the 1820s and sailing ships began to utilise the protected harbour, which was a much safer anchorage than Matavai Bay to the north. By the 1830s it became a regular port of call for whalers, and a number of stores, billiard halls and makeshift bars appeared on the waterfront to handle the business. When the French made Tahiti a protectorate in 1842-43 the military came on the scene, and in their footsteps came French Catholic priests and nuns.

In 1884 a fire destroyed almost half of Papeete, which resulted in an ordinance prohibiting the use of native building materials. Not much of consequence happened until 1906 when huge waves, the result of a cyclone, wiped out a number of homes and businesses. In 1914 two German men-of-war bombarded Papeete, sinking the only French naval vessel in the harbour.

Today the population of greater Papeete is over 80,000. It is French Polynesia's only real city and continues to be a major South Pacific port of call for freighters, ocean liners and yachts. Business and government revolve around the town. It is the site of the High Commissioner's residence, the Territorial Assembly, the Post Office, the Tourist Bureau, the banks, the travel agencies, movie houses, two hospitals, supermarkets, shops, hotels, nightclubs and restaurants.

Since the early 1960s Papeete has undergone a construction boom necessary to support its rising population (about 20,000 immigrants from France and 15,000 from the outer islands of French Polynesia) and modernisation. Although growth was inevitable, much of it can be attributed to the tourism infrastructure and France's nuclear testing programme which resulted in an increased population growth.

Unfortunately, the growth has been at the expense of some of Papeete's beauty. Despite new apartments and offices, the town still has the provincial charm of a French colonial capital – whitewashed houses, buildings of painted wood with large verandahs and corrugated tin roofs, narrow streets, parks, an outdoor market, street vendors and a profusion of odours ranging from pungent copra to the aroma of frying steaks.

Papeete is designed for walking. The sidewalks and avenues are lined with vendors selling shell necklaces, straw hats, sandwiches, sweet fried breads, pastries and candy. The aisles of the Chinese shops are crammed with cookware, rolls of brightly coloured cloth, canned goods from New Zealand and the United States, mosquito coils and imports of every variety. You get the feeling that if you poke around long enough, you might discover a preserved 1000-year-old duck egg.

The best time to explore the narrow streets and browse through the stores is in the cool of the morning. Otherwise, fumes from automobiles and heat from the asphalt can be oppressive. A stroll through Papeete must be done in a leisurely manner and taken with several rest breaks at the many outdoor cafes and snack bars. There you can sit at tables shielded by canopies, sip the local Hinano beer, or eat ice cream and watch the procession of tourists and locals go by. On Sundays after 10 am activities cease and Papeete becomes a sleepy and provincial town.

Information

For information contact the Fare Manihini tourist office on Boulevard Pomare (located on the waterfront). There is also an information office at Faaa Airport but it tends to be manned by taxi drivers waiting for fares, rather than information officers. Best bet is the Fare Manihini office, which has excellent services. Airline offices, banks, the post office and other resources are all centrally located in Papeete, either on Boulevard Pomare or in the Vaima Center.

Foreign Consulates The addresses of the foreign consulates in Papeete are listed in the Facts for the Visitor chapter.

Airlines The addresses of airlines that operate in and out of Papeete are:

Air New Zealand
  Vaima Center, Boulevard Pomare (tel 43-01-70)
Air Tahiti
  Boulevard Pomare (tel 42-24-44)
Air Moorea
  Faaa Airport (tel 42-48-34, 42-44-29)
Qantas
  Shop 54, Vaima Center, Boulevard Pomare (tel 43-06-65, 43-90-90 at the airport)
UTA
  Boulevard Pomare (near Pitate Club) (tel 43-63-33, 42-22-22)
Air France
  Boulevard Pomare (c/o Air Tahiti) (tel 42-44-44, 43-39-39)
Continental Airlines
  Boulevard Pomare (c/o Air Tahiti) (tel 42-24-44, 43-39-39)
Hawaiian Airlines
  (tel 42-44-38)
Lan Chile
  (tel 42-64-55, 42-64-57 at the airport)
Tahiti Conquest Airlines (charter carrier)
  Faaa Airport (tel 43-84-25)

Marche Papeete

The centre of Papeete, the old Marche Papeete (municipal market), covers one square city block and is between Rue 22 September and Rue Francois Cardella. Since July 1986, the 127-year-old market has been undergoing a metamorphosis that has changed it from a dark, crowded, seedy 'casbah' to a modern, well lit, clean place of business. To date, half the old marketplace (which was a charming labyrinth of cramped, shabby stalls flavoured by accumulated tropical filth) has been torn down. The old market, which was one of the last true South Pacific institutions left in Papeete has been replaced by an airy, sunshine filled, double-decked venue that local journalist Al Prince describes as 'something out of the 19th century gaslight era in Paris or the French Quarter of New Orleans'.

The new market has been completely reorganised from the inside out and is much larger than its predecessor. Whereas in the old days fruit, flowers, watermelons and other produce would creep out of the market on major shopping days (like Sunday mornings) all selling now goes on within the market's walls. This is possible because of

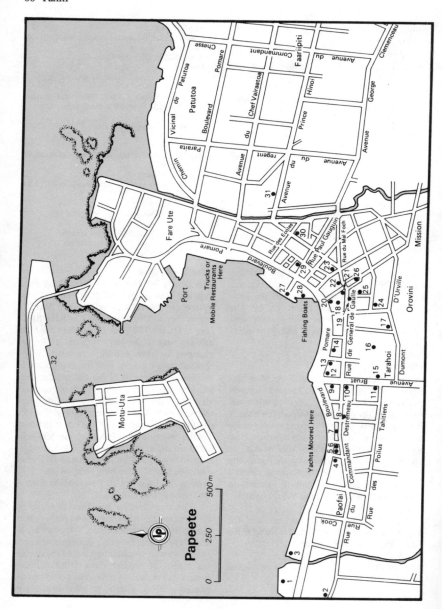

1	Olympic Swimming Pool
2	Stadium
3	Cultural Center & Theatre
4	Foyer de Jeunes Filles de Paofai (Girls Youth Hostel)
5	Church
6	Tahiti Pearl Center & Museum
7	Pizzeria
8	Hospital
9	Hachette Pacifique (Bookstore)
10	Immigration Office
11	Police
12	UTA/Air Polynesia Office
13	Bougainville Park
14	Post Office
15	High Commissioner's Office
16	Territorial Assembly
17	Chamber of Commerce
18	Vaima Center
19	Bank
20	Magazine & Newspaper Kiosk
21	Qantas/Air New Zealand (Vaima Center)
22	Government Offices
23	Market & Bus Stand
24	Clinic Cardella
25	Le Pescadou Restaurant
26	Cathedral
27	Customs, Immigration & Yachts
28	Tourist Office
29	Polyself Cafeteria
30	Town Hall
31	Baie D'Along Restaurant
32	Inter-Island Vessels

and find bananas, pineapples, starfruit, coconuts, oranges, papaya, limes, mangoes, avocados, cassava root, lettuce, tomatoes, onions, carrots, beans, potatoes, cabbage and other items. No doubt there will still be the wary housewives eyeing, squeezing, touching and scrutinising the merchandise.

The upstairs section also offers an ideal place to take market photos without intruding on anyone's territory. In the old days it was very difficult to take shots of this fascinating institution because it was too dark and too jammed. This underlines the most striking improvement in the new regime – the space that now exists both for the consumer and the seller.

The second half of the new market (adjacent to the already completed section) is scheduled for completion in mid 1988. It will also have a mezzanine, and the ground floor will be slightly larger than the completed portion. When completed the new Papeete market will be 3164 square metres, about a third bigger than its predecessor.

The best time to visit Marche Papeete is still early Sunday morning when out-of-towners come to sell their goods, shop and attend church in Papeete. Don't be afraid to sample the exotic-looking fruits, vegetables and fish. The results will be satisfying.

New Bus Stand

Gone from the old market's perimeter is the makeshift bus terminal where Tahiti's entire public transportation system was centred. Amid the cacophonous streets, rumbling diesel powered buses (known as 'le truck') blaring Tahitian music used to line up behind one another like cars on a freight train and inch their way up the road. Though the fume-filled, packed streets could be described as 'colourful', the road and sidewalks in the market area were terribly congested. In its wisdom, the Territorial government has decided to build terminal areas on the outskirts of town. Where this will be (and when it will be built) was not known at the time of writing, but in the meantime the 'terminal' is still in the heart of town, within

the two-tiered construction. The ground floor is reserved for flowers, taro, rootstalks and daily catches of fresh seafood which includes bonito, mahimahi, albacore, lobster, shrimp, clams and other items. These are sold chiefly by Polynesians – the unwritten law here maintains that Tahitians may sell fish, taro, yams and other Polynesian foods; the Chinese sell vegetables; while Europeans and Chinese are the bakers and butchers. Downstairs, on the sidewalk, fruit and vegetables are displayed in the same traditional manner although the sur-roundings are aesthetically more sterile (but undoubtedly leaner). Although the environs are new one can still stroll through the isles several blocks of the market. Visitors should have no problem finding their way around.

Waterfront

Several blocks from the market is the waterfront, known as the quay. Formerly an array of clapboard warehouses and shacks, the area is now dominated by the Boulevard Pomare. On one side of the tree-lined avenue is a row of yachts several blocks long (mostly from the US), beached racing canoes, fishing boats and ferries which deliver goods daily to nearby Moorea. On the other side of the road are business offices, storefronts, hotels, cafes, nightclubs, bars and the new Vaima Center, a luxury residence and shopping centre. Walking along the quay you can see the yachts, watch the fishermen come in with their catch, and in the evening buy a meal from the many food vendors who gather in a huge parking area adjacent to the waterfront.

When the wind blows from the direction of the docks, Papeete's air is filled with the strong aroma of copra (dried coconut meat), the main export of the islands. To find the source of the smell, take a walk past the naval yard to Fare Ute (see map) where the copra boats are moored and where there is a coconut-oil processing plant. Here the vessels unload the crop they have picked up from the outer islands and exchange it for store-bought commodities. Watching the pallets containing beer, rice, drums of kerosene, sacks of flour, cases of canned butter and jugs of wine being loaded on the rusty steamers gives you a feeling of the old days when all travel and trade were done by these boats. Try a sandwich and a bottle of Hinano at the nearby cafe where the stevedores and crew members congregate.

Continuing on past Fare Ute you will cross a bridge to Motu-Uta, which was once an island in Papeete Harbor. Now, joined by two bridges, this area also has mooring spots for copra boats as well as marine servicing and dry dock facilities. This enclosing promontory serves to protect Papeete Harbor during inclement weather.

Territorial Assembly

Constructed in the late 1960s as the chamber of the democratically elected representatives of the French Polynesian government, this modern building is built directly over the source of the Papeete River. (The river has since been diverted to nearby Bougainville Park). In this same area Queen Pomare had her home and eventually a Royal Palace, which in typical governmental fashion was not completed until after her death. Nearby was an exclusive clubhouse for high-ranking military officers and civil servants where Gauguin (while he was still accepted) used to drink absinthe. The other important building occupying these grounds is the High Commissioner's residence.

Pouvanaa a Oopa Statue

Standing directly in front of the Territorial Assembly on Rue du General de Gaulle is a monument depicting Pouvanaa a Oopa, considered the greatest contemporary Tahitian leader. A decorated WW I hero and a courageous Tahitian nationalist, Pouvanaa served as a Deputy in Paris for the Tahitian Territorial Assembly. He was later jailed on what many believe were trumped up charges by the metropolitan French government and exiled from his beloved Tahiti from 1958 to 1970. After his release (at age 72!) he served as a senator in the Territorial Assembly until his death in 1978.

Bougainville Park

Originally named Albert Park after the Belgian king and WW I hero, this park's name was later changed to honour the French explorer. On sunny days people are usually occupying its concrete benches or enjoying the shade of its huge banyan trees. Of the two cannons prominently displayed, the one nearest the post office is off the *Seeadler*, the vessel skippered by the notorious WW I sea raider, Count von Luckner, whose boat ran aground on Mopelia atoll in the Leeward Islands. The other belonged to the *Zelee*, the French navy boat sunk during the German raid on Papeete in 1914.

Melville's Calabooza Beretani

In 1842 this was the site of Melville's celebrated jail, where he gathered the grist for his second book, *Omoo*, and accurately described life during the early French colonial period.

Hats & Church

One traveller wrote to Lonely Planet and suggested that an entertaining way to spend part of Sunday is to go to church, listen to the hymns and study the ladies' hats.

PLACES TO STAY

Hotel reservations are not mandatory but can be made through your travel agent. Those who have booked 'packages' at the more expensive hotels will always get a cheaper rate than those who walk in and get the 'rack rate'. The prices listed are always the 'rack' or walk-in rate. Most prices are listed in French Pacific Francs (CFP) but some are listed in US dollars. Note that the less expensive hotels do not have telex or phone bookings from the US or other overseas countries but bookings can be made by writing directly to the hotel. In most cases there are vacancies year round with the exception of July. During the Bastille Day celebrations (starting the end of June and lasting until August), it is virtually impossible to find a hotel room in Papeete. If you want to avoid crowds, this is not the time to come to Tahiti. Note that *all* hotels except OTAC (the youth hostel) charge the seven per cent tourist tax in addition to the tariff.

I have tried to list all of Tahiti's hotels and pensions in this section. Just because they appear in the book, it doesn't mean they are necessarily good places to stay. Those that I like or those recommended to me are listed with an asterisk (*) and are commented upon.

Places to Stay – bottom end

Just a 10-minute walk from Papeete, the *Mahina Tea* (tel 42-00-97) is your basic family-run, pension-style lodging. There are no frills or luxury about this place, but it is clean, although reports are that local roosters can be aggravatingly noisy. It has 14 rooms with double beds, six 'studios' with bathroom and kitchen, hot water from 6 to 11 pm. Rates are 3000 CFP to 3300 CFP for a single or double depending on the size of room. Rates drop 500 CFP if the guest stays more than two nights. Studios available for monthly rent (60,000 CFP) only. Write to Vallon de Sainte-Amelie, PO Box 17, Papeete.

One of the more reasonable places to stay in Tahiti (though not quite the cheapest) is the *OTAC* (Territorial Hostel Center), (tel 42-68-02). It offers clean, dormitory-style accommodation. There are 18 rooms with three beds in each and three rooms with two beds. The cost is 2200 CFP for the first night, 1600 CFP for each additional night. The centre does not have kitchen facilities but there is a canteen which serves inexpensive meals. The doors are locked at midnight. For reservations write to M Jeffrey Salmon, Office Territorial d'Action Culturel, PO Box 1709, Papeete. You must have a student ID or youth hostel card to stay here. Large groups and organisations should make previous reservations – reservations are not necessary for individuals who are dealt with on a first-come first-serve basis. Office hours are 8 am to 6 pm, Monday to Saturday and 10 am to 12 noon on Sundays.

*Shogun** (tel 43-13-93 daytime, 48-08-75 evenings), located 'conveniently' in downtown Papeete on 10 Rue du Commandant Destremeau, above 'Keiko Boutique'. The 11-unit building has a variety of air-conditioned rooms that will fit the low end pocket book. The daily tariffs are: room with a double bed (known as the 'suite') 5000 CFP for a single and 6000 CFP for double occupancy, apartment with dining and cooking nook is 8500 CFP, and the bargain special is a bed in their 12-cot 'Japanese Inn' for 1900 CFP per night.

Unlike most bottom-end places, Shogun accepts all major plastic (ie VISA, Diners, Mastercard, etc). Reports on Shogun have been satisfactory. There are two apartments with one room containing a double and a single bed, plus cooking facilities, dining area with individual bathroom and toilet.

Hiti Mahana Beach Club* (tel 48-16-13), BP 11580, Mahina, Tahiti. The Papeete area has needed a quality, low budget dorm/camping area for years and Hiti Mahana has become the model in the local tourism industry for this niche. Operated by Coco and Pat Pautu, (he's a Tahitian and she's an American), the beach club is a combination campground and dorm on nine acres adjacent to a black sand beach in the Mahina district. It is highly recommended – the owners appear to be earnest in providing good service and an amiable environment. The 'dorm' is actually a two-story, century-old mansion (once owned by an American) which has both communal and private rooms with bath, as well as cooking facilities, refrigerator, dining room, lounge, and plenty of breathing space. Campers have four acres of lush garden at their disposal as well as amenities such as bath, refrigerator, clothes line, bicycle, reading room and BBQ.

The 'Club' is very accessible by le truck yet far enough from town that one is away from urban blight. The Club also offers good swimming, picnicing, snorkelling, windsurfing and excursions. Banks, grocery stores, inexpensive restaurants and fresh produce can be purchased close by. Reasonably priced sandwiches and hamburgers are available on the premises.

The cost of camping is 700 CFP per person per day. If you lack camping equipment, the Club will rent you all the essentials. Tents are 200 CFP to 400 CFP per day depending on size, and mattress, sheet and pillow are 400 CFP to 800 CFP per day depending on single or double. Dorm accommodation at the White House is 1000 CFP per person per night. Private room with bath is 2000/3000 CFP for single/double, plus daily charges of 300 CFP for linen and 100 CFP for towel.

To get to Hiti Mahana Beach Club from the airport look out for Coco at the visitors information desk. If he's not there take a truck from the airport to the market and

transfer to any Mahina-bound truck. Pay the driver ahead of time (100 CFP to 130 CFP) and tell him to let you off at Hiti Mahana. Though it's a few km off the main road (past the Point Venus turn-off), the driver will take you directly there.

Pensions Staying with families can be an inexpensive and often enriching alternative to hotels. Sometimes it affords you a chance to see a side of Tahiti you would otherwise never experience. Note that the rates and services listed are more subject to change than other types of accommodation. The families marked with an asterisk (*) have been highly recommended.

Chez Mirna, (tel 42-64-11), BP 790, Papeete is a few hundred metres from the Matavai Hotel on the fringes of Papeete in the Tipaerui quarter. They have two rooms with one double bed in each, and a communal bathroom, toilet and shower. The cost is 3500 CFP per day for a single and 4500 CFP for a double (breakfast included).

Chez Michel et Armelle (tel 58-39-18) at PK 15 in the Punaauia district, is on the ocean side just past 'Tahiti Village'. They provide one room with a double bed and private bathroom. Amenities include outrigger canoe, windsurfing, and snorkelling equipment. Rates (with breakfast) are 4000 CFP per day for one person and 5000 CFP for two people. Children aged five to 12 get a 50% discount. The chalet costs 5000 CFP per day for one or two persons, 1000 CFP per extra bed.

Chez Evy, (tel 57-10-58, 57-10-42 office), BP 1453, Papeete, is in the Paea district, 24 km from Papeete, on the seaside. Evy has a Japanese-style bungalow with one double bed, kitchen, private bath (with hot water), television and air-conditioning. Rates are 4000/5000 CFP single/double.

Chez Vaa*, (tel 42-94-32), BP 828, Papeete, is in Punaauia, at PK 8 on the mountain side in the Nina Peata neighbourhood. Her place – one room with double bed, communal bath (hot water) and pool – has been described as 'very clean' and I am

Top: Re-enactment of the crowning of a prince during Tiurai celebrations (RK)
Left: Basket-weaving contest during Tiurai (RK)
Right: Tahitian warrior at Tiurai celebrations (RK)

Top: Le truck at depot in Papeete (RK)
Bottom: Yachts at the quay, Papeete (RK)

told she is a very nice person. The daily rates are 4000/4500 CFP for a single/double which includes breakfast.

Chez Coco*, (tel 42-83-60), BP 8039, Puurai, Faaa, Tahiti is also recommended. Next to the youth hostel and Hiti Mahana, it is probably the cheapest place to stay in the Papeete area and I've never heard a complaint against the operation. Coco Dexter has two bedrooms, each with single beds, and four additional mattresses which can be utilised in the house. There are communal bathroom facilities and a swimming pool. Rates are 1500 CFP per day single and 3000 CFP double. Excursions are also available on request.

Denise & Fariua, (tel 43-54-90), BP 21683, opened on 1 May 1987 and is on Avenue du Prince Hinoi, in the Tabanou quarter, near to the 'Oceanie Occasons' car rental agency. Accommodation is dormitory-style with 16 beds, two communal bathrooms and cooking facilities. There is also one room with a double bed. The dormitory costs 1000 CFP per day and the room is 3000 CFP for a single or double. There is free transport from the airport except on Sunday afternoons.

The same family owns a similar low budget resort in Bora Bora, which has had good reviews. However, reports on the Papeete facility have been mixed. Some travellers have reported bickering over prices and arguments between the owners and guests. On the other hand, there have been no negative comments about the Bora Bora facility which is operated by an employee rather than a family member.

Chez Bennett*, (tel 48-20-65), BP 4279, Papeete is in the district of Arue at PK 8, not far from town. They have one bungalow built on the mountain side having one room with two single beds and one double bed, kitchenette, private bath (hot water), and washing machine. They will also serve family-style meals on request. Free activities include windsurfing, hiking and access to the Tahara'a Hotel beach. This pension is recommended as a friendly place with interesting excursions and activities. The rates are per person per day 3000 CFP single, 2500 CFP double, or 2000 CFP triple.

Chez Christine, (tel 42-54-49), BP 21279, Papeete in the Papeete suburb of Punaauia (at 12.6 PK on the mountain side of the road) provides a room with two beds and private bath. Extra beds are available, linen is provided and there is free transfer to and from the airport. Excursions and meals can be arranged as well. The daily rates for singles/doubles are 3000/4000 CFP and 1500 CFP for children aged from five to 12.

Places to Stay – middle

✓ *Te Anuanua Hotel**, (tel 57-12-54), BP 1553, Papeete, is highly recommended, especially for its excellent food, and is considered one of the best small hotels on the island. Its only drawback is price. Located in the countryside on Tahiti-iti in the district of Pueu, it is far from the hustle of Papeete. They have six bungalows with two rooms per bungalow. The layout includes a double and a single bed, private bathroom and balcony. There is also one 'bungalow suite' with a single and double bed, two bathrooms with tubs and a refrigerator. Amenities include bicycles, windsurfing, lagoon and mountain tours. The daily rates range from 10,000 CFP to 12,000 CFP for single or double occupancy including breakfast. The 'bungalow suite' is 30,000 CFP per day. Credit cards are not accepted so bring plenty of cash.

Hotel Belle Fleur (tel 43-08-01, 42-60-40) is on Punaauia Hill two km from the airport and six km from town. Formerly part of the Ibis chain, it is now independently owned. It has 40 rooms, the ground floor rooms are air-conditioned, while the upper floor rooms have ceiling fans. Each room has a refrigerator and TV. Further amenities include tennis courts and water sports. It is not luxurious but it is decent. The rates for singles/doubles are US$80/100. For reservations the postal address is PO Box 576, Papeete.

Matavai (tel 42-67-67, 42-61-69) was formerly the Holiday Inn but as far as I am concerned, once a Holiday Inn always a

Holiday Inn. The 146-room hotel is on the outskirts of town and is popular with airlines who put their flight crews up for the night there. Awful architecture. Prices are 9000 CFP for a single and 12,000 CFP for a double. The postal address is PO Box 32, Papeete.

*Royal Papeete** (tel 42-01-29) is directly opposite the waterfront or 'quay' in the midst of Papeete's entertainment and shopping district. In its day it was one of the finer hotels but now is known mainly as the home of La Cave, one of the best nightclubs going. The 85-room Royal Papeete is not luxurious but is certainly adequate and is good for business people who need to stay 'in town'. Prices begin at 7200 CFP for a single and 7500 CFP for a double. The postal address is PO Box 919, Papeete.

About two km from the heart of Papeete, the *Hotel Tahiti** (tel 42-95-50, 42-61-55) was also one of the best resorts around in its heyday and still represents excellent (perhaps the best) value in its class. With 92 rooms and 18 bungalows, a swimming pool and an excellent restaurant, cordial English-speaking staff, it is a good choice for the visitor who wants good, clean accommodation but doesn't need the lap of luxury. The rates are US$60 for a single and US$70 for a double. The postal address is PO Box 416, Papeete.

Ibis Papeete, (tel 42-32-77), BP 4545, Papeete has 72 air-conditioned rooms and is located downtown, central to the nightlife and across from the quay. It is Papeete's newest hotel and, keeping in line with Ibis lineage, provides quality at moderate prices. The rooms are on the small side, but have a TV and video. Traffic noise could be a problem. Rates are US$80 for a single and US$100 for a double. The entire hotel is done in pastels.

Princess Heiata (tel 42-81-05) is best known as an after-hours club on the weekends for revellers who don't think the party is over when the nightclubs close down. It has 25 rooms and 11 bungalows and is about five km from Papeete going east towards Pirae near a black sand beach. Prices are around 7000 CFP for a single and 8000 CFP for a double. The postal address is PO Box 5003, Papeete.

Next to the Beachcomber, about seven km from Papeete, *Te Puna Bel Air* (tel 42-82-24) is reasonably priced and adequate. It has 48 modern motel-style rooms and 28 thatched bungalows with overhead fans. The hotel has a freshwater pond-cum-swimming pool with ferocious-looking but perfectly harmless eels. It also has spacious gardens, a good restaurant and is near the beach. Sundays feature a Tahitian feast followed by dancing to a local band. Prices start at 8000 CFP for a single and 9000 CFP for a double. The postal address is PO Box 354, Papeete.

Hotel Pacific (tel 43-72-82) is a recently renovated hotel (formerly the Kon Tiki), moderately priced and located in the heart of Papeete on the Boulevard Pomare. In its former incarnation as the Kon Tiki, it was very tacky but is now quite acceptable. There are 44 air-conditioned rooms; the rates for singles/doubles are 7000/7500 CFP. The postal address is PO Box 111, Papeete.

Puunui (tel 57-19-20) is constructed on a grassy hillside in Taravao, about 65 km from the grime of Papeete. Its 54 'junior suites' are very modern; they were built just a few years ago and command a spectacular view. There are two restaurants on the premises, a pool, two tennis courts and all the water sports. There is also a white sand beach below for use of hotel guests. Rates are US$116 for single or double 'junior suites'. The postal address is PO Box 7016, Taravao.

Hotel Le Mandarin which opened in February 1988 is the newest hotel in downtown Papeete. With 37 air-conditioned rooms, it provides colour TV and direct international dialling from the rooms. Tariffs begin at around US$100 for a single and US$110 for a double. It is within walking distance of Papeete City Hall, banks, boutiques, travel agencies, airline offices and the ferry boat docks.

Places to Stay – top end

*Beachcomber** (tel 42-51-10), a 202-room resort located two km from Faaa Airport and eight km from Papeete, is a compromise between city and town – close enough to enjoy Papeete but far enough away to avoid the hustle. It is considered to be the best large 'resort' hotel on Tahiti. Located on the water and features the usual assortment of water sports and cruises as well as 185 standard rooms and 17 air-conditioned, over-the-water bungalows. Over the past several years management has poured US$5 million into refurbishing the rooms; more recently the bar/restaurant and conference hall have been totally revamped. Prices begin at US$165 for a single and US$195 for a double. The postal address is PO Box 6014, Faaa, Tahiti.

Located about nine km from Papeete (just down the road from the Beachcomber), the *Maeva Beach* (tel 42-80-42) was one of the first luxury hotels in French Polynesia. It has 230 rooms, one of the best restaurants on the island (the Gauguin) and is near the beach. It feels more like a European hotel than any resort on the island. Prices begin at US$130 for a single and US$145 for a double. The postal address is Box 6008, Faaa Airport.

Hotel Tahara'a (tel 48-11-22) is perched

on a summit named 'One Tree Hill' by Captain Cook and overlooks historic Matavai Bay. The hotel is located on the boundary of the Arue district about eight km outside Papeete. Below the Tahara'a is a gorgeous black sand beach and above the view of the bay is spectacular. Despite the lovely locale and a recent US$2 million renovation (which modernised every one of its 200 rooms) the hotel has fallen on hard times. Since 1987, when American Hawaii Cruises (which had a contract to house its guests at the hotel) pulled out of Tahiti, there has been a dearth of guests. In April 1988 the Tahara'a along with its sister hotel, the Hotel Bora Bora, was sold to a Hong Kong businessman. The management of the Tahara'a was transferred to the Hyatt while the highly successful Hotel Bora Bora has retained its management. Rumour has it that the new owner will pour even more money into refurbishing the hotel. The postal address is PO Box 1015, Papeete, Tahiti. The rates start at US$195 for a single or double.

Located in the 'suburb' of Pirae, the *Royal Tahitian* (tel 42-81-13) has 45 rooms with an ocean view and a black sand beach that one guest told me was 'dangerous'. Attractions here are nil with the exception of the hotel restaurant which I am told was 'rather good, but undermanned'. Rooms start at 12,000 CFP for a single and 13,000 CFP for a double. The postal address is PO Box 5001, Pirae.

Tetiaroa* is the name of the atoll resort owned by the iconoclastic Marlon Brando. The string of 12 islands (10 of which are bird sanctuaries) are a 20-minute, 60-km flight from Faaa Airport in Tahiti. In my opinion, they are archetypically beautiful South Pacific islands, complete with blue lagoon, blinding white sand beach, swaying palm trees and warm trade winds. Tetiaroa is also one of the better travel bargains in French Polynesia. If I had a week to spend in French Polynesia with a close friend, this would be one of the places I'd seriously consider.

Though 'resort' is a loosely used term, usually conjuring up images of strangely shaped swimming pools, sickly sweet, red tropical drinks with tiny parasols stuck in them and bored looking waiters, this noun does not apply to Tetiaroa. Brando purchased the atoll in 1965, put a few modest *fares* (local accommodation) up and left it in its natural state. I was told by the manager Alex, a venerable Tahiti hand, that Brando ordered the builders not to use insecticide or chemicals of any kind in construction of the *fares*. They didn't. Since the islands were a bird sanctuary and a former island retreat for the Pomare dynasty (the royal family which sought refuge from the puritanical missionaries) he assumed doing as little as possible to alter the place was the best policy. He was right. To put up fancy digs on Tetiaroa would have destroyed the whole funky atmosphere, which the island still has. However, Brando's private paradise is not for everybody. One gets the feeling he does not want it to be. The island is for self-contained people who like to read fat novels, bask in the sun, or swim. Alex called it a 'decompression chamber', that provides the basic amenities in a superb natural environment.

The biggest attraction is a visit to one of the bird islands where half a dozen species of sea bird nest. The birds (such as crested terns, bobbies, fairy terns, grey terns, frigate birds, etc) seem relatively unafraid of man and one may walk up to their nests.

One of the best things about the island is its proximity to Tahiti. Jump on a plane and 20 minutes from the largest urban centre in the south-east Pacific, you are there. The 'resort' consists of about 12 *fares* constructed from local wood with thatched roofs with simply fashioned furniture, and beds that are comfortable, but not fancy. One is given a kerosene lamp (to use after the generator goes off) and a mosquito coil. Other amenities include a circular, outdoor bar with fishing floats of every nation hanging from the beams and a very orthodox dining hall that serves basic food.

One and two-day excursions are available to the island aboard the *Keke II* and the *Auroch* from Papeete or Moorea. Included in the one-day trip is a visit to Bird Island and archaeological sites on the island. Scuba diving is available at an extra charge. Rates are approximately US$126 per day per person (including three meals) and the air fare is US$220 on Air Moorea. The postal address is PO Box 2418, Papeete (tel 42-63-02, 42-63-03). One can reserve space at Tetiaroa in the US by calling 800-922-6851.

PLACES TO EAT

One of the best things about Tahiti is its restaurants. Thanks to the discerning palate of the French, Papeete is the only town in the South Pacific (with the possible exception of Noumea) where it is actually difficult to find a lousy restaurant. The main cuisines in Tahiti are French, Tahitian, Vietnamese and Chinese or various combinations thereof. Prices range from reasonable to very expensive – US$5 to US$50 per person. The prices listed represent the cost of an average meal.

Good news on the price front is that some restaurants are offering 'tourist menus' – ie special menus which are 20% to 40% less than standard fare. This has come about from a government programme to lower the price of restaurants by decreasing import duties on food and booze for hotels and (participating) restaurants. Unfortunately not all restaurants are going along with the 'programme' thus the lower prices only apply to particular menus at particular restaurants.

Places to Eat – Papeete

La Corbeille d'eau, Boulevard Pomare, French cuisine, considered to be the best French restaurant in Papeete, 5000 CFP.

Le Madrepore, Boulevard Pomare in the Vaima Center, French cuisine, 4000 CFP.

Le Mandarin, Rue des Ecoles, Chinese cuisine, 2000 CFP to 3000 CFP.

Jade Palace, Rue Jeanne d'Arc in the Vaima Center, Chinese cuisine, 3000 CFP to 4000 CFP.

Moana Iti, Boulevard Pomare, French-Tahitian, 2000 CFP to 3000 CFP.

Le Baie d'Along, Avenue du Prince Hanoi, fine Vietnamese food, 2000 CFP to 4000 CFP.

Le Pescadou, one block from Vaima Center on Rue A M Javouhey, Italian food specialising in pizza – lively ambience and the best pizza in town, 1500 CFP.

Scoubie Dou, around the corner from Le Pescadou, fast food Tahitian style, salads, sandwiches, and the like. Owned by same folks that own Pescadou.

Pizzeria, Boulevard Pomare, good pizza but lacks the atmosphere of Le Pescadou, 1500 CFP.

Waikiki, Rue A Leboucher, good and inexpensive Chinese-Tahitian food, 1500 CFP.

Polyself, Rue Gauguin next to the Bank of Polynesia, caters to the lunchtime office crowd – Chinese-Tahitian cafeteria-style food but consistently good, 1000 CFP.

Le Bistrot du Port, Avenue Bruat, an outdoor cafe under shady trees, good seafood, French cuisine and local dishes.

Restaurant Tehoa, corner Rue du Mal Foch and Rue Eduoard Ahnne behind the market, tasty, inexpensive Chinese and European food, 500 CFP to 1000 CFP. Friendly.

Le Snack Paofai, corner of Rue Cook and Rue du Commandante, inexpensive snacks for 250 CFP to 400 CFP and meals at 800 CFP. It is open from 6.30 am to 5.30 pm daily.

Market Area Budget Places Some of the least expensive restaurants are in the vicinity of the market including *Chez Roti*, *Acajou Cafeteria*, *Waikiki* and a few others. They are all quasi-Chinese restaurants/takeaways with prices in the 600 CFP to 1000 CFP range. Their specialty is a dish called 'Maa Tinito', a mixture of red beans, pork, fresh vegetables and whatever else the chef feels like throwing in. These are real local dives and chances are you won't find tourists in there.

The Trucks or Roulettes These places are on

the waterfront parking lot opposite the upper end of Pomare Boulevard. These vans serve up the best, inexpensive meals in town with prices in the 600 CFP range. Best time to go is in the evenings. Dishes include grilled chicken, steaks and fish piled high with 'pommes frites' (chips). There are also vans specialising in Chinese food, omlettes, and one that serves only crepes with toppings that include Grand Marnier, chocolate and honey. They are open after 5 pm every day and are very popular with locals as well as visitors.

The Outdoor Cafes or Al Fresco Bars These places are at the upper end of Pomare Boulevard, opposite the Moorea Boat Dock. Near the sleazier discos on Boulevard Pomare these are the hangouts of what travel guides refer to as 'colourful' people – soldiers, sailors, French Legionnaires, prostitutes (of all persuasions), transvestites, pimps, transexuals and perhaps a lost tourist. These charming places are also great to hang out and watch the world go by while sipping an expresso, a glass of wine or perhaps a Hinano. Typical of the bars in this category are *Tiare Tahiti Bar*, *Jasmin Cafeteria* or the *Taina Bar*. They are a must for aspiring novelists and post-beat poets.

'Tourist Menu' Restaurants The following restaurants in Papeete have adopted the governments policy of a 'tourist menu': *Acajou*, *Le Baie d'Along*, *Le Bougainville*, *Le Jade Palace*, *Le Mandarin*, *La Pizzeria*, *Le Gillardin* and *Le Manava*

Places to Eat – Around the Island
Pirae *Le Belvedere*, a 'tourist menu' restaurant, is perched on a mountainside near Papeete – great view day or night. It serves French food at 2500 CFP and specialises in Fondue Bourguignonne (meat fondue). For free transportation call 42-73- 44.

In Pirae there is another 'tourist menu' restaurant, the *Le Lion D'Or*.

Pamatai *Maribaude* has an oceanside view.

They offer French cuisine at 3000 CFP to 5000 CFP. Excellent.

Punaauia *Coco's* serves seafood at 3000 CFP to 6000 CFP and it is near the ocean (PK 13). There is also an American-style bar, *L'Auberge du Pacifique*, offering seafood from 3000 CFP to 5000 CFP (PK 11.2).

In Punaauia, two restaurants that have adopted the 'tourist menu' are *Acajou* and *L'Auberge du Pacifique*.

Faaa *Le Gauguin* is at the Sofitel Maeva Beach (PK 7.5). The cuisine is French at 3000 CFP to 6000 CFP. Excellent.

Papara *Le Petit Mousse*, (PK 32.5) constructed on the water, makes for a nice Sunday afternoon dining outdoors. It serves North African food at 2500 CFP.

The *Nuutere* and *Vahine Moena* restaurants in Papara have adopted the 'tourist menu'.

Mataiea *Vahoata* (PK 42.9) is famous for its Tahitian feasts on Sunday. The restaurant is a 'tourist menu' one and the food is Tahitian at 2500 CFP.

Papeari *Restaurant-Bar Musée Gauguin* (PK 60) has good French food and pleasant surroundings at 2500 CFP to 4000 CFP. It's another 'tourist menu' restaurant.

NIGHTLIFE
Moonglow and a freighter's lights reflect from the rippling waters of the harbour. A warm south-east trade wind blows through the narrow streets and ruffles the bright print dresses of vahines as they walk in pairs towards the neon signs.

On the street, young sailors with crew cuts and tight-fitting jeans leer at the girls, banter in French and puff away at Gauloises cigarettes. Behind them, the pulsating disco beat of the Blackjack Club blares into the night. A painted, mini-skirted Tahitian in stilt-like platform shoes stands at the doorway and peers into the street.

Across the Boulevard Pomare, on the quay, the American yachts are moored neatly in a row. Inside the lighted cabins you can make out the figures of people eating dinner and sipping wine from plastic cups. Occasionally a denim-clad youth will slip out of a darkened yacht, cross the street and disappear into the maze of lights and people.

Down the Boulevard Pomare, near the bus stop, several old women with sleeping babies at their sides sit cross-legged on pandanus mats and weave crowns of pungent Tiare Tahiti beneath fluorescent street lamps. Later they will peddle their fragrant creations in restaurants, night clubs, bars and streets.

Over at the Pitate Club, across from the Monument de Gaulle, the band has started to play a Tahitian-style fox trot and couples are slowly filing in. At the bar sit four crew members of a Chilean naval ship. The young men, who have been two months at sea, ogle the women and squirm self-consciously on their orange plastic seats. The Tahitian women eye them; some whisper to their boyfriends that they will try to hustle a few drinks from the *popa'a* (foreigners).

Clubs range from sleazy servicemen's clip joints to posh discos. However, before you step out, prepare to spend some cash. The cheapest beer in town is at least 300 CFP, and the price for a cocktail ranges from 1000 CFP to 1500 CFP. On a weekend night most clubs will extract a cover charge of about 1000 CFP, which includes a drink. Papeete is a small town, and most places are within several minutes' walking distance of each other.

Undoubtedly the friendliest places in town are the rollicking, working-class bars where the common people come to unwind with conversation and a few beers. The bars are noisy, crowded, smoke-filled dens that usually have a trio or quartet hammering away on ukuleles and guitars. These places will seem formidable at first because of the mass of people packed inside. Once you're in and flash a few smiles, however, the locals will be quite amiable.

Someone will most likely buy you a beer and ask where you're from and if you're married. For some reason, Tahitians are extremely curious about one's marital status. If you have no spouse, they will shake their heads and say, 'Aita matai (no good), maybe you find a nice vahine from Tahiti'. You might also be questioned about a person they have met from the same area. 'You know Jimmy from Los Angeles? He come here two years ago. He nice man.'

Expect to be chided a little if you go to working-class bars. Tahitians are generally polite, but often the visitor bears the brunt of their jokes. Laugh along. One evening at a local dive, several Americans were fortunate enough to be entertained by one drunken Tahitian comedian who alternately plunked away at a ukulele and told outrageous jokes. He was bringing the house down. The routine was entirely in Tahitian, and the Americans were the butt of every joke.

Dance Halls

For the average Tahitian, the dance halls (as opposed to the discos), are the most popular places to go. All the dance halls have amplified sound systems and bands that play the same Tahitian waltzes, fox trots, rock 'n' roll and music for the sensual *tamure*, the hip-shaking dance which has been known to cause palpitations in otherwise healthy men. Watching the tamure being performed by the bronze-skinned, sultry-eyed Tahitian beauties for the first time is a memorable experience. The Tahitians have a way of gyrating their hips to a breathtakingly rapid beat while their feet and shoulders remain perfectly still. Though originally an Eastern Polynesian (Tahitian and Cook Island) dance, the tamure has become a Pan-Polynesian phenomenon.

Of the dance halls, the classiest and certainly the one with the prettiest vahines is *La Cave*, beneath the Royal Papeete Hotel. La Cave has more of a ballroom atmosphere than the dance halls. Virtually everyone in Tahiti dances, sings, plays guitar, or does it all. Music and dance play an extremely important role in Tahitian culture. To not take part in this is to miss a large slice of the Tahitian experience. The *Maeva Beach Hotel* has a free music and dance performance.

Continuing on the dance hall circuit, down the socio-economic ladder from La Cave is *Le Pub* on Avenue Bruat and adjacent to it, the *Pitate* on Boulevard Pomare. Sporting garish red lights and movie posters on the ceiling, the Pitate is the most popular club among working-class Tahitians. At the door sits a bouncer with fists the size of hams. During the course of the evening couples file past him and disappear into the parking lot across the street, only to return several minutes later. 'There is', as one local put it, 'very little pretension at the Pitate'.

Discos

They seem to have a universal character – flashing lights, a pulsating beat and a high decibel level. There are three types of discos in Papeete: the seedy B-girl hangouts frequented by French sailors; those popular with transvestites (and French sailors); and the posh 'straight' discos.

The first category, located on the waterfront near the naval yard, should be avoided. The second variety, which includes the *Piano Bar*, its neighbour, the *Topless Club* and the *Bounty Club*, have the 'loosest' ambience in town and attract a mixed crowd of tourists, locals, servicemen, gays and straights. Everyone is accepted here, and you can spend the evening dancing or watching the assorted types filter in and out through the swinging doors. The Piano Bar and the Topless Club are meeting places for the *mahus* (transvestites), and features strip shows with female impersonators. The Topless Club specialises in transvestites who have had hormone injections and like to show off their acquired charms. The Piano Bar, however, is the older, more famous institution. When it's time for the show to begin, the music stops and patrons gather in a semicircle before the mirrored wall of the stage like school children awaiting a puppet show. With a vaudeville flair, the owner announces the entrance of Gigi, and the disc

jockey cranks up Donna Summer or Michael Jackson to a deafening level. From stage left emerges Gigi, knees pumping and bottom swaying, making her way to a solitary bar stool in the middle of the dance floor.

She stands over six feet tall in her five-inch chromium-plated shoes and is wearing a skimpy leopard-skin outfit. Strands of hair from her wig fly in all directions as she bumps and grinds her way across the stage and contorts her body on the stool. Meanwhile, the audience is in rapt attention. The women giggle, the French sailors leer, and the American tourists try hard to be nonchalant. Within a few minutes into the next song, Gigi's clothing has been peeled off and a drunk Tahitian teenager is sitting near her groping for her G-string. He is harmless and nobody pays attention to him. With a casual but deft flick of the wrist, Gigi removes even the G-string and disappears backstage.

At the tables, the hum of conversation resumes. Several uniformed sailors, still covered with acne, are animatedly flirting with a mahu. Although her demeanor and husky voice mark her as a transvestite, there are other mahus who are not so obvious. Often the transvestites rival women in their beauty; an occurrence which, since the time of Cook, has led to some surprising discoveries by the unwary visitor.

Leaving the Piano Bar behind, you can try the 'straight' discos which include the *Lido, Star Circus, Le Retro, Club Too Much* (formerly the Rolls Club) and the ultra-posh *Mayana* – all places to be seen for the young and the restless. The Mayana caters to a younger, 'teenybopper' crowd while Le Retro's patrons are usually older. All the clubs are near the waterfront or the Vaima Center area, within a few minutes' walk from each other.

Drinks

On a Saturday night, a quiet cocktail can be had at *La Jonque*, a remodelled boat anchored across from the Pitate Club. Likewise the major hotels in the area like the

Beachcomber or the *Tahara'a* provide a tranquil ambience if you are not up to the nightclubs. When the bars close down (after 2 am), the *Princess Heita* in Pirae picks up the after-hours crowd. There you can either continue drinking and dancing or head to the 'trucks' for a bite to eat.

GETTING THERE & AWAY

Travellers arriving in French Polynesia by air will all arrive in Papeete. See the Getting There chapter about flying to Tahiti. Papeete is also the central travel point for all of French Polynesia. From here flights fan out to the other islands and it is also the main port for copra boats which service the more remote islands. See the Getting Around chapter for details of domestic flights and copra boat schedules. Or see the individual island sections for details of transport there from Tahiti.

GETTING AROUND

Short of renting a car in Tahiti, there are three other modes of transportation: le truck, taxis and hitch-hiking.

Le Truck

The bus system, known as le truck, is the most practical and widely used form of transportation on the island. The trucks, which are somewhere between jitneys and buses, have wooden benches that run the length of the vehicle, no shock absorbers, and speakers that blast Tahitian music and rock 'n' roll. Each driver is an owner-operator, who, like all independent truck drivers, must hustle to survive. The trucks have a few official highway stops (with canopies and benches), but generally they will pull over along any stretch of the road if you wave them down.

The trucks run on weekdays from the first light of dawn until about 10 pm. On Saturday they operate until midnight, and Sunday is the drivers' day off. The main departure point for all trucks is the central marketplace in Papeete. To go west (towards Faaa Airport) you must catch le truck on the west side of the market. To go east (towards Pirae), catch a truck on the opposite side of the market. Drivers are always paid after the trip is completed. The fares range from 100 CFP (if you're going from Papeete to the airport – just under six km) to a maximum of 300 CFP to the other side of the island. Unlike a taxi one does not have to fear being 'taken'. The fare within a 20 km radius of Papeete is around 160 CFP.

Taxis

Compared to those in other locales, taxis in French Polynesia are expensive. The government regulates taxi fares and rates have been established from Papeete to virtually every hotel and restaurant.

Inside the greater Papeete area the taxi fare should not exceed 500 CFP so be suspicious of anything much more than that for a ride within town. The tariff from town to the airport or vice versa is 800 CFP, except after 10 pm when the price goes up 50%. All other fares *double* from 10 pm to 6 am and on holidays and Sundays the minimum rate may go up 25%. Any complaints should be directed to OPATTI (the Visitors Bureau). Note that taxi fares (like everything else) are subject to change.

Hitch-hiking

Hitch-hiking is also possible with varying degrees of difficulty for foreigners. The idea is to be as conspicuously non-French as possible. Tahitians enjoy meeting foreigners.

Car Rental

For the visitor spending any appreciable time in Tahiti or the person wishing to do an around-the-island tour solo, renting a car is a necessity. Aside from the the big names like Budget, Hertz and Avis there are smaller, good quality rentals – but consumer beware. Scrutinise the vehicle before you drive it away, lest you find nonexistent brakes or flat tyres. Depending on your choice of model, prices range from US$60 to US$100 per day or more. Rates are generally based on time plus distance and an insurance charge of 600

CFP to 1500 CFP. Gas is not included and it ain't cheap. A valid driver's licence issued in your country of residence is required.

Tahitian motorists can be uncommonly courteous but they do have their own rules of the road and when in doubt, drive very defensively. Watch out for French and Tahitian motorists who may insist on passing on blind curves, tailgating and turning without signalling. Beware also of children playing on the street, pedestrians who seem oblivious to traffic, and drunks on the weekends. The agencies are at the following locations:

Andre
    Boulevard Pomare opposite the naval base in Fare Ute (tel 42-94-04)
Avis Polynesie
    Rue Charles Vienot (tel 42-96-49) and at the airport (tel 42-44- 23)
Budget
    Avenue Georges Bambridge (tel 42-66-45)
Daniel
    near the airport, PK 5, (tel 42-30-04)
Europcar
    Boulevard Pomare (tel 42-46-l6)
Hertz
    Rue Cdr Destremeau opposite the sports stadium (tel 42-04-71) and at the airport (tel 42-55-86)
Pacificar
    Rue des Ramparts near Pont de l'est in Papeete (tel 42-43-04, 42-43-64)
Robert
    Rue Cdr Destremeau (tel 42-97-20)

Airport Transport

Faaa Airport is 5.5 km from Papeete. Le truck takes 15 minutes into town and costs 90 CFP. There are also plenty of taxis. Taxi rates are set by the government and are fixed from the airport to each hotel. The taxi fare from the airport to Papeete is 800 CFP.

Airport Facilities The amenities at Tahiti's International Airport include: two banks that are open an hour before international flights depart and an hour after arrival; a post office which is open regular buisness hours; an OPATTI (Office of Tourism) information booth which opens for arriving international flights; and a snack bar with restaurant.

There is a consign (storage area for luggage) and shower facilities for transit passengers; three duty-free shops and a (non-duty-free) boutique, Manureva, which has fashions, souvenirs and a newsstand. The Gallerie Leonard da Vinci is an art gallery.

There are two car rental offices (Hertz and Avis); and offices for Air New Zealand, Qantas, Lan Chile, Continental, Air France, Hawaiian Airlines, Air Moorea, and Air Tahiti. In separate buildings are offices for Tahiti Helicopter and Tahiti Conquest Airlines, both charter carriers. Note that the office for Air Moorea is in a separate wing from the international and Air Tahiti offices and is adjacent to Tetiaroa's office.

Across from the airport is a *fare* where old women sell purses, hats, shells, flower and shell leis for departing friends and relatives.

Tours

Tahiti's interior is one of the most beautiful (and seldom seen) attractions, making an inland tour a high priority. Tahiti Rainbow Tours and Terai Tours provide four-wheel drive tours to the interior of Tahiti as well as standard 'Circle Island Tours'.

Tahiti Rainbow Tours (tel 43-56-30) has two inland excursions – the 'West Coast' and the 'Mountain & Waterfall' tours, both of which are half-day trips. The West Coast Tour (which appears to be more coast than inland oriented) visits both the 'Gauguin' and 'Tahiti & its Islands' museums, the Vaihpahi garden and waterfall, the black sand beach at Papara, the Fern Grotto of Maraa and a visit to a residential area. Times are 8.30 am to 12.30 pm and 2.30 to 6 pm and cost is 3000 CFP. The 'Mountain Tour' utilises an eight-seat capacity, four-wheel drive Jeep wagon and visits Faarumai Falls, passing through thick jungle to the highest road accessible by vehicle to Mt Marau (1400 metres). This is the real 'bushwhacker' tour and takes in some spectacular scenery. The owner/driver, William Leteeg is said to be an entertaining and informative guide, familiar with local legends as well as flora and fauna. The price is 4000 CFP and times are 8.30 to noon and 2.30 to 6 pm

Terai Tours (tel 42-27-50) has a similar itinerary to Tahiti Rainbow Tours, visiting Mt Marau and Faaruumai Falls.

Charter Boats Revatua Charters (tel 43-28-21, 48-04-39) has trips to Brando's private island (Tetiaroa), Moorea, sightseeing tours of Papeete's harbour area, and deep-sea fishing expeditions. Those of more modest means interested in renting a dingy or outrigger for fishing, diving, or lagoon exploration should call Tac Boat (tel 42-28-65). They also rent fishing gear, snorkelling equipment, and underwater cameras. The office is next to the Maeva Beach Hotel.

Horseback Riding The Equestrian Club Te Anavai, (tel 57-20-20, 57-15-67), PO Box 7186 Taravao, Tahiti, is directed by Wendy Offers and has a whole range of outings including a trail ride up the hillside of Papeari which has great vistas of Tahiti's isthmus and peninsula; rides along streams that border the club; visits to swimming holes; and riding lessons. Prices are 1400 CFP per hour, per person or 1300 CFP per hour for a party of four or more. Day trips (lasting from 10 am to 3 pm) are 3500 CFP; riding lessons are 6000 CFP for 10 sessions and a five day riding workshop is 20,000 CFP. The school is at PK 53 in Papeari (the opposite end of the island from Papeete).

Club Equestre de Tahiti, (tel 42-70-41), is in the Papeete suburb of Pirae. Open Tuesdays through Saturdays 8 am to 7.30 pm and 8 to 11.30 am on Sundays. The cost is 1800 CFP per hour for riding and 1150 CFP per hour for lessons.

Club Equestre de Tahiti l'Eperon, (tel 42-79-87), is also in Pirae. It is open every day except for Monday from 8 am to 7 pm and has a mountain and lagoon ride lasting two hours. Cost for mountain rides are 2600 CFP and 3000 CFP for the lagoon rides. Lessons are 1300 CFP per hour or 1100 CFP per hour for 10 lessons.

Skydiving Yes, folks, one can even skydive in paradise. For information call Club de vol Libre Polynesien (tel 43-72-04) in Pirae.

Around the Island

In the pre-European days Raiatea and Huahine were the most important islands in the Society Islands group. It was only after the Europeans came that Tahiti became the centre of trade and eventually the focus for colonisation. Consequently Tahiti is the most densely populated, the most developed, and with the exception of archaeological sites (mostly on Huahine), has the most to see.

Tahiti has one main road that circles the major part of the island (Tahiti Nui), but dead-ends in the outer reaches of the smaller part of the island (Tahiti Iti). The main roads are well maintained, but tend to be narrow and overcrowded.

When driving around the island, you cross the halfway point at the Isthmus of Taravao (PK 60). From there you may either complete the circle or explore one of three dead-end roads in Tahiti Iti.

For the reader interested in an in-depth overview of the historical sights around the island, Bengt Danielsson's *Tahiti Circle Island Tour Guide* is the definitive book on the subject. Most of the information for this section was gleaned from it and I owe the author a tremendous debt for compiling facts that would otherwise be very difficult to come by. The guide is available at most bookstores in Tahiti.

The starting point for the (clockwise) tour is Papeete. The location of all sites listed on the tour is determined by their distance to or from the capital. You can pinpoint your position on the map from the red-topped 'PK' km stones along the inland or 'mountain side' of the highway. Each description of the points of interest includes the 'kilometreage' to help orient the (perhaps confused) map reader.

BEACHES NEAR PAPEETE

One naturally associates Tahiti with beaches, and there is no shortage of sand on this tropical island. Just two miles north of Papeete, near the Royal Tahitian Hotel in Pirae, is a black sand beach fringed with ironwood trees, palms and shrubs. Offshore is a beautiful view of Moorea. Further north, at the foot of the Tahara'a Hotel in the Arue district, is one more black sand beach, perhaps the loveliest on the island. Just a few km further north of the Tahara'a is the Point Venus/Museum of Discovery area, popular with picnickers because of a shady grove of palm and ironwood trees and an excellent beach.

To find a white sand beach you must go south of Papeete – about 10 to 15 km – to the 'high-rent' district of Punaauia. Access to the beach is through the former Hotel Tahiti Village. Although there are fine homes adjacent to the hotel area no one will chase you off their frontage – the general public has sunbathing and swimming rights to practically all the beaches in Tahiti. A few more km down the road will put you in Paea, which has more beaches and some of the best surfing conditions on the island. Surfing was the ancient sport of Polynesian kings, who rode the waves in to these very shores 1000 years ago. In fact, it was none other than the Tahitians who brought surfing to Hawaii, when they migrated there in the 11th and 12th centuries.

Aside from Paea other surfing areas can be found just south of Pomare's Tomb, south of Point Venus and beyond the Papenoo River towards the Arahoho Blowhole. (All these areas are on the north coast highway).

NORTH COAST: PAPEETE-TARAVAO
Pirae
(1.5 km, Papeete)

As you drive out of Papeete on Avenue George Clemenceau (the beginning of the north coast road) you will enter Papeete's suburb of Pirae, home of Tahiti's former President Gaston Flosse. Pirae is also headquarters for the Centre du Experimenta-

tion de la Pacifique (CEP) the agency responsible for nuclear testing on the island of Muroroa in the Tuamotu Group. The massive complex is on your left. This huge bureaucracy, which employs thousands of French Polynesians and metropolitan French, is a source of French pride, though perhaps the sentiments are not shared by all Tahitians. France's independent nuclear arsenal known as 'Force Frappe' was developed during the days of de Gaulle and French Polynesia was chosen as a testing ground when Algeria (a former French colony used as a nuclear testing ground) became politically unsuitable.

Unlike the many vocal nuclear activists in the United States or Great Britain, French people of all political persuasions accept the policy of an independent nuclear striking force and the CEP has not been a centre of controversy since the mid 1970s when many Tahitians rallied round the cries of independence from France. On the contrary, many Tahitians are paid quite well for their work in this often hazardous form of employment.

Fautaua River & Pierre Loti's Pool
(2.5 km, Papeete)

Pierre Loti was the pen name for Julien Viaud, the French merchant marine whose book *The Marriage of Loti* describes the love affair of a Frenchman and a native girl (see the Tahiti Literati in the Facts for the Visitor chapter). The pool where he first saw the enchanting Rarahu (the novel's heroine) is several km up the Fautaua River Valley. Unfortunately this romantic spot on the river is now covered with concrete but is marked by a bust of the author. The Bain Loti also is the trail head for a three-hour hike to the Fautaua Waterfalls (see Trekking section later on in this chapter).

Tomb of King Pomare V
(4.7 km, Arue)

A sign on the ocean side of the road marks the access road to the tomb. The Pomare line rose to power as a direct consequence of the

European discovery of Tahiti. The first of the lineage, Pomare I, utilised members of the ex-*Bounty* crew who were armed with guns to defeat his enemies. Pomare I's son and successor, Pomare II, was crowned at a temple just a few feet away from the site of the present-day tomb where the Protestant Church now stands. During the ceremony a *Bounty* crew member, James Morrison, reported that three human sacrifices were made on behalf of the new king.

In 1812 Pomare II became the first Tahitian convert to Christianity and after three years managed to convince the populations of Moorea and Tahiti (if necessary with the use of arms) to follow his example. In his religious zeal Pomare II constructed a temple larger than that of King Solomon out of breadfruit tree pillars, palm fronds and other local materials. The 'Royal Mission Chapel', as it was called, was about 230 metres long (longer than St Peter's in Rome!), 18 metres wide and had the capacity to hold 6000 people. Pomare II died in 1821 at the age of 40 from the effects of alcohol and soon afterwards the Royal Mission fell into disrepair. Today a 12-sided chapel built in 1978 stands where the Royal Mission once did.

The tomb itself was constructed in 1879 for Queen Pomare, who died in 1877 after a reign of 50 years during which her country became a French colony. The Queen's remains were removed a few years later by her son King Pomare V who, feeling that his end was near, apparently wished to occupy the mausoleum by himself. Pomare V lived on a stipend supplied by the French government, and died in 1891 at the age of 52; in true Pomare tradition, he drank himself to death. (An account of his funeral is given by Paul Gauguin in *Noa Noa*.)

Local tradition has it that the object on the tomb's roof – which misinformed guides say represents a liquor bottle (which would have been a fitting memorial to Pomare) – is actually a replica of a Greek urn.

Home of James Norman Hall
(5.4 km, Arue)
Look for the old Hall residence on the mountain side of the road. Nordhoff and Hall (see Tahiti Literati section), authors of the *Bounty Trilogy, Hurricane* and *The Dark River*, probably did more to publicise Tahiti in the 20th century than did any other writers. Hall died at his Arue home in 1951 and is buried on Herai Hill just above.

Tahara'a Hotel & One Tree Hill
(8.1 km)
Pull into the hotel parking lot and walk a few metres to the cliff, which affords a magnificent view of Moorea and Matavai Bay where Wallis and Cook once anchored. Wallis originally called this piece of real estate 'Skirmish Hill' because he bombarded the Tahitians gathered here with cannonballs from his ship. Cook later changed the name to 'One Tree Hill' because of the solitary *'atae* tree that grew here at the time. When the hotel was built in 1968 the owners kept the Tahitian name. The Tahara'a Hotel, which hugs the bluff like a gull's nest, has recently been refurbished.

Point Venus, Museum of Discovery & Matavai Bay
(10 km, Mahina)
Turn left towards the ocean at the sign marked 'Point Venus' (on the same corner as a large store). Drive about a km to the parking lot. This area has all the natural amenities – shady trees, a river, beach and exposure to cooling trade winds – and makes a wonderful picnic ground.

In the early days of Tahiti's history this tiny point of land was utilised by some of the most important visitors of that era – Captains Wallis, Cook and Bligh. Until the 1820s, when Papeete became a more popular port of call, all visiting ships anchored in the area. Although Wallis, Tahiti's discoverer, landed here in 1767, it was Captain Cook's expedition in 1769 that was to give this piece of land its name.

Cook was sent by the Royal Society of

England to record the transit of Venus, which would theoretically enable scientists to compute the distance between the earth and the sun – a figure that would be an invaluable tool for navigators. On 3 June 1769 the weather was good and the transit was recorded by the best instruments available at the time. Unfortunately the best equipment of the day was not accurate enough and Cook's measurements were for nought. His journey was still a success, however, because of the many new species of flora and fauna gathered by the other scientists on the trip. Cook also anchored off Matavai Bay in 1773, 1774 and 1777 during his second and third voyages of exploration.

During the *Bounty* episode in 1788, Captain Bligh also landed here, collecting breadfruit plants to use as a cheap source of food for the slave population in the West Indies. His landing became grist for Hollywood, which over the years came up with three different cinematic interpretations in 1935, 1962 and 1983. According to Danielsson, during the shooting of the 1962 *Bounty* version with Trevor Howard and Marlon Brando a sequence was filmed on Matavai Bay featuring thousands of Tahitian extras welcoming the visitors ashore. The director, wishing to portray the Tahitians in their former glory, had the Tahitian extras don long-haired wigs and false teeth before the filming to compensate for attributes most of them no longer possessed.

Wallis and Cook are honoured by non-figurative wooden sculptures placed at Point Venus in 1969. Bligh, the third navigator to visit the area, is not remembered by any monument though Bougainville is – and he never saw Matavai Bay.

In the same area you will also note another abstract monument which Danielsson describes as a 'needle pointing to heaven'. This commemorates the arrival of the first Christian missionaries on Point Venus in 1797. Dispatched by the London Missionary Society, they abandoned their mission in 1808 and did not re-establish themselves until 1817. Though they worked actively for the British annexation of the islands, the British missionaries were eased out of Tahiti after the French takeover in 1842. The missionary era came to an end in Tahiti in 1963 when an independent Protestant church run by Polynesians was formed.

About 50 metres north-east of the Missionary Society memorial is a monument enclosed by an iron railing. According to the text on its bronze plaque, the column was erected by none other than Captain Cook in 1769 and refurbished in 1901. However, not only was the monument not built by Cook (it was a product of the local public works department), it is not on the spot where Cook made his astronomical observations (which took place between the river and the beach).

In this area is the Museum of Discovery, which is housed in a thatched bamboo hut. Pay a few francs at the door and step inside to see the wax figures of Wallis, Cook and Bougainville meeting various native dignitaries. There are also memorabilia and period pieces such as a ballast bar from the real HMS *Bounty* and the hat worn by Charles Laughton in the 1935 MGM *Bounty* production. Among the more impressive artefacts is a Spanish cannon dated 1576. Unfortunately most of the artefacts are poorly documented in fading type. Finally, the most visible landmark on Point Venus is the lighthouse, constructed in 1868 despite the 1867 date perhaps over-optimistically inscribed on the entrance.

Hiti Mahana Beach Club & Campground
(10.5 km, Mahina)
This campground/dorm is the best thing to happen to low budget travel in Tahiti. It is run by a savvy couple (Coco & Pat Pautu), and the operation offers inexpensive and clean lodging. The atmosphere is friendly, international in flavour, and about half an hour (depending on traffic) from downtown Papeete by le truck. Highly recommended. (More information in the Places to Stay section).

Orofara Leper Colony

(13.2 km, Mahina)

Prior to WW I victims of leprosy were ostracised from communities and chased into remote areas away from the population. By government decree, in 1914 the Orofara Valley was set aside as a 'leper colony' for all those in Tahiti who suffered from the dreaded disease. Until the development of sulphur drugs there was little the French Protestant mission treating the lepers here could do. Nowadays it is possible in most cases to cure the disease and allow patients to go home. According to current statistics, approximately two out of 1000 French Polynesian citizens suffer from leprosy.

Papenoo Village & Valley

(17.1 km)

Papenoo is a typical rural village, the type that has rapidly disappeared since the end of WW II. Many of its homes are built in the old colonial style, with wide verandahs. The Catholic and Protestant churches and 'Maire' (city hall) are all along the highway. Past the village, a new bridge (the longest in Tahiti) spans the Papenoo River. The Papenoo Valley, the biggest on the island, was formed by an ancient crater. The river's mouth (where the bridge is located) is the only hole in the crater wall. Continuing up the Papenoo Valley you will come to the trail head that leads across the island. (See the Trekking section.)

Blowhole of Arahoho

(22 km, Tiarei)

Located beneath a steep cliff about 200 metres before the road turns towards Tiarei is one of Tahiti's biggest roadside attractions, Arahoho Blowhole. Perhaps it does not rate as one of the world's great blowholes, but it is clearly the most accessible (if not the only one) in Tahiti. Through countless years, battering surf has undercut the basalt shoreline and eroded a passage or tube to the surface. When waves crash against the rocks, the result is a geyser-like fountain of sea water and a shower for the onlooker.

Faarumai Waterfalls

(22.1 km, Tiarei)

Just past the blowhole is a marked 1.3 km dirt road leading to the three Faarumai Waterfalls. Park in the lot near a bamboo grove and walk the several hundred muddy metres to Vaimahuta, the first fall. Bring a swimsuit and some insect repellent, and try standing under the falls – an exhilarating experience. The other falls are accessible but necessitate a good hike. (See the Trekking section.)

Gardens & Copra Plantation

(25 km, Tiarei)

This is a private reserve but you can park and from the road see the lily ponds and accompanying flora that thrive in the area. The coconut plantation here, only one of many around Tahiti and its neighbouring islands, was once an important source of cash for the average Tahitian. Although harvesting copra (dried coconut meat) is still a vital occupation for islanders outside of Tahiti, it is of secondary importance in an economy that now relies on tourism, governmental bureaucracy and small businesses as money-earners.

Battlefield

(32.5 km, Mahaena)

The annexation of Tahiti by France in 1843 sparked armed resistance among Tahitians and guerrilla warfare continued until the rebellion was crushed in 1846. The most important battle of this war was fought at Mahaena on 17 April 1844. The battlefield stretched from the beach southward to the present-day church and city hall. Heeding the advice of British sailors and French army deserters, Tahitians dug three parallel trenches and awaited their French adversaries. Two French warships did appear and a force of 441 men stormed the Tahitian position which had approximately twice the defenders but lacked the weapons of the French. When the dust cleared 102 Tahitians were dead while the French lost only 15 men. After this blow the natives realised guerrilla warfare was the only alternative and they continued to operate from bases in the bush until their main stronghold was captured in 1846.

Bougainville's Anchorage

(37.6 km, Hitiaa)

Look out to sea and note the two islets, Variararu and Oputotara. The former has a few trees and the latter just brush. Bougainville anchored at Oputotara in April 1768; a plaque at the bridge in the nearby village commemorates the event. Although cultured to the bone, Bougainville was not much of a sailor. His choice of this particular anchorage, which lacked the proper shelter and wind conditions, was not the best. He managed to lose six anchors in 10 days and nearly lost the ships as well. Believe it or not, soon after this debacle some Tahitians actually salvaged one of the anchors and gave it to the King of Bora Bora as a gift. Captain Cook later took possession of it in 1777. Bougainville will probably be best remembered for his glowing account of Tahiti, later published in France, where he lauded the Tahitians' hospitality and sexual freedom. Well versed in the classics, he called Tahiti 'New Cytheria', after the island birthplace of the Greek goddess of love, Aphrodite. To this day, the myth lives on.

Vista of Peninsula

(39 km, Hitiaa)

Splendid view of Tahiti Iti, Tahiti's panhandle.

Fa'atautia Waterfall

(41.8 km, Hitiaa)

Pause at the bridge and take a few photographs. This site was chosen by American film maker John Huston to make a cinematographic version of Herman Melville's *Typee* but due to his first commercially unsuccessful Melville flick, *Moby Dick*, the scheme was abandoned.

Military Base & Junction

(53 km, Taravao)

Military and police installations have existed here since 1844 when the French guarded the isthmus to prevent marauding guerrillas from filtering down from the peninsula to the main part of the island. The old fort (located within the army camp) still stands. Since then, the site has served as a gendarmerie, an internment camp for Germans fortunate enough to be on the island during WW II and, most recently, as a military base. Nearby is a large Catholic church with a most imposing facade and also the junction for the two roads leading to the peninsula. Note that the north and south coast roads do not meet – to get around the far end of the island you must hike.

PENINSULA: TARAVAO-TAUTIRA
Detour to Vista Point

(0.6 km, Afaahiti)

Take the turn-off at the sign on your right, just before the school. There are pastures complete with grazing cattle and the seven-km road leads to a summit. Hike the rest and take in a gorgeous panorama of Tahiti.

Te Anuanua Hotel

(9.8 km, Pueue)

This is a highly recommended, inexpensive hotel run by a local family.

Vaitepiha River

(16.5 km, Tautira)

Great place for a swim.

Vaitepiha Bay

(18 km, Tautira)

Captain Cook's second expedition almost met its doom near Tautira in 1773. One morning the esteemed navigator awoke to find his two ships drifting perilously close to the reef. Apparently the crew had been too busy entertaining Tahitian visitors the evening before to notice. The ships eventually did run aground, but were saved by smaller boats that kedged the larger vessels off the reef. Cook lost several anchors in the confusion. In 1978, by sheer luck, one of the anchors was located and brought to the surface. The event was properly celebrated by locals and the crew of movie producer David Lean who was on location to promote a new version of the *Bounty* episode. Although the film was never made, the anchor can be seen at the Musee de Tahiti et des Isles.

This bucolic setting was also the scene of a confrontation between the British and the Spanish. Angered at the English presence in the Pacific (which the Spanish felt was theirs to plunder) the Viceroy of Peru was ordered by his King to send a ship to Tahiti. He promptly sent the *Aguila*, commanded by Boenecha, which after having the misfortune of striking a reef, anchored in a lagoon about three km from Tautira village and formally 'took possession' of Tahiti for the King of Spain. Less than a year later Cook, on his second voyage of discovery, wound up in the same vicinity and soon heard about the landing of the dastardly Spanish. In 1774 Boenecha returned to the area with two Franciscan priests in an effort to give the savages a little religion. The mission failed miserably. Captain Boenecha soon died and the priests, scared witless of the Tahitians, erected a veritable fortress to keep the curious natives away. The *Aguila* returned at the end of 1775 with provisions but the priests would have none of the missionary life and gladly sailed back to Peru.

Cook came back to Tautira on his third voyage in 1777 and found the padre's quarters still in good condition. The house was fitted with a crucifix which bore the inscription 'Christus vincit Carolus III imperat 1774'. On the reverse side of the cross Cook ordered his carpenter to carve 'Tertius Rex Annis 1767, 69, 73, 74, & 77'. By this time, Bengt Danielsson writes, 'both England and Spain had realised that Tahiti was an economically as well as strategically worthless island and gave up their costly shows of force'.

One hundred years later Tautira was the temporary abode of Robert Louis Stevenson, who anchored the *Casco* here in 1888 (see Tahiti Literati). He was taken in by local royalty and stayed for about two months, calling Tahiti a 'Garden of Eden'. Although on assignment for the *New York Sun* to write about the cruise he spent his time in Tautira working on 'The Master of Ballantrae', a Scottish horror story. Upon returning to England, Stevenson's mother sent a silver communion service to the local Protestant church, where it is still being used.

PENINSULA: TARAVAO-TEAHUUPOO
Research Station

(0.5 km, Afaahiti)
This atmospheric research station was constructed during the 'International Geophysical Year, 1957-1958' to study the ionosphere.

Zane Grey's Fishing Camp

(7.3 km, Toahotu)
Although the author of *Riders of the Purple Sage* and 60 other pulp westerns spent his life cranking out stories about the old American West, his real passion in life was deep-sea fishing. From 1928 to 1930 he spent many months in Tahiti with his cronies catching marlin, mahimahi, sailfish and other sport fish. Like Melville's protagonist in *Moby Dick*, Grey dreamed of landing his own version of the white whale and on 16 May 1930 he finally did – a 14-foot, 1000-pound-plus (four-metres, 454-kg) 'silver marlin' that probably would have weighed 200 pounds (91 kg) more had not the sharks ripped off so much flesh. Describing this episode in *Tales of Tahitian Waters*, Grey gives us an insight into French colonial mentality. Grey relates that French officials had the local chief spy on the Americans because they thought the fishermen might actually be surveying the area for the US government which perhaps had designs of taking over Tahiti as a naval base. Said Grey, 'The idea of white men visiting Tahiti for something besides French liquors, the native women, or to paint the tropical scenery had been exceedingly hard to assimilate'.

Maui's Footprints on the Reef
(8.5 km, Vairao)

Tradition has it that on this very spot the great Polynesian hero Maui slowed down the sun in order to provide time for the Tahitians to cook their food before it got dark. Maui accomplished this by braiding a rope of pubic hair from his sister Hina, lassoing the sun, and tying the unwieldy ball down to a boulder on the beach. To prove the tale Maui's footprints are still visible on the reef.

CNEXO Oceanographic Research Station
(10.4 km, Vairo)

The ponds you see here are for breeding shrimp – one of the many ambitious projects of CNEXO (Centre National pour l'Exploitation des Oceans), a French government agency.

Last Refuge of the Nature Men
(18 km, Teahuupoo)

Years ago the 'nature men', as Danielsson refers to them, were a common fixture throughout Tahiti, but as civilisation marched on this remote area became their last refuge. The most well-known of these rugged individuals, who perhaps bore a strong resemblance to the American underground comic book character 'Mr Natural', was Ernest Darling. According to Danielsson, Darling 'lived stark naked, slept on the ground with his head pointing north, and produced an endless stream of pamphlets, extolling the virtues of nudism, vegetarianism, abstinence, pacifism, Christian Socialism and phonetic spelling'.

WEST COAST: TARAVAO-PAPEETE
Home of Robert Keable
(55.5 km, Papeari)

Look carefully among the mango trees on the hill and you will see the former home of English writer Robert Keable. Although not a household word today, Keable produced two religious novels, *Simon Called Peter* and *Recompense*, which sold a combined total of 600,000 copies in the 1920s. Obsessed with the question of why Tahiti and Tahitian women held so much attraction for white men, he provided his own answers in two more books *Tahiti, Isle of Dreams* and *Numerous Treasure*. Keable's well-maintained home is in its original 1920s condition.

Debarkation Point of Ancient Tahitians
(52 km, Papeari)

Traditional accounts say that this was the first place the ancient Polynesians settled over 1000 years ago. Because of this, families chiefly from this district have always had the highest prestige among their counterparts in the other districts of Tahiti. The present-day village is known for its beautiful gardens and roadside produce stands. The Papeari inlet has a number of oyster beds and fish traps.

Botanical Gardens & Gauguin Museum
(51.2 km, Motu Ovini)

The gardens were established in 1919 by Harrison Smith, a physics professor who at age 37 left the Massachusetts Institute of Technology to dedicate the rest of his life to botany in Tahiti. He introduced a variety of tropical shrubs, trees and flowers from throughout the world to the islands, some of which became important local products. My favourite among these is the huge, delectable grapefruit known as the pomplemousse, which originated in Borneo. Smith did not merely putter around in his own garden but generously gave seeds and cuttings to Tahitian farmers to help them improve their own crops. After his death in 1947 the garden was willed to another botanist and through the help of American philanthropist Cornelius Crane was given to the public.

The massive garden is laced with footpaths that wend their way through acres of well-tended palms, hibiscus, elephant ears, bamboo, bananas and many other species. There were also several Galapagos turtles brought to Tahiti in the 1930s which were given to author Charles Nordhoff's children.

In the garden grounds is a modern, circular building – the Gauguin Museum – with exhibits chronicling the life of Tahiti's most famous former resident. The walls are covered with documents and photographs from the Gauguin era, along with reproductions of his works. Ironically, in the Gauguin Museum there are very few original works or objects from Gauguin's own life. The finest original paintings exhibited are those by Constance Gibbon Cummings, an English woman who stayed in French Polynesia for six months in 1877. She has left us with some exquisite landscapes of Tahiti and Moorea. For sale at the gift shop are excellent reproductions of her paintings and the works of other artists who resided on the island.

Outside the museum note the two-metre-tall *tiki* (statue) from Raivavae in the Austral group. Those in the know say it has a curse attached to it, as do many tikis removed from their original surroundings.

Although modern-day Tahiti is very different than it was during Paul Gauguin's time, the joyous and perplexing moods of Tahitians that he captured on canvas are still displayed today on every street corner in Papeete.

Those taking le truck to the Museum from Papeete and its environs should start their trek early in the morning. The last le truck heading back towards town is at 1 pm and believe me, it's a long walk back. Entrance fee to the Botanical Garden/Museum is 350 CFP.

Gauguin Museum Restaurant
(50.5 km, Papeari)
Located on the ocean side, the restaurant is excellent but somewhat expensive.

Vaihiria River & Lake
(48 km, Mataiea)
The Vaihiria River originates from the lake of the same name – Tahiti's only lake. At 500 metres above sea level, it is bounded on the north by 1000-metre cliffs which make up the southern wall of the Papenoo crater. The lake is known among locals for its large eels and nearby plantations of *fe'i* (mountain bananas). It is accessible with the aid of a guide, but there are cascades visible from the road. (For more information, see the Trekking section.)

Mataiea Village
(46.5 km, Mataiea)
After living briefly in Papeete, Paul Gauguin moved to this village in October 1891 and lived here until May 1893. He rented a bamboo hut, found a vahine and painted such masterpieces as *Hina Tefatou* (the Museum of Modern Art, New York), *Ia Orana Maria* (the Metropolitan Museum of Art, New York), *Fatata te Miti* (the National Gallery of Art, Washington, DC), *Manao Tupapau* (Albright-Knox Art Gallery, Buffalo), *Reverie* (the William Rockhill Nelson Gallery of Art, Kansas City) and *Under the Pandanus* (the Minneapolis Institute of Art).

Twenty-three years later, when Somerset Maugham came to the village culling information about Gauguin's life for his novel *The Moon & Sixpence*, he discovered three painted glass doors in the wooden bungalow belonging to Gauguin's landlord. These paintings by the great artist had never been discovered. Most of the paintings had been mutilated by children's play but Maugham picked the best one up for 200 francs and painstakingly shipped it back to Europe. Near the end of his life he sold the forgotten door at Sotheby's for a cool UK£13,000.

Rupert Brooke's Love Nest
(44 km, Mataiea)
Shortly before WW I Rupert Brooke jumped on a boat in San Francisco and headed for Tahiti 'to hunt for lost Gauguins'. He ended up in Mataiea, rented a bungalow, and instead of discovering lost French painters found his first and only true love. Mamua inspired one of his best poems, 'Tiare Tahiti'. Brooke eventually left Tahiti with a heavy heart and several years later died on a hospital ship off Gallipoli, a casualty of the

war. His beloved Mamua fell three years after that, a victim of Spanish influenza.

Atimaono Golf Course

(41 km, Papara)

Though today this area is a golf course (see Sports section); the cotton plantation that once covered what today are fairways and sand traps had a tremendous impact on Tahiti's population and history. The story begins not in Tahiti but in the United States which in the early 1860s was in the midst of a bloody civil war. This war not only caused bloodshed in the States but in Europe created a shortage of the cotton that usually came from the southern USA. The demand for this commodity gave Scottish wine merchant William Stewart, who made a living importing liquor to the South Pacific, the idea of growing cotton in Tahiti. He acquired land in Atimaono, the only area in Tahiti capable of large-scale agricultural development, and with the help of blackbirders (slave traders), he recruited labour. This did not work too well, so coolie labour from China was used and thus the seeds of the powerful Chinese community in Tahiti were planted. Working conditions were atrocious and violence tempered by the guillotine was the rule of the day.

Despite the awful circumstances, by 1867 1000 hectares of high-grade cotton were planted and the harvest lived up to Stewart's dreams. In the meantime he had built a huge villa and spent his evenings as the king of the roost, entertaining Tahitian high society. However, there was a catch. The American Civil War had ended and with it the shortage of cotton from the United States ended. Stewart could not compete with his American counterparts who were geographically much closer to Europe, and he plummeted into bankruptcy. He died at the young age of 48. About half the Chinese coolies elected to stay and the rest is history.

Duffers will be interested to know that the golf course is being renovated to the tune of 100 million CFP. Improvements will include a new club house, restaurant, pro shop, pool, tennis courts and driving range.

Site of Marae Mahaiatea

(39.2 km, Papara)

The access road to the ruins of this once great temple is posted on the highway. Today it is only a huge pile of boulders but early European visitors (such as Captain Cook) were astounded by its dimensions (about 90 metres long, 29 metres wide and 15 metres high) and its architecture. Not only did the builders need a considerable amount of skill to construct the temple, they had to do so without the benefit of iron tools. Danielsson claims it was once the most spectacular monument in Tahiti. The temple's fall into decay is not only the fault of nature – apparently the old temple was used by William Stewart as a source of stones for his building projects down at the cotton plantation a few km away. In the words of J C Beaglehole, the great biographer of Cook, whom Danielsson quotes in describing the fate of the marae, 'Nature and human stupidity combine as usual to wipe out the diverse signs of human glory'.

Protestant Church & US Civil War Memorial

(36 km, Papara)

In the graveyard of this Tahitian church lie the remains of a former US Consul and Yankee hero of the Civil War. The inscription on the stone tells the story of Dorence Atwater who at age 16 joined the Union Army, was captured by rebel scouts and served time in three Confederate prisons until he was sent to a hospital where he ended up as a clerk recording the deaths of Federal prisoners. Fearing the Confederates were not keeping accurate records, he copied the lists and escaped, bringing them to the attention of the Federal government. Atwater was buried here because in 1875 he wed the beautiful 'princess' Moetia of the local chief's family which had ruled the district for generations.

Border Between Papara & Paea

(29 km)

The districts of Paea and Papara have the least amount of rainfall and are among the most desirable areas in Tahiti to live. Note the fine homes on the coast (mostly owned by whites) and the quiet lagoon and beaches, sheltered by a barrier reef. Just prior to Paea is the Maraa Fern Grotto.

Paroa Cave

(28.5 km, Paea)

This cave, always a stop on the visitor's itinerary, has no traditional importance. Its only meagre significance is that it is an optical illusion – it seems to be smaller than it is.

Marae Arahurahu

(22.5 km, Paea)

Danielsson writes that this particular marae (located 400 metres off the main road from a Chinese grocery) had no great historical importance, but it did capture the imagination of Dr Sinoto of the Bishop Museum enough so that he completely reconstructed the shrine. The rectangular pyramid is about the size of a tennis court and has a flat top with a wooden platform where animal and human offerings were left for the gods. The marae is now used during the Tiurai festival in July as a stage for re-enactments of ancient rituals such as the 'Crowning of a King' ceremony or similar events. The temple is in a lush valley bordered by steep cliffs.

Irihonu Craft Center

(20 km, Paea)

At the mouth of the Orofero River are three buildings housing the workshops of artisans (all members of the Paea Craft Association) who still practice the traditional arts of the islands, woodcarving and mat-weaving, as well as a skill introduced by missionaries – quilting. The varied arts and crafts are on sale at the centre, which is supported by the local Paea government. In the past few years there has been a resurgence of interest in the old Polynesian arts, a trend that will hopefully check the disappearance of traditional skills.

Near the crafts centre is a popular surfing spot. Surfing is a sport the Tahitians have practised since time immemorial and brought with them to Hawaii. During the missionary years surfing was prohibited (surfboards were ridden naked in those days) and it wasn't until the 1960s, after Tahitians had visited Hawaii by plane, that the sport actually made a comeback. The same beach was also the site of a marae where in 1777 Captain Cook witnessed a human sacrifice.

This area was also the scene of an important battle in 1815 that pitted Pomare II, by then a Christian convert, against the heathen forces of the Teva i Uta clan. Pomare's well-armed Christian soldiers, aided by white mercenaries, overran their adversaries but with true Christian mercy spared the enemy from unbridled revenge. Pomare spared human life but unfortunately all of the artistic treasures – the wooden and stone carvings – were either tossed into the fire or destroyed, leaving future generations with very little in the way of Tahitian art. One of the results of this episode is that modern-day artisans carve tikis which are copies of works from the Marquesas Islands or those of the New Zealand Maoris.

Musee de Tahiti et des Iles

(15.1 km, Punaauia)

Opened in 1978, the museum is an excellent introduction to Tahiti and the entire spectrum of French Polynesian culture. You can get there by taking a right turn (coming from Papeete) at the sign posted at the junction of the gas station and market and continuing toward the beach for another km or so. Though damaged in the cyclone of '83, it was later revamped and remains the finest and most modern museum in the South Pacific. It consists of four sections:

1) Milieu Natural – flora, fauna, geology and Polynesian migration exhibits. Many of the displays include sophisticated, electrically operated diagrams and instructional aides.

2) Traditional Polynesian Culture – homes,

costumes, religion, games, dance, musical instruments and ornaments.

3) Post-Contact Era — displays illustrating Cook, Bougainville, Wallis, Pomare dynasty, missionary period and Chinese population.

4) Outdoor Exhibits — botanical garden consisting of plants that Tahitians brought with them (such as taro, 'ava, yams, medicinal herbs) and the Canoe Room displaying traditional outrigger and dugout canoes.

In addition to the museum's exhibits of traditional arts and crafts there is a wonderful collection of paintings and prints. Most of these will be available for viewing in the Exhibition Building which has rotating shows ranging from artists like Webber (Captain Cook's artist) to modern-day Tahitian painters, sculptors and potters who otherwise would not have the means of displaying their works. Exhibitions will not be limited to local art but will show works from throughout the Pacific and the rest of the world.

The building will also be the home of special events programming such as demonstrations of tapa-making, mat-weaving, instrument-making, traditional dances and exhibits illustrating the latest archaeological excavations.

No visitor to Tahiti with an interest in the island's culture should miss the museum. Hours are 9 am to 6 pm daily except Monday. Entrance fee is 300 CFP.

Punaru'u Valley

(14.8 km, Punaauia)

Beyond the bridge was once a fortress built by the French during the Tahitian uprising of 1844 to 1846. The site is now used as a TV relay station. The road up the valley leads to a trail (see the Trekking section) to the Tamanu Plateau where oranges grow in profusion. In the 19th century Tahiti was a large exporter of oranges to New Zealand and — believe it or not — to California.

2+2=4 Primary School & Site of Gauguin Home

(12.6 km Punaauia)

A 19th-century French landowner donated the land for the school and had the above mathematical equation inscribed at the entrance. According to Danielsson, the planter, dubious about the propriety of introducing the French educational system to Tahiti, figured that if nothing else the children would learn at least one thing of value.

Just south of the school, in an area now subdivided, Paul Gauguin lived in a fine home from 1897 to 1901 and produced about 60 paintings. Among these are *Where Do We Come From* (the Museum of Fine Arts, Boston), *Faa Iheihe* (Tate Gallery, London) and *Two Tahitian Women* (the Metropolitan Museum, New York).

Captain Bligh Restaurant

(11 km, Punaauia)

Formerly known as the Lagoonarium, this is a decent restaurant which used to be combined with a small aquarium. The aquarium end of the attraction was shut down but the restaurant thrives. It's open daily, except on Monday, from noon to 2 pm and after 7 pm.

Yachties and other visitors needing large quantities of groceries should be aware of the new 'Euromarche', a huge new supermarket located off the freeway, in Punaauia. This discount mart, along with a similar new market called 'Tropic Import', in Pirae are the cheapest places in French Polynesia to purchase groceries. These new stores are such bargains that it is actually less expensive for residents of the outer islands to take a ferry (with automobile) to Tahiti, stock up on groceries and return to their home island, than to buy from a local grocer. Due to the lack of competition, the retail mark up in Tahiti was horrendous until the supermarkets entered the scene.

Sofitel Maeva Beach
(8 km, Punaauia)
Just beyond the super highway entrance Maeva Beach is a popular 'local' beach. Nearby is the Sofitel Maeva Beach, one of the largest and oldest hotels on the island.

'Super Highway' Entrance
(7.8 km, Punaauia)
At this point the motorist can either take a modern four-lane freeway and zoom back to Papeete, or travel down the old coastal highway.

Tahiti Beachcomber
(7.2 km, Punaauia)
The site of the present-day Beachcomber (which has one of the best cuisines on the island) is called Tata'a Point. In times past it was a holy place where the souls of the dead were said to depart to the nether world.

Tahiti – Faaa International Airport
(5.5 km)
Tahiti's Faaa Airport is as modern as any in the world, but still has distinct Tahitian touches like barefoot kids, rotund Tahitian women selling shell *leis* (necklaces) and perhaps an unattended dog sleeping near the ticket counter. The airport's 3.5-km runway was constructed by filling in a lagoon. Prior to its completion in 1961 Tahiti was served by passenger vessels and New Zealand TEAL flying boats. See the Getting Around section in this chapter for more information about the airport.

TREKKING
Upon your arrival in Tahiti the verdant hills beckon but venturing into the bush can be a dangerous proposition unless you know what you are doing and where you are going. Torrential rain can swell streams into rivers and 'easy-to-find' trails can be overgrown with vegetation in no time. It's always best for the serious hiker to be accompanied by a guide. In many instances it's also best to rent a four-wheel drive to get to the trail head.

Despite the requirements, Tahiti has a variety of excellent trails and guides for hire. Here are seven treks of varying difficulty. Many, but not all, require guides.

Mataiea / Lake Vaihiria / Papenoo
This two-day, across-the-island hike via Lake Vaihiria (Tahiti's only lake) begins on the south coast, crosses the island's ancient volcanic crater and ends in Papenoo on the north coast. Allow 45 minutes by four-wheel drive to the Mataiea trail head. Hikers should be in good physical condition and a guide is required.

Mt Aorai
The trek begins at the end of the Belvedere restaurant road (near Papeete). This is a two-day hike and a guide is required. Small *fares* have been built for hikers along the trail.

Fautaua Waterfall
For this day trip up the Fautaua Valley take an ordinary car to Bain Loti (of Pierre Loti fame) and walk three hours to the waterfall. A guide is not necessary but permission is needed from the Service des Eaux et Forets.

One Thousand Springs Hike
This is a comparatively easy hike and no guide is required. Take Mahinarama Road (near the Tahara'a Hotel) to the end (about five km) and walk two hours to the springs. From this junction it is possible to climb Mt Orohena (Tahiti's highest) but naturally a guide is required for such an undertaking.

Plateau of Oranges (Punaru'u Valley)
Take a car to Punaauia (about 15 km from Papeete) and enter the Punaru'u Valley road to the trail head (one to two km by car). Walk to Tamanu Plateau – an eight-hour hike. Trekkers should be in good shape and a guide is required.

Lava Tubes
Start at PK 40 (east coast) and four-wheel it about eight km. It's a two-hour walk to the Lava Tubes. The walk is easy but a guide is required.

Moorea

Lying 19 km west of Tahiti is Moorea, the only other major island in the Windward group. It covers an area of 132 square km and has a population of nearly 6000. After Tahiti, it is the second most popular tourist attraction and, aside from Tahiti and Bora Bora, it is the island slated for the most tourist development over the next few years. Moorea is quick and easy to reach from Tahiti – shuttle flights leave every 30 minutes from Faaa Airport and ferries depart from Papeete daily.

Moorea, which means 'yellow lizard', is a name taken from a family of chiefs which eventually united with the Pomare dynasty. The island is serrated with sharp peaks that command deep cleft valleys, which were once centres for vanilla cultivation. Nowadays pineapple has replaced vanilla as the biggest cash crop. Seen from the air, Moorea is encircled by a lagoon of translucent green and is fringed by an azure sea. It has a triangular shape, one side with two large but shallow bays (Cook's Bay and Opunohu).

Archaeological evidence in the Opunohu Valley suggests that people were living on the island as early as 1600 AD, which corresponds with the oral history of the valley. At the time of Cook's arrival in 1774, there was internecine fighting among the islands' chiefs and warfare with tribes on neighbouring Tahiti. The battles continued for many years and the arrival of the missionaries in 1805 actually helped the Pomare dynasty gain power in Tahiti by supplying arms and mercenaries in return for support. After Pomare I conquered Tahiti, Moorea (which had been his refuge) became no more than a province of the Tahitian kingdom. During the latter half of the 19th century, colonists arrived and cotton and coconut plantations began to spring up. Vanilla and coffee cultivation came later, in the 20th century.

Moorea is famous for its tie-dyed pareus which are sold on the island or in Tahiti.

AROUND THE ISLAND

I recommend staying a few days in Moorea to get the feel of the place. The visitor will immediately note that the pace is much slower than in Tahiti and people tend to be friendlier. The thing to do is take an around-the-island tour by renting a car or scooter, or by going with one of the many organised groups advertised by every hotel.

The following guide begins at PK 0, at the airport. For ease of reference there are (as on Tahiti) km posts along the road, which start at PK 1 going in both directions from the airport. Thus there will be posts PK 1 at Temae Village (heading west) and at the Hotel Kia Ora (heading east). In this guide we will go west, in an anti-clockwise direction.

As a common courtesy visitors should take care not to trespass on private land, whether it's someone's front yard or the Biological Research Station near Pao Pao, in order to take photos. After all you wouldn't want some tourist doing the same to you back home.

Temae Village
(1 km)
It was here that novelist Herman Melville persuaded the chief to have the vahines perform the erotic 'Lory-Lory' for him; a dance forbidden by the missionaries. The author came here after his release from jail in Tahiti where he and other crew members of the *Lucy Ann* were punished for their participation in a mutiny. Temae Village is still famous for its dancing troupes that perform regularly for the island's dance revues.

Cocotier Restaurant
(3 km)
This is possibly the best relatively inexpen-

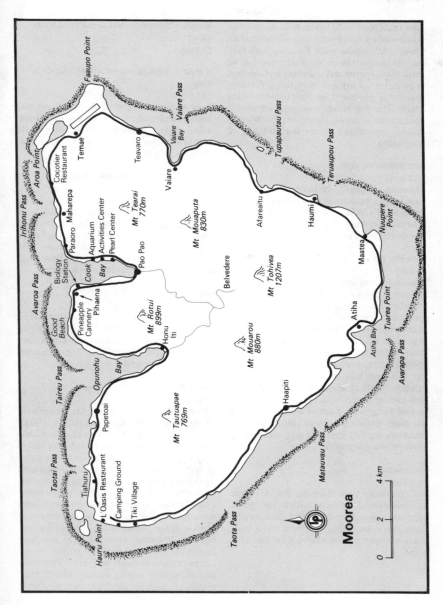

Moorea

0   2   4 km

sive restaurant in Moorea. It is in an older whitewashed home with a lovely verandah, about a 10-minute walk from the Bali Hai, on the mountain side of the road. The restaurant is petite and charming and the food is straightforward and very tasty. Friendly service is proffered by the hostess Maea Flohr. The big hotels (are you listening?) could take a lesson from Ms Flohr who knows something about the lost art of hospitality.

Maharepa Village
(3.5 km)
Maharepa Village, just before the Bali Hai Hotel, has a bush track which begins behind the Jehova's Witness church that runs deep into the mountains. The beach just before the hotel offers good snorkelling.

Bali Hai Hotel
(4 km)
The hotel environs include the Coconut House Restaurant, Michele & Jackie (another restaurant) and 'Maison Blanc'. The latter is a renovated, turn-of-the-century plantation house owned by one of the principals of the Bali Hai Hotel. With the vanilla boom during the latter part of the 19th and early 20th centuries a number of homes like this were built in Moorea, but none are in such excellent shape. With a careful eye you can still see other plantation houses tucked away in the bush or along the side of the road. Style consists of clapboard construction, roofing iron and a verandah with white wooden fretwork.

Patisserie
(4.5 km)
A five-minute walk from the Bali Hai is a patisserie/outdoor cafe which has good pastries and serves breakfast and lunch. Great place for coffee, croissant and a look at a newspaper, or a nice break from the hotel scene.

Moorea Supermarket & Bank of Indo Suez
(5 km)

Paraoro Village – Entrance to Cook's Bay
(7 km)
Paraoro has a number of shops, car and bike rentals, and a wharf. Galerie van der Heyde, a fine art shop is also here. The area was also one of the sites for the recent production of *Return of the Bounty*.

Hotel Kaveka/Activities Center
(7.8 km)
At the front of the Hotel Kaveka is the Moorea Activities Center, the unofficial visitors bureau. This is also the place to book local tours, yacht charters, four-wheel drive excursions, water sports and visits to 'Tiki Village', a quasi amusement park. Best of all, it is good for information about Moorea.

Aquarium
(7.9 km)
Combination aquarium/boutique that has 36 tanks filled with marine life. Although an aquarium-cum-boutique sounds tacky, they do an excellent presentation. The admission is 300 CFP and well worth it.

Bali Hai Club & Pearl Center
(8 km)
The Bali Hai Club is also the site for a branch of the Bank of Tahiti, Chez Albert, Hakka Restaurant, a gas station, and the Aimeo Boutique. Next door to the Club Bali Hai is the Pearl Center, brought to you by the same man (Teva) who constructed the Aquarium. Teva has a knack for combining culture and capitalism which he does equally well at the Pearl Center. Here he combines a jewellery store, art gallery and museum. You can browse in the jewellery department for free but the Museum costs several hundred francs. It has an excellent collection of artefacts from throughout French Polynesia including tapa cloth, adzes, tikis, feather necklaces, a large outrigger canoe, photos

and a great many other items. Naturally the jewellery department specialises in pearls and pearls set in precious metal. If you are interested, the price of pearls range from US$70 to US$30,000.

Te Honu Iti Eatery
(8.2 km)
Good and inexpensive food. A cross between a fast food outlet and an outdoor cafe.

Pao Pao Village & Junction for Belvedere Vista Point Road
(9 km)
This village is the site of the main dock used by trading vessels and services include a pharmacy, Chinese stores, a school, an infirmary, Bank of Polynesie, and a doctor's surgery. This is also the turn-off for the Belvedere vista point and Pao Pao Valley. One can follow the interior road through the Pao Pao Valley to the Belvedere vista point and the many ancient temples or marae. Halfway from the main highway to the Opunohu junction (see map) is a small boutique and botanical garden called 'Opuhi Plantation' owned by the 'old Tahiti hand', Alex Duprel. It's worth a visit.

Catholic Church
(10 km)
This Catholic church has an altar inlaid with mother-of-pearl. The mural in the church features brown-skinned, Polynesian versions of St Joseph, the Virgin Mary, the Archangel Gabriel and the infant Jesus. The background landscape is that of Moorea.

Richard Gump South Pacific Biological Research Station
(10.9 km)
With land donated by San Francisco jewellery magnate Richard Gump, the University of California at Berkeley has established a biological research facility for terrestrial and marine life. The station consists of two buildings, a dormitory, a lab and several boats. Open to researchers from around the world whose interests may range from insects to dolphins, the facility is definitely *not* open to the general public.

Pineapple Cannery
(11 km)
Located several hundred metres off the main highway (on the mountain side of the road) is a cannery which naturally specialises in canning the island's number one agricultural product, pineapple. A local girl greets you and gives a well rehearsed monologue describing the various stages of the canning process. On the grounds is a small kiosk where visitors are served shots of fruit liqueur derived from what is produced locally. Ironically, it is impossible to get a sip of fruit juice from these people, yet, booze is given away freely!

Opunohu Bay
(14 km)
Opunohu Bay has good snorkelling. The coral, however, is infested with crown-of-thorns starfish and there are dangerous stonefish in the vicinity so take heed.

Robinson's Cove
(17 km)
A popular yacht anchorage.

Opunohu Valley Entrance
(18 km)
This road which winds through the Opunohu Valley is the second way to reach the interior of Moorea. This road eventually links up with the Pao Pao Valley road and dead ends at the Belvedere vista point. It's worth the detour. Just prior to the road's junction on the main highway are several prawn ponds.

Papetoai
(22 km)
Papetoai was formerly the seat of the Pomare I government and the scene of his conversion to Christianity. An octagonal church built by the London Missionary Society still stands here – it is the oldest European building in use in the South Pacific. (In 1811, years before Moorea's importance as a vanilla-

growing region, the island was the London Missionary Society's centre for evangelical work for the entire Pacific.) The church is built on the site of the 18th century Marae Taputaputea. All that remains of the Polynesian temple is a slim monolith outside the octagonal church. In the back of the churchyard is a solar energy panel. Also in the area are Chinese stores, a post office and a school.

Tiahuru

(26 km)

Tiahuru is the community where the Club Méditeranée is located. Nearby there is a gas station; the new Sofitel Tiare Hotel, the Rupe Rupe riding stables, the Climate de France (hotel), Les Petit Village (a shopping centre including a grocery store, bank, doctor's surgery, restaurant, jewellery shop and other amenities); Les Tipanier Hotel/Restaurant which has moderately priced accommodation and fine Italian food; and L'Oasis, another excellent restaurant, however, expensive. This is also the beginning of a long sandy beach which stretches for about five km.

Campground & Hibiscus Hotel

(27 km)

Adjacent to the Hibiscus Hotel is Moorea's only campground and although it has spartan facilities is quite adequate. Nearby is the Captain Cook Beach Hotel, Moorea Village, a good low budget hotel, and Tiki Village, a quasi amusement park that purports to be a replica of a precontact Tahitian village. They have regularly scheduled dance performances, feasts, and (naturally) a boutique.

Varari

(28 km)

Here the 'sauvage' side of Moorea emerges, with fewer people and gives one a foretaste of life on the outer islands of French Polynesia. It is where, until just a few years ago, the pavement ended on the main road. There are scattered copra plantations and the feeling is more rural. Varari is also the site of

the Nuurau Marae, a Polynesian temple used by the Marana royal family from which the Pomare dynasty originated. (The Pomare family ruled Tahiti when the Europeans arrived.) The marae is in a coconut grove at the mouth of a small creek and covers several hectares. The surrounding walls of the temple and the *ahu* or central platform are made of coral. Much of the structure is standing but restoration is needed. At this point there is a gap in the km posts and the next marker is PK 24.

Haapiti Village

(24 km)

The village has a soccer field, Chinese store and a huge Catholic church. The church was formerly the centre of the island's Catholic mission.

Atiha Bay

(20 km)

Pirogues (canoes) are set on blocks along the side of the road and nets hang from poles or ironwood trees giving the area a pleasant, bucolic atmosphere. There is also a fine view of Tahiti. This bay has a double reef and sometimes young boys can be seen surfing from the inner reef on home-made plywood surfboards.

Maatea Village

(14 km)

Maatea, perhaps due to its rural setting, is a close-knit, friendly village with charming homes draped in flowers. There is a Chinese store, school and movie house. Maatea is also the site of Marae Nuupere, which is on private land but is accessible from the beach. The temple is on a small man-made coral hillock directly on the shore.

Haumi Village

(12 km)

Afareatiu Village

(10 km)

This is where you'll find Moorea's administrative centre, shops, a church, accommodation (Hotel Pauline), a school and a road to an interior waterfall. Like other Moorean communities of Papetoai, Haapiti and Maharepa, Afareatiu was built around ancient temples and chiefs' dwellings of former times. There is quite a bit to see around here if you have the time to ferret them out.

Chez Pauline has a wonderful collection of prehistoric stone tikis, no doubt imbued with 'mana' to spare. There are also other artefacts such as adzes and grinding stones and several wooden relics. All have been collected around the village. Pauline's pride are the tikis and I was told by a friend that if you offend her the easiest way to be pardoned is to ask her about the tikis.

The Umarea Marae, which is the oldest (900 AD) in Moorea is on the shore about 100 metres towards Maatea from Chez Pauline. Adjacent to it is a lovely coral garden ideal for a snorkel or a swim. At the other end of Afareatiu, just before the hospital, is an unpaved track leading to the waterfall. The four-km track crosses or passes near several ancient structures which are part of Marae Tetii as well as a few cascades. The trail gradually becomes a narrow, slippery, overgrown path for the last two km before reaching the waterfall. Recommended for stalwarts.

Vaiare Bay
(5 km)

Here you will find the dock for cargo boats and the passenger cruiser *Keke III*, the *Moorea Ferry* and the *Tamarii Moorea Ferry* which sail daily from Papeete. If you have the opportunity, watch the embarking and disembarking of passengers and loading of cargo at the dock. There is also a track which begins in Vaiare at the Chinese store just beyond the harbour over the mountains to Pao Pao.

Sofitel Kia Ora Hotel & Teavaro Beach
(1 km)

The hotel offers the most luxurious accommodation on the island and there is excellent snorkelling nearby as well as a lovely beach called Teavaro. At the opposite end of the beach from the Kia Ora topless bathing is considered *de rigueur*.

Bali Hai Story

It is impossible to write about tourism on Moorea without mentioning the Bali Hai Boys: Jay Carlisle, Muk McCallum and Hugh Kelly. After arriving in Moorea in 1961, the three invested in a run-down vanilla plantation and inadvertently became owners of a ramshackle hotel. Their timing was impeccable. Airlines were just beginning to land in Tahiti, and when a journalist discovered their dumpy but charming hotel, success was just around the next coconut tree. Since then, the 'boys' have established hotels on Raiatea and Huahine, and have turned the original plantation into a successful experimental farm and egg-laying facility. The Bali Hai Boys are known to be free-spending good-timers. They have left their mark on the island in many ways.

Lumbering Hugh Kelly is fond of telling the story of the return of Moorea's missing tikis. The two stone reliefs were in an ancient religious shrine on the vanilla plantation and were left undisturbed by the three Americans. A week after Kelly showed them to a wealthy Honolulu businessman, the tikis disappeared. Kelly denied rumours that he had sold the priceless artefacts and vowed to somehow get them back. Several years passed with no trace of the relics, until an American woman approached Kelly with some startling news. She had seen the tikis at the Honolulu home of the same businessman who was the last person to see them in Moorea. Apparently this man was an avid collector of Polynesian artefacts.

Hugh Kelly decided to take the matter into his own hands. He flew to Honolulu and questioned the teenage son of the businessman about the tikis. The son insisted he knew nothing until Kelly blurted out a tear-jerking tale of a dying Tahitian woman who supposedly owned the tikis. With mock anguish, Kelly claimed the woman was shivering on her deathbed because she thought the tikis were in a cold place. The boy broke down and assured Kelly the tikis were in a warm place – on the balcony of his father's apartment. That was all the wily Kelly had to know. He confronted the businessman and threatened to spread the word to the Honolulu papers if the man didn't return the tikis. Faced with an embarrassing situation, the businessman consented. Several months later, amid pomp, press coverage from Tahiti and Hawaii, and incantations by Moorea's *tahua* (shaman), the sacred tikis were returned intact to their age-old shrine.

OPUNOHU VALLEY

The Opunohu Valley, with its reconstructed marae (temples), excellent vista and lush meadows, is well worth the detour off the perimeter road. In the precontact era this valley was teeming with people but is now largely deserted and devoted to agriculture. Its population declined in the early 19th century, soon after the abandonment of the traditional religion.

Over 500 ancient structures have been recorded here, including religious and secular stone buildings and agricultural terraces. The complexity of the remains indicates a highly developed social system. The chief remnants of these buildings are six marae, reconstructed by Y H Sinoto of the Bishop Museum in Honolulu in 1967. A council platform and two archery platforms have also been rebuilt. From the junction at Pao Pao (nine km) it is several winding km to the marae. All are an easy walk from the road.

Marae Ahu-o-Mahine

This marae has the most elaborate form and features a three-stepped *ahu* (platform). It was once the community marae for the Opunohu Valley and was built some time after 1780 AD. Note that it is constructed with hand-crafted, round dressed stones, similar to those of Marae Arahurahura in Paea, Tahiti.

Archery Platforms

Archery was a sacred sport in ancient Tahiti, practised only by people of high rank – chiefs' families and warriors. As is clearly visible from the map, archery platforms have distinct crescent forms at one end. Archers perched on one knee to draw their bows and aimed for distance rather than accuracy. Of the three archery platforms in the Opunohu Valley, two have been restored. As in other parts of Polynesia, bows and arrows were not used as weapons of war. The tracks to the two archery platforms and the connecting Marae Afareaito are not easy to follow. Look for any small parting of the scrub between Marae

Titiroa and the nearby parking area and the Belvedere Lookout. The view from here is great.

Marae Afareaito

Between the two restored archery platforms is Marae Afareaito, similar to Marae Titiroa further down the trail. A small *ahu* near one end is the principal structure of the marae, which was reserved for the gods. The upright stones near the *ahu* were the gods' backrests and stones in the court area marked the positions of worshipers. On the perimeter of the marae are small shrines, one attached and one detached from the main temple. Some of these independent shrines are associated with agricultural terraces and suggest that crop-fertility ceremonies were held on the structures.

View Point

A few more km up the road is Belvedere, the finest vista of the valley. This was part of the setting for the latest film version of the *Bounty* story with Anthony Hopkins and Mel Gibson (which gave much-needed temporary employment to the locals). Continue back down the road, this time taking a left towards Opunohu Bay. On this route you will pass scenery that but for the coconut trees might belong to a Swiss valley – you'll see verdant pastures with fat, contented cattle grazing. A few more km along and you are once more on the main drag that circles the island.

PLACES TO STAY

Places to Stay – bottom end

Fairly new on the scene is the *Hotel Residence Tiahura**, (tel 56-15-45) in Haapiti. There are 24 bungalows, 18 with kitchenettes. Other amenities include a pool, snorkelling gear and good restaurant. Prices start at 3500 CFP for a single and 5500 CFP for a double. Reports on the accommodation here have been mixed.

Chez Albert* (tel 56-12-76), in the village of Pao Pao, is one of the best in the bottom-end category. It is a small, family-run

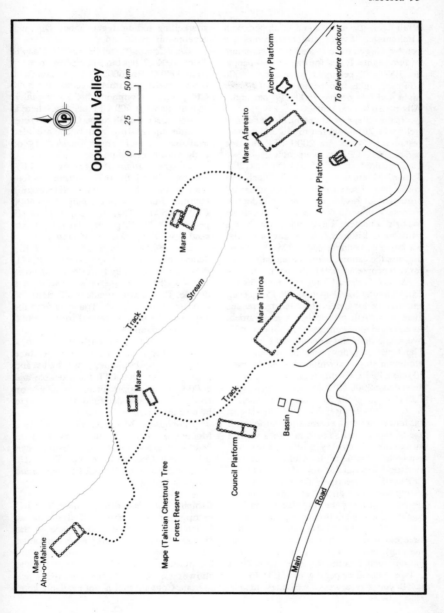

Opunohu Valley

affair with 19 units some equipped with kitchenettes. Stores and restaurants are nearby. Guests have to stay for a minimum of two nights. Rates for one or two people are 3000 CFP per night, three people 4000 CFP per night, four people 6000 CFP per night and five people 7000 CFP per night. Albert also has car rentals.

In the village of Afareatiu, *Hotel Pauline* (tel 56-11-26) has seven rooms and a small restaurant. Prices are 2000 CFP for one person, 3500 CFP for two people.

*Linareva** (tel 56-15-35) PO Box 205, Temae, Moorea, has 12 units which can house two to seven people. Recommended primarily for divers, they require a deposit for reservations 15 days in advance; contact M Eric Lussiez. Each bungalow has a bathroom, kitchen, plates and utensils, washtowels, bedding and a TV. Occupants may use the canoes, barbecue and raft. Rates for two people are 6800 CFP per night.

*MUST Lodging** (tel 56-17-32, 56-15-83), Opunohu Bay, Papetoai, PK 15, is set up exclusively for divers. Located by the sea there is a small private beach and garden. Accommodation consists of two rooms with two single beds and a communal bathroom. The tariff includes three meals, and the minimum stay is six nights. A single costs 30,000 CFP for six nights and a group of six divers cost 2000 CFP per person per night. Call Philippe Molle for more information.

*Chez Nicole** (tel 56-15-66) in Haapiti has four rooms with a common bathroom and use of the kitchen. There is also a seaside bungalow. Bicycles and a canoe are available. Double/triple/quadruple accommodation is available for 3500/4500/5500 CFP per day respectively. Reports from Chez Nicole have been good – accommodation is clean and she is apparently a nice person. The postal address is PO Box 6619, Faaa, Tahiti.

Chez Dina, (tel 56-10-39), Pao Pao has three bungalows with one double bed and one single bed in the mezzanine, kitchenette, and communal bathroom. The cost is 4000 CFP per bungalow per day or 3500 CFP per day if you stay a week. Activities include snorkelling and outrigger canoes. Dina will accept your credit card.

*Chez Josiane**, (tel 56-15-18), Haapiti, Tiahura PK 27, has three bungalows ranging from 5000 CFP to 6000 CFP per night (with private bath) and smaller rooms for 3000 CFP per night (communal bath). Camping is also available at 500 CFP per day. There is enough space for 30 tents. Other activities include snorkelling and bikes are also available for rent. It is recommended as good budget accommodation.

*Village Faimano**, (tel 56-10-20), Papetoai, PK 14, BP 1676 Papeete, has four bungalows with two rooms and cooking facilities. Bungalow prices range from 4000 CFP to 6500 CFP. A big bungalow for six people is 9500 CFP per day. There is a white sand beach and excellent swimming.

*Chez Madou**, (tel 56-31-04, 56-17-16), Temae, two km from the airport, BP 371, Papeete, has two fully furnished bungalows at 5500 CFP for single or 8500 CFP for a double. It is a two-minute walk from the bungalows to the beach. Transfers from the airport to the lodging (round trip) cost 600 CFP. Well recommended.

*Chez Nani**, (tel 56-19-99, 42-97-67), Papetoai, PK 14, BP 67, Papeete, has three bungalows with kitchen, two baths and prices start at 7000 CFP for a double and 8000 CFP for a triple. Food is available on request. Recommended for those wanting to be near the water.

*Fare Bahia**, Maharepa, PK 3.5, BP 166, Moorea, has one bungalow with two twin beds, kitchen and private bath with hot water. It is close to Cocotier Restaurant, the beach, and stores. Rates are 7000 CFP for single and 8500 CFP for double.

Camping There is one of only three 'official' campgrounds in French Polynesia, in Moorea. The campground is next to the Hibiscus Hotel and is run by a woman named Anna. A bus service is available from the campground to the dock. Except for the shower and toilette, the amenities are spartan. Cooking fuel is not available here,

Top: Beach at Tetiaroa (RK)
Bottom: Tetiaroa (Bird Island) (RK)

Top: Moorea from the air (TTB)
Bottom: Pineapple Plantation, Moorea (RK)

however, the campground is near a store. There is an excellent beach nearby. Cost is 500 CFP per night.

Places to Stay – middle

Climat de France Moorea (tel 56-15-48) Haapiti, Moorea, is a quite newly constructed 40-room, 46-bungalow hotel near Club Med on the beach. It has modest bungalow-style accommodation which is rather spartan but seems to be adequate. Other amenities include a restaurant, bar, windsurfing, snorkelling, swimming pool and tennis. Tariffs begin at 9500 CFP for a garden bungalow with kitchen and 15,000 CFP for a beach bungalow with kitchen.

An excellent, moderately priced hotel/restaurant/bar is *Les Tipaniers* (tel 56-12-67), run by a very nice Italian woman who doubles as a fine chef. The hotel is near Club Med. Some of the 21 units are equipped with kitchenettes. There are free outrigger canoes and excursions. Prices start at 7500 CFP for a single and 10,000 CFP for a double. This place deserves an A-1 recommendation. The postal address is PO Box 1002, Moorea.

Hibiscus (tel 56-12-20) has 30 bungalows (without kitchen) and double rooms with space for an extra cot. Located in Haapiti, it has a restaurant, snack bar, pool and beach. Rates (single or double) begin at around 8000 CFP. The address is 1009, Moorea.

Kaveka Village (tel 56-18-30) at the foot of Cook's Bay, has been renovated and is now under Canadian management. There are 25 bungalows, water sports (including scuba diving), a white sand beach and a bar/restaurant. Hotel rates are 8000 CFP to 9000 CFP for a single or double. The postal address is PO Box 13, Moorea. The most important development at the hotel is the founding of the 'Activities Center', a booth at the entrance (just off the road) which provides information and books tours on the island. Since there is no official government tourist office on the island, this serves an important role. On Sundays the Activities Center invites newcomers to a 'happy hour'

which includes a slide show/lecture on Moorea and an all-you-can-eat dinner for 1500 CFP. For more information about the Activities Center call 56-21-40.

Just down the road from Captain Cook is *Moorea Village* (tel 56-10-02). It has 50 recently renovated Tahitian-style bungalows, (15 with kitchenettes), a pool, bar, restaurant, tennis and volleyball facilities and a beach. Prices begin at 6000 CFP for a single and 7000 CFP for a double. The address is Haapiti, Moorea.

On the beach about four km from the village of Pao Pao is *Moorea Lagoon** (tel 56-14-68, 56-11-55). The atmosphere on the property, which has been completely renovated is friendly and very Tahitian. During the holiday periods and sometimes on weekends, much of the clientele is local. There are 45 rooms and four bungalows, suites with a jacuzzi, five hectares of gardens, a pool, bicycles, a bar/restaurant, a boutique and conference facilities. You can take advantage of a full array of water sports including an 'Aqua 6' – a sort of surface submarine used for viewing underwater life without getting wet. There's also a fire dancing show every Saturday night. Rates begin at 11,000 CFP for a single and 12,000 CFP for a double. Postal address is PO Box 11, Moorea.

Places to Stay – top end

At the entrance of Cook's Bay and close to the air strip is the *Bali Hai Moorea* (tel 56-13-59) established by three Americans who came before the Tahiti tourist boom to run a vanilla plantation and wound up as hotel magnates. The hotel has a restaurant, two bars, a white sand beach, water sports, Liki Tiki cruises, tennis, pool, and scuba facilities. There are 63 units; try to avoid the ones by the road because of sounds of passing autos at night. On Wednesdays there is an excellent dance review open to all. The best features in the hotel are the landscaped plants that grow in the bathrooms, watered by clients' showers. A great touch. Prices start at around US$85 for a single and

US$100 for a double. Postal address is PO Box 415, Papeete.

In addition to the Bali Hai Moorea there is a second location, *Club Bali Hai** on Cook's Bay, which operates a time-sharing programme and occasionally rents rooms that start at US$110 for a single and US$125 for a double. Accommodation is older bungalows but they are charming.

Situated on a white sand beach facing Tahiti and only two km from the airport, the *Kia Ora Moorea* (tel 52-86-72) is the most luxurious and perhaps the most beautiful of the hotels on Moorea. Its famous disco, aboard an old, converted inter-island schooner, unfortunately sunk during a hurricane. There are three bars, two restaurants (one of them an exceptional gourmet restaurant) and all the amenities you could want such as a boutique, car rental, outrigger canoes, tennis, windsurfing, sailboats and scuba diving. Prices for singles or doubles begin at US$140 for a single or US$155 for a double. The address is PO Box 706, Papeete.

Club Méditerranée Moorea, (tel 56-15-00), is a focal point for the young, the hip and the restless. On Moorea it is the only nightspot on the island. Though refurbished, the property seems to have lost its old charm by doing away with thatched roofs. As in all Club Meds this one has planned activities (a sort of summer camp for adults) located on many motus (islets) to explore. Rates are US$700 per week per person including three meals and all sporting activities. This does not include the US$65 membership fee to join the 'club'. The Club Med at Moorea is the larger of the two French Polynesian CM facilities with a capacity of 700 people. The address is PO Box 1010, Papeete.

The newest hotel on the island is the 150 room *Sofitel Tiare-Moorea* (tel 56-19-19). This was to be Sofitel's jewel in the French Polynesian crown but it's having growing pains. Though food is reportedly excellent and water sports are well provided for, one gets the feeling that the hotel is still under construction and may have opened prematurely. One can clearly see that sand has been brought in to create a beach where there was none and that the shrubs and coconut palms planted by the landscapers haven't quite taken root. One can't help but be impressed one way or another by the Sofitel-Tiare. Upon entering the hotel grounds the visitor is met by a guy in a headdress (I guess an ancient Tahitian headress), carrying a walkie-talkie. The reception area is covered by a huge canopy and the accommodation is striking – thatched-roof bungalows painted in pastels. The whole hotel is done in pastels giving one the impression that the architect spent quite a bit of time in Miami Beach before making it to French Polynesia. Prices begin at US$175 for a single and US$190 for doubles.

PLACES TO EAT

It is hard to go wrong at any restaurant in French Polynesia. Price ranges listed here for Moorea's restaurants do not include wine.

Cocotier, only one km from Bali Hai, this is my favourite restaurant. The food is tasty and reasonably priced. Nice surroundings and friendly Polynesian hospitality. What more can one ask for? Try the fish braised in soya sauce. Prices range from 500 CFP to 1200 CFP for an entrée. Practice your French with Maea, the hostess.

Coconut House, near Bali Hai, is a 'tourist menu' restaurant and has local Tahitian and French cuisine priced from 1000 CFP to 3000 CFP. Reports have not been the greatest.

Hakka Restaurant, Cook's Bay, serves Chinese food, 1500 CFP to 2500 CFP. Mixed reviews.

Manava Restaurant, Cook's Bay, has good, basic Chinese and Tahitian food, 1000 CFP to 2000 CFP. Another 'tourist menu' restaurant and it is recommended.

Michel et Jackie, near Bali Hai, serves French and local cuisine, 2000 CFP to 3000 CFP. Mixed reviews on this one.

Tipanier, near Club Med, has Italian and French specialities, including pizza, 1000 CFP to 2500 CFP, recommended.

L'Oasis, near Club Med, has excellent seafood and French cuisine. Although it's a 'tourist menu' restaurant it's pricey (up to 4000 CFP for a meal), but considered among the best upscale restaurants on the island.

Low Budget Restaurants

Several decent, inexpensive cafes have sprung up in Moorea since I last visited. They include *Honu-Iti* (which means 'small turtle' in Tahitian) in Cook's Bay just on the fringes of Pao Pao. It's run by an engaging Australian woman who cooks up a mean American-style hamburger, good sandwiches, fish burgers, breakfast, shakes and steaks. It's a sort of combination hot dog stand/outdoor cafe. Prices range from 200 CFP to 800 CFP. The best bet.

Near the Bali Hai (about a half km towards Pao Pao) is a *Patisserie* which has good breakfasts, lunches and of course good pastries. It has an outdoor cafe feel as well. *Snack Rotui*, at the foot of Cook's Bay is a 'local' style takeaway which has Chinese food, sandwiches and soft drinks in the 200 CFP to 800 CFP price range.

NIGHTLIFE

There isn't much nightlife except at the swinging *Club Med* which has nightly entertainment and local dances on the weekends. On Moorea it's best not to expect much nightlife or bring your own.

WATER SPORTS
Diving

Divers are well looked after in Moorea. MUST (Moorea Under Water Scuba Diving), (tel 56-17-32), run by Philippe Molle has exploratory dives for experienced divers, night diving and has the facilities for teaching novices.

The other operation, Scuba Piti, (tel 56-15-35), owned by Jean-Luc and Cathy Arnau also teaches beginners the basics as well as taking out the experts. Their forte is underwater photography.

Snorkelling & Shelling

Here Moana Moorea Snorkelling &

Shelling, (tel 56-11-10), run by Ron Hall teaches those with an interest in marine biology the basics of shellfish, coral, currents and the like. He will gladly teach you how to clean the shells once you've discovered them. Getting the stinky things home is your problem.

William Haring's Snorkelling & Shelling (tel 56-14-68) has a similar operation. He provides a huge dugout canoe that seats 25 people for his snorkelling excursions.

Other Water Sports

Reva, (tel 56-15-00), located at Club Med has a motorboat suitable for tours of Moorea's bays, sunset cruises, shopping tours to Tahiti or rentals.

Seer a luxury yacht operated by Peter Ringland (tel 56-21-40) over at Hotel Kaveka has similar outings to the lagoon, island tours, barbecue and sunset cruises and trips to the motus (small islets).

Deep-sea fishing enthusiasts can arrange boat rentals or half-day trips by speaking to Alain Hequet at Club Med.

Those interested in water-skiing, jet skiing and aqua six activities can contact the Kia Ora Hotel (tel 56-16-41) or the Sofitel Tiare (tel 56-12-90) for information on these watersports.

GETTING THERE & AWAY
Air

Air Tahiti flights depart every 30 minutes from Faaa Airport. Recently the airport in Moorea was improved, allowing direct service from Moorea to the outer islands on Air Tahiti's spiffy new ATR 42 aircraft. A regular service from Moorea is provided to Bora Bora, Huahine, Manihi, Maupiti, Raiatea and Rangiroa. See the Getting Around chapter for more information on air fares.

There is also a helicopter service between Moorea and Faaa Airport on Tahiti Helicopter (tel 43-34-26) and Pacific Helicopter Service (tel 43-28-90).

Sea

At the time of writing, there are four boats you can take from Papeete. They are docked on the quay several hundred metres up Boulevard Pomare from the tourism office, Fare Manihini, (where the food vendors park at night). While on the water keep an eye open for flying fish propelling themselves off the crests of the waves and dolphins swimming up to the bow. The ferries are crammed to the scuppers with men, women, children, animals, cars, cases of Hinano beer and every other provision imaginable. They include the *Tamarii Moorea II* and the *Tamarii Moorea VIII* (tel 43-76-50) which hold 300 passengers and cost 700 CFP one-way. The *Tamarii Eimeo* (tel 42-83-79, 43-82-48) holds about 250 passengers and can carry 35 automobiles. It departs three times daily with an extra departure on Sundays and costs 700 CFP one-way. The *Moorea Ferry* (43-73-64) is the largest vessel with a capacity of 350 passengers and also carries cars. It departs from Papeete every morning, with additional trips during the weekend afternoons. The one-way fare is also 700 CFP.

Due to the frequency of the ferries one generally need not worry about reservations. Just go down to the dock. Upon landing at Vaiare (the administrative centre), le truck can be taken free of charge to any hotel around the island. Taxis are available as well. They are most definitely not free. Round trip for most ferries is around 700 CFP which includes the le truck ride to your hotel.

GETTING AROUND

The author's big 'beef' with Moorea is that there is no public transportation, except for the regularly scheduled trucks that are coordinated with the ferries and of course taxis, which are brutally expensive. (I paid 800 CFP, about US$8, for a four-km cab ride). Would be explorers on the cheap must get their hitch hiking thumb out or (gasp) spend the money to rent a motorscooter or car. Fortunately for those on the cheap, hitch hiking is good on most days except Sunday.

As on most of the outer islands, the larger hotels will supply guests with bicycles and can arrange car rentals.

Independent rental agencies on the island include Benjamin Transports (tel 56-11-59) in Temae for those interested in Mercedes, trucks, or minibuses; Arii Rent A Car (tel 56-10-01) (the local Hertz representative) in Haapiti, the airport (tel 56-15- 06), Vaiare (tel 56-16-02) and Temae (56-1-03); Billy Ruta Rent A Car (tel 56-16-98) in Haapiti; Moorea Rent-A-Care (tel 56-16-20) (next door to Billy's which has motorcycles as well); Maeva U Drive (tel 56-10-46) at the Kia Ora; Moorea Transports in Haapiti (tel 56-11-13); and Urbain Petit in Haapiti (tel 56-11-13); and Albert's Rentals (tel 56-13-53) which has cars, motorcyles and scooters, next to the Bali Hai in Pao Pao. One reader reported that he arranged for a rental with Albert's and the agency failed to show up at the hotel with the automobile. Without picking unfairly on Albert's, it's unfortunately typical of the way of doing 'business' in French Polynesia.

It is difficult to see Moorea without a motorised vehicle (or a guided tour) so you may well find yourself in the position of renting something. Be sure and check your car or scooter for minor details like inflated tyres and brakes that work. Expect to pay at least US$65 for an auto per day and about half that for a scooter. This does not include other items like insurance, gas and perhaps a deposit on the vehicle.

Trekking & Overland Tours

Bruno Excursions, (tel 56-18-96), operated by Bruno Meunier will take hikers through the mountains and bush of Moorea. His treks are designed for three levels of difficulty ranging from novice to expert and range in time from $1^{1}/_{2}$ to seven hours. Activities include picnics, swimming in mountain streams, visits to ancient marae and great landscapes. The cost is 2000 CFP to 3500 CFP.

For those less physically inclined, Moorea Safari Tour, (tel 56-20-41, 56-19-13), run by Ronald Sage takes visitors on excursions through the interior with his Land Rovers. The itinerary includes a swim in a river, visit to a bamboo forest, vanilla, coffee and pineapple plantations deep in the highlands. The trip is well worth it for the individual who wishes to see the interior. Safaris can be booked through the Activities Center. 'Safari' departs morning and evening and the cost of the tour is US$40.

Horseback Riding

Rupe Rupe Ranch (tel 56-15-31) near Club Med has equestrian activities for those so inclined.

Huahine

Huahine, 176 km north-west of Papeete, has a population of approximately 4000. It is actually two islands, Huahine-Iti and Huahine-Nui (Little Huahine and Big Huahine) which are part of the same land mass and are connected at low tide by an isthmus. (For the convenience of motorists, there is a bridge.) The island is verdant and rugged and along the coastline there are several gorgeous bays.

The residents have a long tradition of fierce pride and independence. According to a Tahitian proverb, 'Obstinacy is their diversion'. To this day, their cockiness is intact and their practical jokes could very well be a memorable part of the visitor's experience.

Huahine is also a landmark for surfers. Although it does not have the kind of waves that will bring people flocking from Hawaii or Australia, it does have the best surfing in French Polynesia.

Pouvanaa

Huahine is the birthplace of Pouvanaa a Oopa, the greatest contemporary French Polynesian leader. Pouvanaa, a decorated WW I veteran, was the son of a Danish sailor and a Polynesian woman. In 1947 he was jailed by the French for advocating Polynesian veterans' rights, and became the spokesperson for the Tahitian Independence Movement. Blessed with charismatic oratorical skills and well versed in the Bible, Pouvanaa established himself as the most powerful politician in the French Polynesian Territorial Assembly. Known as Metua – 'beloved father to the Tahitians' – he lambasted the colonial system for its treatment of Polynesians as second-class citizens and fought for legislative reforms that would grant Polynesians greater autonomy.

At the zenith of his power, Pouvanaa was convicted of conspiracy in a plot to burn down Papeete and was sent to the notorious Baumette prison in Marseilles. At the age of 64 he was sentenced to eight years of solitary confinement and banished from Polynesia for another 15 years. Ten years later he was pardoned for the crime many felt he did not commit and returned to Tahiti. Eventually he went back into politics and again served in the Territorial Assembly. He died in 1976. For an excellent account of Pouvanaa's life, Bengt Danielsson's *Moruroa Mon Amour* is recommended.

FARE

The small community of Fare, which faces the waterfront, is the island's main settlement and has the usual Chinese shops, a quay to accommodate the copra boats and several pension-style hotels. Fare is almost 'Wild West' in character with its one main street shaded by huge trees and its old-fashioned clapboard stores. It is a slow-moving town in the heat of the day. An occasional auto may pass and kick up some dust or the air may be disturbed by the sounds of school children giggling or bicycle tires gliding across the road. Occasional buses provide transportation to such far-flung communities as Parea at the opposite end of the island or the village of Maeva, a 35-minute, 24-km ride from Fare. The environs of Parea are dense rainforest and two km out of town there is a lovely golden beach. At Marae Anini itself there is another excellent beach. The roads are excellent and follow the often steep contours of the terrain, making it very worthwhile to rent a car for an around-the-island trip.

MAEVA

In ancient times Huahine was a centre of Polynesian culture and was ruled by a centralised government instead of by warring tribes as most of the other islands were. Archaeologically, Huahine is the richest island in French Polynesia and is sometimes referred to as an 'open-air museum'. In the village of Maeva alone there are 16 restored marae, the ancestral shrines of local chiefs. The stone slabs of these ancient temples jut out like phalluses on the landscape and are eerily reminiscent of the Druid ruins of Stonehenge. In the nearby lagoon, rich in crab and other seafood, are nine ancient fish traps constructed from

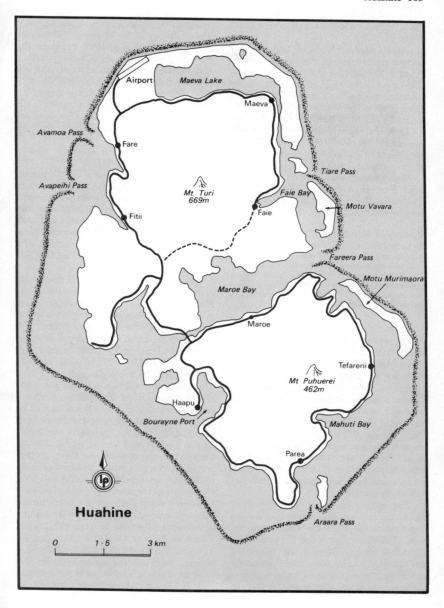

Huahine

0   1·5   3 km

stone, some of which have been rebuilt and are in use today.

Above Maeva village, on Matairea Hill, is the second most important temple in all of French Polynesia and more recently discovered archaeological sites, such as the foundations of priests' and chiefs' homes, more temples and a huge wall guarding the mountain sanctuary from sea raiders.

Opposite Maeva, just across the bridge near Marae Manunu (No 15 on map) is a monument to the Battle of Maeva in 1846. The monument, marked by seven cannons, commemorates the unequivocal French rule over Eastern Polynesia, even though constitutionally it was only a 'protectorate' until formal annexation in 1880.

Mystery of Matairea Hill

The coastal flats of Maeva – where the majority of the reconstructed temples are located – was according to royal tradition, subdivided by the eight royal families of Huahine for purposes of worship. That all the royal families would have their temples in the same area is extremely unusual and suggests a large number of retainers living nearby.

According to tradition, the second most important temple in French Polynesia, Marae Matairea-rahi, is on Matairea Hill above Maeva. Dr Y H Sinoto (the world's authority on Eastern Polynesian archaeology) of Honolulu's Bishop Museum, familiar with the temple ruins, surveyed the area and upon noting the presence of a number of stone structures assumed he had found the remains of the retainers' homes. Upon further investigation, however, instead of retainers' residences he found 40 previously unrecorded marae and realised the area was much more important than had previously been thought.

The survey of Matairea Hill proved significant because they uncovered for the first time marae of the Leeward group that were of similar construction to those of the Windward group. Although the Windward and Leeward islands were allied politically and culturally, marae found in both groups had always been of greatly different

construction – an archaeological mystery. The discovery of the Matairea Hill temples provided a 'missing link' between the cultures of the Leeward Islands (Huahine, Raiatea, Bora Bora and Maupiti) and the Windward group (Tahiti, Maio and Moorea.) The excavations indicate that marae in the Windward group probably originated in the Leeward Islands, such as Huahine, reinforcing the early cultural importance of the island.

ARCHAEOLOGICAL SITES

Along with the very many visible marae, underground excavations reveal that Huahine has the oldest known settlement in the Society Islands. The Vaito'otia/Fa'ahia site came to light in 1972 when a war club (similar in design to artefacts found in New Zealand) was dragged from the bottom of a pond during the construction of the Bali Hai Hotel near Fare. Archaeologist Sinoto happened to be in Huahine at the time of the club's discovery and was called to the scene. Realising it was a significant find, he coordinated subsequent excavation with the owners of the hotel. Between 1973 to 1984 Dr Sinoto unearthed the remains of an entire village, believed to be have been settled between 650 to 850 AD – the oldest remains ever found in the Society Islands.

From tool-making areas at the site, workers unearthed habitations, canoe-making areas and a chief's house as well as numerous wooden, stone and shell artefacts – adzes, fish hooks, pendants, scrapers, canoe bailers and canoe parts. Sinoto theorises that around the year 1000 AD this particular village – whose inhabitants most likely came from the Marquesas (as indicated by the style of the artefacts) – was faced with a natural catastrophe. Either a hurricane or tsunami destroyed the village, creating a sort of Polynesian Pompeii. In all probability the villagers had to evacuate their homes quickly, leaving behind most of their possessions. This was unfortunate for the residents but was a stroke of luck for future archaeologists. Many of the otherwise

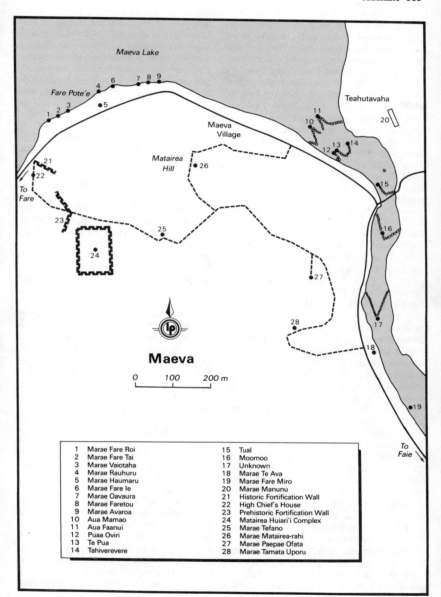

Maeva Lake

Fare Pote'e

Teahutavaha

Maeva Village

Matairea Hill

To Fare

To Faie

Maeva

0   100   200 m

1 Marae Fare Roi
2 Marae Fare Tai
3 Marae Vaiotaha
4 Marae Rauhuru
5 Marae Haumaru
6 Marae Fare Ie
7 Marae Oavaura
8 Marae Faretou
9 Marae Avaroa
10 Aua Mamao
11 Aua Faanui
12 Puaa Oviri
13 Te Pua
14 Tahiverevere

15 Tual
16 Moomoo
17 Unknown
18 Marae Te Ava
19 Marae Fare Miro
20 Marae Manunu
21 Historic Fortification Wall
22 High Chief's House
23 Prehistoric Fortification Wall
24 Matairea Huiari'i Complex
25 Marae Tefano
26 Marae Matairea-rahi
27 Marae Paepae Ofata
28 Marae Tamata Uporu

perishable wooden materials were buried and preserved in the mud – literally in the back yard of the future hotel. The Bali Hai has a display of artefacts in the hotel lobby.

The excavation buttresses Sinoto's theory that early Polynesian settlers came from the Marquesas to the Society Islands, eventually migrating to New Zealand. Artefacts uncovered on the Bali Hai site continue to come to the surface but Sinoto feels his work on this particular spot is '90% complete'. The inventory of artefacts leaves little doubt as to the Marquesan/Huahine/New Zealand link. Sinoto has no evidence that the area was ever resettled after the natural calamity, but it remained an important religious site. Near the entrance of the Bali Hai is the reconstructed Marae Tahuea where Tapaea, the native priest who led Captain Cook to Huahine, is thought to have prayed after his visit to the island with the English explorer.

Touring the Marae

Grab a bus, taxi or bicycle and make your way to the Fare Pote'e, an old-style meeting house in Maeva. The 100-year-old meeting house, which had fallen into disrepair was rebuilt in 1972 by Sinoto. This is where the oceanside marae (constructed mostly in the 16th century) begin. Here the individual chiefs worshipped their ancestors at their respective temples. Heading further south down the road, you will be able to see stones piled in a 'V' shape inside the lagoon, an area particularly rich in fish, crab and other sea life. These stone structures are ancient fish weir traps, which have also been rebuilt by Dr Sinoto and work as well now as they did hundreds of years ago. Fish enter the traps by means of incoming and outgoing tides.

Professor Sinoto initiated the intensive survey of Matairea Hill in 1979 with funding from Earthwatch, a nonprofit organisation in Watertown, Massachusetts. Fonds d'Entralde aux Iles de la Polynesie Francaise have also provided generous financial support. Three sessions with volunteer assistance were needed to complete the mapping of over 200 structures. In 1986, clearing, partial repairs, and test excavations were undertaken in this area. Charcoal samples were collected from test excavations to determine the dates of the occupation of this complex. The excavation revealed that the local people raised dogs and pigs while also consuming a great deal of clams and fish.

New Maeva Discoveries – New Trail

Past Fare Pote'e opposite the Protestant Church is one of the trail heads for the many marae reconstructed by Sinoto on Matairea Hill. The trail head is not obvious; it is set behind a house so ask a local to show you. The 400-metre hike to the main section of the trail is a bit steep at the beginning. At the summit the trail opens up, and the area is covered with ferns and manioc patches. (At this point the mosquitoes begin to attack so bring some repellent along.) In former times this was a vanilla plantation and you can still see the vines spiralling up the trees and bushes.

Beginning in 1984, new excavations by Dr Sinoto revealed that Matairea Hill was occupied (according to the newly discovered cultural layers) from 1450 to 1700 AD. In his efforts to uncover the past, Sinoto has a new historical trail which begins from the shore and goes to Marae Tefano (see map). The trail begins at the fortification wall built in 1846 (when the French marines attacked Maeva) and up the hill adjacent to the latest Sinoto site. A few metres away (22) is a large stone pavement which was part of a round-ended house foundation that most likely belonged to a supreme chief. Interestingly, the front terrace with the large flat stone pavement is oriented inland, facing the sacred mountain of Moua Tapu. The trail goes through the old fortification wall (No 23 on map) which protected residents from invaders from Bora Bora. Just up the trail, at the Matairea Huiari'i complex (24) was occupied by chiefly families who in fact occupied the entire inland slope of the Hill. Each residential unit had one or more marae.

To have a density of so many chiefly families in one place was very unusual.

The most significant marae on the hill is Matairea-rahi (26), the most important temple in the Society Islands prior to the building of Taputaputea in Raiatea. Oral tradition says that when Taputaputea was to be built, stones from Matairea-rahi were transported to the building site to ensure that the new temple would retain the old temple's mana (power). Matairea-rahi consists of two structures: in the first, nine upright stones (a) represent 10 districts – the tenth stone is missing. There are also stone posts that serve as intermediaries to the gods. In the rear is a raised platform called an *ahu*, which was a throne for the gods. Below the *ahu* is a lower platform where sacrifices (some human) were placed. On the other structure (b) stood a house built on posts where the images of gods were kept. The house was actually seen in 1818 by a missionary, Rev William Ellis who saw a building perched on stilts, guarded by men day and night to protect the holy images inside. Captain Cook's painter was also supposed to have seen the temple.

Just a few hundred metres from Matairea is Marae Tefano (25), also an impressive sight. Its *ahu* is huge and the temple basks in the shade of a huge banyan tree, probably planted there around the time the marae was constructed.

A km or so from Fare Pote'e, cross a small bridge and continue to your left on the motu (coral islet) to another very impressive temple, Marae Manunu. This became the marae for the community of Huahine Nui after Matairea-rahi. Next to the low offering platform is the grave of Raiti, the last high priest of Maeva. When he died in 1915 one of the huge marae slabs fell. He was buried at the marae at his request.

Marae Anini, on the southernmost tip of Huahine Iti, served this community as a worshipping place for the deities of Oro and Hiro. The last priest of the temple told Rev Ellis in 1818 that he remembered 14 cases of human sacrifice. The principal feature of the marae is its *ahu*. Small platforms, *ro'i* were

said to be for the gods Oro or Hiro. The upright stones are backrests for priests and chiefs, or memorials for deceased chiefs. A small marae was built when a royal family adopted a child of lower rank. A platform far out on the court was where the house of Oro stood. Under each post of the house a human sacrifice was rendered.

A thorough tour of the marae near Maeva will take several hours and a bit of walking so it is suggested you do it in the early morning or late afternoon. There is also a fine beach near Anini.

The archaeological complex is the core of a planned historical/ecological 'living' museum to be organised by Dr Sinoto and the French Polynesian government. Eventually, with the cooperation of the local population, scientists and the local government hope to create a master plan that will ensure the integrity and maintenance of the archaeological treasures. Ideally, Sinoto feels that agriculture can be revived by practising age-old Polynesian ecology (such as taboos against over-fishing, etc) and combining it with modern agricultural and aquacultural techniques. Sinoto would also like to rebuild the chiefs' and priests' houses near the marae and have families and caretakers occupy them on a full-time basis. The master plan would in addition provide zoning recommendations as to where restaurants, hotels and commercial buildings should be built so as to protect the archaeological zone.

PLACES TO STAY
Places to Stay – bottom end

Hotel Bellvue* (tel 68-82-76, 68-81-70) has bungalows and is in the Fitii district seven km from the airport and five km from Fare. It is one of the better bottom-end hotels on this island, though it is a bit far from town. The Bellvue is on a bluff overlooking a gorgeous bay. The hotel is not fancy but it does have all the amenities including solar heated hot water, restaurant, bar, steam bath (!), horse riding and fishing. The deposit for one night is required. There are 15 bungalows each with a double bed, single bed, bathroom, terrace and private parking. There are also eight rooms each with a double bed and single bed, private bath and balcony. The hotel offers a number of day trips throughout the island as well as fishing expeditions. The rates for one night are 3500 CFP, 4500 CFP and 5000 CFP for one, two and three people respectively. If you stay for two nights the rates go down by 500 CFP per room. Bungalow rates for one night are 6000 CFP, 7000 CFP and 8000 CFP for one, two and three people respectively and go down by 1000 CFP per room for two nights or more.

Hotel Huahine (tel 6-82-69) in Fare has 10 rooms, a restaurant and a bar. It is clean and simple; each room has an individual toilet and shower. The deposit for one night is required. Prices with meals are 5000 CFP per person per night, or, 1700 CFP for a single, 2500 CFP for a double and 3500 CFP for a triple per night. Lunch or dinner is approximately 2000 CFP; you must inform the proprietor if you plan to eat there. Excursions an nsportation to the airport are available

Pensions Known for its fine cooking, *Pension Enite* (tel 68-82-37) is often full to capacity. It is in Fare and has six clean rooms and a common bathroom – no hot water. There is also a restaurant/bar. The minimum stay is two nights. Cost is 5500 CFP per person per night, including three meals or 4800 for room and continental breakfast. Meals are priced from 2000 CFP to 3000 CFP and can also be ordered by nonpatrons but must be reserved. Though Enite is famous for its food, be warned, the owners can be moody and the domestic scene may spill over to the visitor's scene. The pension also provides windsurf rentals (2000 CFP for half day), bicycle rentals (1000 CFP for half day), airport transfers (600 CFP round trip), and island tours on a minibus. Enite has special 'ferry package' rates for those arriving on the bi-weekly ferry – Wednesday breakfast to Thursday dinner or Saturday breakfast to

Sunday dinner (two days and one night) for 10,400 CFP. Finally, those reserving rooms at Enite's must give one night's deposit.

Pension Huahine (tel 68-82-69) is in Fare, directly across from the quay. It is a two-story structure with 10 rooms, eight of which have one double bed and a single, the other two with two double beds and a single. Each room has a private bath (cold water). There is a restaurant/bar on the premises. Rates with breakfast are 2500 CFP, 4000 CFP, and 5000 CFP for single, double and triple respectively. Auto tours of the island are available at 1000 CFP per person.

*Pension Guynette** (tel 68-83-75) is recommended for the budget traveller. Situated in Fare, across from the quay, it has six rooms each with a double bed and private bath, and a dorm with seven cots (communal bath). Kitchen facilities are available. The rates are 3000 CFP for double, groups of four to six are 1000 CFP in rooms and dorms are 800 CFP per night.

Pension Rine, (tel 68-82-79), PO Box 19, Fare, Huahine, is in Fare, above the post office. It has four rooms, each with double bed and private bath. Rates are 2500 CFP for single or double with breakfast.

Pension Tarapapa, (tel 68-12-52, 68-81-23), PO 80, Fare, Huahine, is in Maeva, nine km from the airport. It has two buildings, one a four-room structure on the lagoon, and the other, with six rooms on the 'mountain' side of the road. All rooms have one double bed, kitchenette and private bath. Extra cots can be added if necessary. Round trip transfers from the airport are included in the rates which are 5000 CFP for single or double, 7000 CFP for triple.

Places to Stay – middle

*Hotel Huahine Nui** (tel 68-84-69), at Maroe Bay, a half-hour drive from the airport and quay at Fare, is a good hotel but isolated from the main community. There are six spacious bungalows overlooking the bay, a restaurant, marina, pool, and tennis court. Four of the bungalows have double beds and one cot, the other two have simply one double bed. Rates are 7000 CFP for single or double (including breakfast). Round trip transfer is 1000 CFP. MAP also available. The postal address is PO 121, Fare, Huahine.

Places to Stay – top end

The *Bali Hai Huahine* (tel 68-84-77, 68-82-77) offers the most luxurious accommodation on the island. It features the usual hotel provisions: dining room, two bars, pool, snorkelling, canoes, windsurfing, bicycles, cruises, tennis, white sand beach and beautifully manicured garden. There is a historical, reconstructed temple on the premises; the hotel is on the site of the oldest discovered habitation in the Society Islands. Artefacts on display in the lobby were recovered during construction and subsequent archaeological excavation.

The Bali Hai is within walking distance of Fare, the main village on Huahine, and a 15-minute bicycle ride from the village of Maeva, site of many reconstructed temples. The postal address is PO Box 415, Papeete. Rates begin at US$85 single and US$100 double.

As this book is being updated two hotels are under construction on Huahine. They include the 60-unit *Sofitel Heiva* (tel 42-80-42) and the 50-unit *Hotel Te Tiare No Huahine*.

PLACES TO EAT

Food is available at all of the hotels. The *Bali Hai* has the classiest food and is the most expensive. The restaurant at the Huahine Nui has a 'tourist menu'.

There is only one restaurant on the island not attached to a hotel, *Snack Bar Temarara* in Fare. This 'tourist menu' restaurant is a cozy cafe/bar set directly on the water and features seafood dishes (including lobster), steak and hamburgers. The food is reasonably priced (500 CFP to 2500 CFP) and the mix of tourists and locals provides an interesting ambience.

When the copra boats come in it is always a good time to eat. Their arrival is usually accompanied by vans selling chicken, brochettes, or other goodies for around 600 CFP per plate. The nearby *Enite* is also worth checking out, but reservations are necessary. If you happen to be on the far side of the island try *Ralais Mahana* which is at the southernmost tip of the island near Marae Anini.

GETTING THERE & AWAY

There are air connections between Huahine and Tahiti, Bora Bora, Moorea and Raiatea. There are flights to and from Papeete two to four times daily. Most flights connect with Bora Bora and Raiatea.

The *Temehani II*, the *Taporo IV*, and the *Raromatai Ferry* also sail to Huahine on a regular basis. See the Getting Around chapter for more details.

GETTING AROUND
Car Rental

Kake Rent-a-Car (tel 68-82-59) is adjacent to the Bali Hai. Prices range from 6000 CFP to 7000 CFP per day and 4000 CFP to 5000 CFP per half day, depending on the vehicle. Kake also has scooters and small Hondas available from 3000 CFP to 4000 CFP per day. Bicycles are available for 800 CFP.

Budget (tel 6-81-47) is in Fare and has vehicles for 6500 CFP per day or around 4000 CFP per half day.

Dede, in Fare, has Hondas available for 3000 CFP per day and 2000 CFP per half day.

Note that gas can be purchased at the Faremiti or Mobil stations in Fare.

Horseback Riding

Le Petite Ferme Stable, (tel 68-82-98), halfway between the airport and Fare, has 10 horses and an able 'wrangler', Mme Colette Sioratt. Mme Siorat takes group camping tours of two days or more as well as shorter rides. The cost is around 2500 CFP for two hours, 4400 CFP for four hours, 8200 CFP for day rides including a picnic. The two-day camping trips go for 12,500 CFP (including food) and day-trip mountain rides to visit the marae for 4400 CFP.

Raiatea & Tahaa

One hundred and ninety-two km (120 miles) north-west of Papeete and 40 km (25 miles) west of Huahine are the sister islands of Raiatea and Tahaa. The two share a common coral foundation and protected lagoon. Tahaa is three km north-west of Raiatea – roughly a 20-minute boat trip between the islands.

Legend has it that Raiatea and Tahaa were originally one island but a giant eel swallowed a young girl. Possessed by her spirit, the raging eel broke through the earth and caused the sea to flow, cutting the one island of Raiatea into two – creating Raiatea and Tahaa.

Raiatea

Raiatea is the largest of the Leeward Islands with an area of 170 square km and has about 6500 inhabitants. The island is totally surrounded by a reef but has several navigable passes and the only navigable river, the Faaroa, in French Polynesia. There are no beaches on the island. Raiatea receives plenty of rainfall to irrigate its fertile soil and has a lagoon rich in sea life. Its main products are copra and vanilla. Scientists are also developing oyster breeding in the town of Uturoa.

One of the nicest things about Raiatea is that it remains 'undiscovered' by most visitors to French Polynesia and does not have a well-developed tourist infrastructure. From the visitors standpoint, this is very good. Hotels and pensions are few, thus Raiateans are not inundated by tourists, and are still relatively friendly. However, it is a 'major' community by French Polynesian standards, there are all the amenities – shops, rental cars, hospital, etc.

Like Huahine, Raiatea is an archaeologists's delight. Scientists have unearthed artefacts linking the island with Hawaii,

which corresponds with local tradition that says Raiatea was the great jumping-off point for ancient Polynesian mariners. There are also a significant number of marae, including Taputaputea, considered the most important temple in the Society Islands and a national monument.

Culturally, one of the most unusual aspects of Raiatea is that it is the last bastion of fire walking in French Polynesia. Unfortunately, one rarely sees fire walking on the island. Raiatean fire walkers are generally seen in Tahiti during 'Tiurai', the Bastille Day celebrations.

Omai

Raiatea is the home of Omai, the first Polynesian to visit Europe. When Captain Cook arrived in the Society Islands on his second voyage in 1773, Omai expressed a fervent desire to see 'Britannia'. His wish was granted and he soon became the darling of English society. Although a simpleton, Omai was friendly and charming. Dressed by his benefactors in velvet jackets, he dined in London's best homes, met the king, learned to shoot and skate, and became a favourite with the ladies.

En route back to Tahiti, he served Captain Cook as a translator in the Society Islands and Tonga. He returned to Tahiti in 1776 bearing gifts of firearms, wine, tin soldiers, kitchenware and a globe of the world. The hapless Omai was cheated out of many of his treasures by Tahitians, so Cook saw to it that he was moved to Huahine. Cook's carpenters built Omai a house there and supplied him with pigs, chickens and tools. Omai bid farewell to the crew, who had become his close friends, and held back his tears until it came time to say goodbye to Cook.

MT TEMEHANI

The highest point on the island is Mt Temehani (1033 metres), and it can be climbed. According to tradition one of the principal Polynesian gods, Oro, was born of this volcano. Temehani is also the home of

Tupenu Point
Punape Point
L'Isle
Patio
Hipu
Morifenuo
Tapuamu
Tapuamu
Bay
Raai Bay
Mt Ohiri
Faaaha
Tahaa
Tiva
Haamene
Faaaha
Bay
Niua
Haamene
Toahotu Pass
Bay
Tiamahana Pass
Apu
Poutoru
Puhi Point
Vaitoare
Marina Iti
Toamaro Point

Moorings
Yacht
Airport
Harbour
Swimming
Hole
Uturoa
Pension
Surfing
Marie-France
Teavapiti Pass
(Raiatea Scuba)
Surfing
Rautoanui Pass
Mt Temehani
Avera
Utafara
Point
Surfing
Raiatea
Maire Pass
Tevaitoa
Pension
Opeha
Green Hill
Point
Faaroa
Marae Tevaitua
Tehurui
Bay
Marae
Taputaputea
Mt Tefateaiti
Te Ava
Moa
Pass
Toamaro
Pass
Vaiaau
Opoa
Vaiaau
Vista
Bay
Point
Faatemu Bay
Punaeroa
Pass
Puohine
0   3   6 km
Fetuna
Rauroro Point
Taurere
Point
Motu
Naonao

the *tiare apetahi*, a white flower found only on this mountain. Legend has it that the blossom's five petals represent the five fingers of a young Tahitian maiden who fell in love with a Tahitian prince but was prohibited from marrying him because she was a commoner.

UTUROA

Uturoa is the capital and main port of Raiatea and it is also the administrative centre for the Leeward Islands. It consists of one main drag flanked by two-story cement structures, interspersed with a few old-style clapboard buildings. One block from 'main street' is a quay lined with fishing boats. Uturoa is the second largest town in French Polynesia and although it is not a metropolis it has its own electrical power station, a hospital, gendarmerie, courthouse, Chinese groceries, several small hotels, two restaurants, hardware stores, three banks, boutiques, post office, pharmacy, Air Tahiti office, schools and a barber shop. There is also a plant which makes the ice used to refrigerate fish exports to Papeete and a small municipal market. The market comes alive at the crack of dawn on Wednesdays, Fridays and Sundays. If you feel bored or want companionship, there are always yachts moored at the 'Moorings' yacht harbour whose occupants are eager to trade stories and consume beer. Animal lovers may not be in attendance but for those interested there are cock fights every Sunday at 2 pm.

AROUND THE ISLAND

The newest tourist developments on Raiatea are the Moorings, the largest yacht harbour outside of Papeete (see Yacht Rentals); Green Hill, an excellent, low budget pension; and Pension Marie-France, a low budget hotel that specialises in scuba divers and has limited room for camping. The major 'upscale' hotel in the area is the 36-unit Bali Hai (just outside of Uturoa) which is small by industry standards.

Most of the hotels and pensions organise excursions up the Faaroa River (traditionally the departure point for the ancient Polynesians who settled Hawaii and New Zealand). The river trip is a relatively short excursion into Faaroa Bay a fjord-like inlet with steep verdant cliffs on either side and up the river about a km or two into a 'Heart of Darkness' jungle with thick foliage. The trip lasts until the river becomes too shallow to navigate. Day trips may also include canoe rides to Raiatea's sister island of Tahaa or a trek to Mt Temehani to see the apetahi flower.

Near Uturoa is Tapioi Hill where in 1974 a television relay station was installed. The short climb to the top provides an excellent view of Raiatea and her neighbouring islands.

The tumbled-down ruins of the great temple Marae Taputaputea are just past the village of Opoa, about 35 km from Uturoa. To get to Opoa in order to see the temple you can travel by road or take a motorboat ride down half the length of the lagoon to the marae site.

On the west side of Raiatea is Tevaitoa (about 15 km from Uturoa) where another temple, Marae Tainuu, is located. Continuing south along the road to Fetuna (about 45 km) one can see gorgeous landscapes the entire length of the journey. Those wishing to drive the 96 km circumference of the island will be pleased to know that a road circling the island has recently been completed.

At the southern end of the island, just across from Fetuna Village, is a large motu called Naonao which has a nice beach and is great for picnics. The best motu is off Opeha Point, near the mouth of Faaroa Bay.

Places to Stay – bottom end

*Greenhill**, (tel 66-37-64), PO 598, Uturoa, Raiatea, is my favourite pension in all of French Polynesia. It provides great scenery, modest prices, good food and a comfortable atmosphere. Perched on the side of a ridge overlooking Faaroa Bay, the view it affords is superb and archetypally Polynesian. It is about 12 km out of Uturoa, approximately 20 minutes by car. The pension is run by a charming, cultured, French woman, Marie-

Isabelle, and her equally accommodating husband, Jason, who create a family-style ambience. The cooking is good and all visitors eat at a common table, making one feel as if they are guests at someone's home rather than at a hotel. Accommodation includes one large family bungalow which can house up to nine people, an apartment that houses up to three people and two units for two people. All lodging has a private bath and gorgeous views.

Marie-Isabelle is an entertaining hostess who has lived throughout the world and is definitely an attraction in her own right. The grounds are manicured and lodgings are clean and modest. What is most unusual at Greenhill is that all excursions and day trips are included in the tariff. Thus there are no extra charges for airport transfer, trips up the Faaroa River, round-the-island tours, snorkelling and beach trips to a nearby motu, or use of a bicycle. Whereas many hoteliers attempt to extract every Franc out of the guest, here one gets the feeling that the owners of Greenhill have not succumbed to one of French Polynesia's greatest sins, excessive greed. The cost of accommodation plus three meals per day is a modest 4000 CFP per day, per person. Greenhill requests that visitors make reservations at least two days prior to arrival and a minimum two-day stay is required. Greenhill is often a weekend retreat for local government dignitaries and it's a good idea to make reservations well in advance. You must pay with cash as credit cards are not accepted.

Pension Yolande Roopinia (tel 66-35-28) is in Avera at PK 10, next door to Raiatea Village on the water. The clientele are mostly local as Yolande does not speak English. The pension consists of one long barracks-like building with four, self-contained units, each with single beds, kitchenettes, and private baths. Frankly, it looked sort of dumpy. They offer the usual excursions. The rates are 5000 CFP for a single and 9000 CFP for a double (includes meals). Transfer is 1000 CFP.

Pension Ariane Brotherson (tel 66-33-70) does quite a bit of business with the French military who take their R&R on Raiatea. Though the two-room pension does not have an outstanding reputation as a lodging, Mr Brotherson is renown as the best guide in the area and is very knowledgeable regarding the island's history/archaeology. He does give tours of various archaeological sites such as Taputaputea and treks to Mt Tapioi and Temehani, which he charges 5000 CFP as a guide. Rates are 4500/8000 CFP single/double per day. The address is PO Box 236, Raiatea. It is in the Avera district, about 10 km from the airport.

Pension Marie-France* (tel 66-37-10) specialises in accommodation for divers but they do take in nondivers and they have limited room for camping, literally in their back yard and at another locale. The pension, one km outside of Uturoa (a few hundred metres past the Bali Hai) is ideal for those who wish to stay close to town. It is located directly on the lagoon and has a private dock for swimmers. Patrice Philip, the owner, is the island's only dive operator. He also leads tours to all of the island's attractions including Temehani, Faaroa River, snorkelling and picnics on a motu, and custom tours on his large outrigger canoe. His wife, Marie-France, is quite a good cook and both do their best to make the visitor feel at home. There are four rooms on the premises for 4000 CFP per night (single or double) and tent space is 500 CFP. Add another 300 CFP to rent a tent. Cooking is family style and the cost for three meals per day is just under 3000 CFP. Both campers and lodgers are advised to reserve space by phoning the pension. Patrice will provide free transfer to and from the airport and furnish rental bicycles.

Places to Stay – middle

Hotel Raiatea Village (tel 66-31-62, 66-33-60) has six seaside bungalows and six 'garden' bungalows (all with kitchenettes). The hotel is near the Avera area, at the foot of Faaroa Bay, a 10-minute auto ride from town. The atmosphere is nice but accommodation is over-priced, especially when compared to Green Hill, a km down the road.

Though on the water, swimming may not be advisable due to the presence of a particular type of algae nearby which causes extreme itching. (The owners shrugged off the danger which made me uneasy.) Bicycle, canoe and car rentals are available. Tariffs for the seaside bungalows are 5885 CFP per day for a single, 8239 CFP for a double, 9416 CFP for a triple and 11,770 CFP for four people. Three meals are available with accommodation for an additional 3000 CFP to 4000 CFP per day. The postal address is PO Box 282, Uturoa.

*Hotel Apooiti** (tel 66-33-47) gets a high rating, and would be ideal for families or those wishing to cook for themselves. Two km from the airport and five km from town, it has 12, very modern, comfortable self-contained bungalows in a former copra plantation adjacent to the lagoon. Kitchenette with utensils, television, free transfer, parking space and outrigger canoes are provided. The staff are very friendly. Fruit in season is also freely given to guests. Bungalows are set in an expansive grassy area and afford a great deal of privacy. Rates are very reasonable – 5000 CFP for a single or double, 6000 CFP for a triple or 7000 CFP for a couple with two children. Scuba diving is also available through Patrice Philip. The Apooiti does not accept credit cards. The postal address is PO Box 397, Uturoa, Raiatea.

Hotel Le Motu (tel 66-34-06) is in the centre of town and appears to be the local 'businessman's' hotel. The rooms appeared to be clean and comfortable and there is a good restaurant/bar on the premises as well as a pool hall and disco. The hotel would be recommended except for the disco and pool hall which are noisy and unacceptable for those desiring tranquillity (especially over the weekends). The hotel also provides tours, picnics, boating excursions and free transfers for guests. VISA card is accepted. The rates are 5000 CFP per day for a single or double and 6500 CFP for a triple.

Places to Stay – top end

The *Bali Hai* (tel 66-31-49) is on a lagoon five minutes from the airport about one km from the town of Uturoa. This is the largest and most luxurious hotel on the island and has nine over-the-water bungalows and 27 garden bungalows. There is also a pool, boutique, bar, swimming dock and all the usual excursions. Prices begin at US$70/85 for a single/double

Places to Eat

There is one local bar in Uturoa, the *Three Stars*. Just outside of town is the Bali Hai Hotel which also has a bar and a restaurant. Other eateries include *Le Motu* (part of the hotel with the same name) which is a 'tourist menu' place; *Jade Palace*, which has Chinese food; *Quai du Pecheurs* serves pizza, beer, and good French food on the waterfront; and *Chez Remi*, has excellent French and Tahitian cuisine.

There are also several snack bars such as the *Coconut House* and *Snack Moemoe* which is more of an outdoor cafe serving coffee, sandwiches and beer. Both are near the waterfront. The action doesn't begin until after 10 pm on Saturday because of an important weekly event, the TV show *Dallas*.

Nightlife

In Uturoa the *Vairahi* is a rollicking local disco, basically for the younger crowd.

Scuba Diving

The lagoon offers excellent diving and the local scuba operator, Raiatea Scuba, (tel 66-37-10), run by Patrice Philip, PO 272, Uturoa, Raiatea provides equipment, rentals, transportation and lessons for diving enthusiasts. Aside from pelagics, soft coral and an essentially 'virgin' lagoon, the Raiatea/Tahaa area has unusual blue and purple coral. Lagoon dive sites are numerous, and many are less than 10 minutes by boat from Philip's Pension Marie-France (a few hundred metres from the Bali Hai Hotel). For an extra charge Philip will also pick up divers from yachts or other hotels on the island. Philip has a large outrigger canoe that serves as a dive boat and can seat up to 10 people. Rates are 4000 CFP per dive (including gear) or 3000 CFP for those staying at Pension Marie-France.

Getting There & Away

Flights with Air Tahiti are available to Raiatea seven days a week from Papeete and flying time is 45 minutes. There are also regular flights to and from Bora Bora, Huahine, Maupiti, Moorea and Rangiroa.

Raiatea and Tahaa can be reached by inter-island steamer from Papeete. The *Temehani II* and the *Taporo IV* take about 19 hours. The *Raromatai Ferry* also sails regularly from Papeete. See the Getting Around chapter for more details.

Getting Around

On Raiatea, taxis are available as is le truck service to all the outlying districts between 5 am and 6 pm. Trucks regularly travel from one end of the island to the other two or three times per day. The fare is from 100 CFP to 200 CFP.

Car rentals are available from Hotel Le Motu (tel 66-34-06) or Motu Tapu, a few km outside of town in the same direction as the airport. Expect to pay at least 7000 CFP per day for rentals.

Yacht Rentals

The construction of a yacht harbour by the Moorings Ltd, an internationally known purveyor of 'sailing vacations', is one of the more exciting tourism developments in the Society Islands. Only five minutes from town, the yacht harbour has moorings for private vessels as well as 19 of its own 'boats' ranging in size from 37 to 51 feet in length.

The Moorings have two options for nautical adventurers: 'bareboating' which applies to those who already have the skill to sail a yacht and 'crewed' yachts in which experienced seamen are provided (at a much greater cost). In either case the Moorings people will supply all provisions from bread

to booze, and if necessary, crews. Due to Raiatea's geographical position in the Society Islands, cruising to nearby Bora Bora, Huahine and Maupiti is easy. As one might imagine, cruising is not for everyone's pocketbook but for those that can afford it, it is the best way to see the islands. Prices begin at US$255 per day or US$1785 per week for a *Endeavour 37* to US$550 per day or US$3850 per week for a *Moorings 51*. Call 66-35-93 or 66-20-94; or write to PO 65, Uturoa, Raiatea for more information. From the US call (800) 521-1126.

Tahaa

The area of Tahaa is 90 square km and the population numbers approximately 3500. Tahaa is not as fertile as Raiatea, doesn't have as much rainfall, is more isolated and consequently is less economically developed. Being somewhat of a backwater, it is even more tranquil and off the beaten track. It used to be when travelling to Tahaa one stayed at a local's home but now there are several excellent lodgings. The island is surrounded by a reef with two passes and is served both by regularly scheduled inter-island boats from Papeete and local ferry boats from Raiatea. The travelling time by boat from Raiatea is about 20 minutes.

Agriculture is mainly in the form of subsistence farming although vanilla and copra are produced commercially. Livestock and chicken ranches are also important. Local crafts such as hand-woven hats, baskets, place mats, bedspreads, shell necklaces and wood sculpture are a cottage industry for many.

Parts of Tahaa are still only connected via a footpath but this makes for pleasant walks from Patio (the main community) to Hipu and on to Faaaha. One can also trek from Tiva to Vaitoare along a path that traverses the cliff's edge along the shoreline. One story about the island, recently substantiated, concerns the survivors of a Chilean slave trader wrecked near the village of Tiva in 1863. Before the rescue party arrived, several of the crew members disappeared. They hid in the village, married islanders and became the ancestors of Tahaa's 'Feti Panior' – the Spanish clan. To this day, their descendants live in Tiva and are renowned for their beauty.

PATIO
The capital of Tahaa is Patio, on the northern portion of the island. It has a gendarmerie, an infirmary, a post office (with radio telephone) and school. Excursions to points of interest can be arranged with locals, including visits to spots where the mythical Polynesian hero – appropriately named 'Hiro' – left his mark. These landmarks consist of Hiro's bowl, file, left footprint, crest and boat. The tiny islet of Hipu off the coast of Tahaa is the home of Hiro's shark. There are some strikingly beautiful bays on the island, including Haamene and Hurepiti, which a local guide will be glad to show you.

Places to Stay
The good news is that four new hotels have sprung up in Tahaa, the most interesting being the *Hotel Marina Iti* (a hotel-cum-yacht mooring) and a tiny resort which is more a collection of bungalows called *L'Ile*, located on a remote motu. There is even a good low-budget accommodation *Chez Pascal*.

Chez Pascal* (tel 65-60-42) is in the Tapuamu district of the island a km away from the quay. It consists of one home with two clean rooms each with double bed and private bath. Cooking facilities are available and the electricity is solar powered. Activities include picnics at a nearby motu for 5000 CFP. Single or double rooms are 3000 CFP including breakfast. Write to Pascal Tameahu, Tapuamu, Tahaa.

Pension Hibiscus (tel 65-61-01) in the Haamene district is 20 minutes by boat from the quay at Uturoa. It has three 'traditional'

bungalows. Prices are 5000 CFP for a double without meals and 6250 CFP per person per day with food. There is a small seafood restaurant on the premises. Write to Mrs Teaere Aritu, PO Box 184, Haamene, Tahaa.

Marina Iti Hotel* (tel 65-61-01) is on Toamaro Point, the southernmost tip of Tahaa, 10 minutes by boat from the Raiatea Marina. It combines a marina/nautical atmosphere with three comfortable bungalows. Amenities include bar/restaurant, electricity and transfers from the airport or dock at Raiatea. Activities are diving, cycling, canoeing, sailing, fishing, water-skiing, windsurfing, boating trips to Bora Bora or Huahine and excursions to Raiatea's attractions. Diving rates are 5000 CFP per person per dive (including equipment). The hotel has two bungalows with double beds, single bed, private bath, and terrace, and one bungalow with a double bed, private bath and terrace. The tariff is 11,700 CFP per person which includes three meals. Marina Iti does not accept credit cards. The postal address is PO 888, Uturoa, Raiatea.

L'Ile*, PO 119, Uturoa, an upmarket getaway run by Diego Paterlini and Fancoise Burdinet, is highly recommended. Tucked away on a tiny motu off the north-western shore of Tahaa, it consists of 3.5 hectares of land bounded by long stretches of white sand beach. There are three bungalows for two guests each and common bath. Each bungalow has its own private beach and there are canoes available. Bicycles are also provided for tours of Tahaa. Transfers to Tahaa are free but transportation to Raiatea is 1000 CFP. The cost of lodging and meals is 9000 CFP (single), 16,000 CFP (double) and 30,000 CFP (four people). At the time of writing a phone is being installed.

Getting There & Away
Refer to the Getting There & Away section of Raiatea for this information.

Bora Bora

Located 264 km north-west of Tahiti and just 16 km west of Tahaa lies Bora Bora. Dominated by two towering volcanic peaks and by locals who have learned a thing or two about capitalism, the island has been the subject of much publicity. Formerly a quiet retreat, it is now a mecca for American tourists, hotel entrepreneurs and at one time, Italian film-makers. It has been the subject of a great deal of tourist development over the past few years and perhaps has reached saturation level.

Bora Bora is also a microcosm of the extremes French Polynesia has to offer. No superlatives can adequately describe the spectacular beauty of its emerald-green hills and crystalline blue lagoons. At the same time, visitors may find that locals sometimes have an understandably jaded attitude towards tourists (of whom perhaps they have seen too many). The lesson has not gone unnoticed on other islands. Residents of neighbouring Maupiti shake their heads when they speak of changes on Bora Bora and vow that the same thing will not happen on their island.

Through the years, Bora Borans have learned to cope with an ebb and flow of foreigners. During WW II, 4500 American troops were stationed on the island. In 1977 the island was again occupied, this time by an army of Italian film-makers shooting Dino De Laurentiis' production of *Hurricane*. Again the economy boomed – local merchants turned a handsome profit and many of those hired by the movie-makers were riding new motorbikes or playing new cassette decks. When the Italians left, business as usual became the order of the day. Women returned to work in the hotels and men returned to their fishing boats. The islanders' flexibility is both admirable and a matter of survival.

American author James Michener has written a great deal about Bora Bora and in his epic *Hawaii* offers the theory that the island was a jumping-off point for Polynesian mariners who settled Hawaii. Michener's novel suggests that the reason for this migration was religious persecution. The current population is about 2600.

Bora Bora & the War

In January 1942 the United States was still shaken by the Japanese raid on Pearl Harbor. With much of its Pacific fleet out of commission, the Pentagon had to reappraise the perimeter that could be defended until a counter offensive against Japan could be mounted. The arc 3200 km south from Hawaii, to the Free French Society Islands (now French Polynesia) and westward through Samoa and Fiji to New Zealand was believed to be defensible in those sombre, early days of the war. Bora Bora, 264 km north-west of Tahiti and 6400 km along the direct route from Panama to New Caledonia and Australia, was selected to be the first chain of refuelling bases across the South Pacific. It was code-named Bobcat.

On 8 January 1942 Admiral Ernest King and General George C Marshall approved a joint US Army-Navy plan for the occupation of Bora Bora. Bobcat became the first joint expeditionary force sent into the Pacific. It was composed of a 4000-man army garrison force, comprised of Army National Guard; a navy seaplane squadron of eight OS2U single-engine float planes; a 250-man naval construction detachment (known as 'Seabees'); and a naval base command for harbour defence, waterborne services and fuel depot.

By 21 January 1942, the Bobcat convoy consisting of four cargo vessels and two recently converted passenger ships was being filled with disassembled seaplanes, spare parts, bombs, ammunition, trucks, bulldozers, pontoon barge sections, landing craft, prefab buildings as well as the army

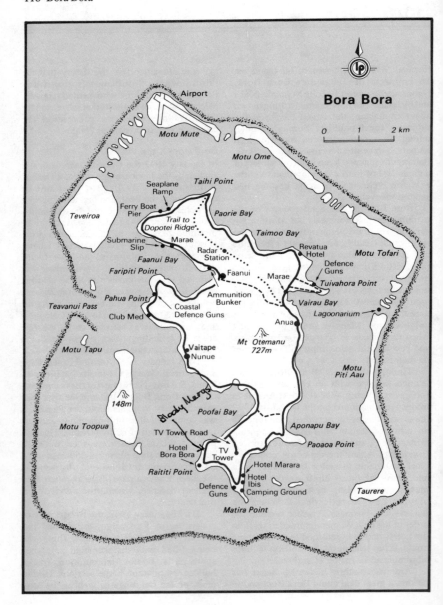

and navy personnel. It was reported that the senior naval officer, Captain Jack Roudebush, had many 'unprintable comments' about the condition of the two passenger vessels. Nevertheless, the six-ship convoy set sail for Panama on 24 January. From Panama onward, the convoy was protected by five other US men of war. They arrived in Bora Bora on 17 February without incident. The convoy was met by the Free French Navy's schooner, *Oiseau des Iles*. Meanwhile a navy hydrographic survey team has charted the only channel into deep water anchorage Teavanui Harbor.

According to an article by Jack Roudebush and Donald I Thomas, both US Navy captains who were on hand:

The island was virtually unspoiled by civilisation; no vehicles; no roads except coral paths for bicycles and pedestrians and coconut log bridges across streams; and no utilities except a minimal water supply ....

The only non-Polynesians on the island were Hank and Connie Hedges, a retired American couple from Illinois who had come to Bora Bora to get away from civilisation. It seemed, however, that 'civilisation' had caught up with them. Paradise was soon filled with some 4500 US servicemen, a seaplane squadron, coast and anti-aircraft defence artillery, trucks, bulldozers, tents, prefab buildings, and thousands of tons of other equipment and supplies.

Though isolated, Paradise had its good points. The locals were friendly, hospitable and an 'extremely handsome lot' according to Captains Roudebush and Thomas. 'The younger women were strikingly beautiful – until they smiled or spoke – nearly all had already lost their front teeth,' they continued. Elephantiasis was common among the older people and the medical and dental staffs of the cruisers spent many hours ashore treating this and other various ailments.

After much initial confusion the multitude of equipment was sorted and unloaded. The main problem was off-loading the pontoon bridges so as to ferry the cargo ashore. Naturally, the 'jewellery' (the fittings) to string the pontoons together had been inadvertently stowed deep in the holds, making the pontoons useless without them. Eventually the ingenius Americans welded a few pontoon barges together and managed to ferry enough cargo out of the hold to get at the jewellery.

The Seabees eventually figured out where to put their seaplanes, bombs, etc and improvised shelters for engines, radio shops, photo labs, and all the other wonders of war. In addition, an aviation machinist's mate who had been a well digger in civilian life made sure that the seaplane base had the first freshwater showers on the island.

The face of Bora Bora quickly changed. Army camps and artillery sites sprang up throughout the island and according to Captains Roudebush and Thomas, the 'din created by heavy trucks and bulldozers shattered its tranquillity, to the delight of the young natives who had never seen these mechanical monsters'. All footpaths and bridges had been destroyed by the vehicles and the Seabees set about construction of heavy duty *American* roads.

The isolation sought by the retired American couple, the Hedges, was gone forever. But life went on. Hank Hedges, a retired civil engineer, assisted in building the waterworks and his wife Connie became mother to 4500 servicemen.

As part of the island's defence, the seven-inch guns were painstakingly unloaded and hauled up the hills. Three of the four original batteries can still be seen today as can the remains of many of the other military paraphernalia. The guns were never fired in anger – the Battle of Midway eliminated any threat of hostility. In either case, they were of little military value – their range hardly went beyond the outer reef.

The fuel depot in Faanui Bay was completed in June 1942 and a signal station on Bora Bora's highest peak Otemanu, was installed. The American signalmen never failed to be amazed at the capability of the 'kibitzing natives' to spot ships in the distance and describe their features long before they were visible by the lookouts who had binoculars.

By 1943, the Seabees had constructed an airstrip on the northern side of the island as a staging base for use of aircraft being ferried to the forward areas. This now serves as Bora Bora's commercial airport. This was not the only legacy of the Americans. By the time the island was handed back to the French in June 1946, the local stock had been invigorated with the addition of several dozen children fathered by Americans. Most of the information in this section was furnished by a fine article which appeared in the March 1986 issue of *Shipmate*, by Captain Jack Roudebush USN (Ret) & Captain Donald I Thomas USN (Ret).

AROUND THE ISLAND

Bora Bora is about 32 km in circumference and the best way to see it is from a bicycle seat. Bikes can be rented from many places and some hotels lend them to visitors as part of the tariff. Depending on what form of conveyance you use, the round-the-island tour can take from 90 minutes to several hours. The tour starts from the Hotel Bora Bora and goes anti-clockwise around the island.

Martine's Creations

(0.5 km)
Martine's small boutique began as a roadside stand and is now a 'chic' shop selling black pearls, tye-dyed T-shirts and air brushed T-shirts that are of her own creation. It's a good place to start looking for souvenirs and cheaper than hotel gift shops. It is one of many boutiques and family run crafts stands, an important cottage industry on the island.

Restaurant & Hotel Matira

(1 km)
A good basic Chinese cafe serving moderately priced food. The same proprietor has over priced bungalows with kitchen facilities.

Coastal Defence Guns

(1.1 km)
Less than 100 metres past the Matira Restaurant (on the hillside) are the most accessible coastal defence guns. The trail begins opposite cabin No 18 on the Matira property. It is best to ask the proprietor of the restaurant if you can see the site since the track begins on his land. It takes about five to 10 minutes to hike the trail depending on what kind of shape you are in. Just be glad you weren't one of the 400 GIs who literally dragged the 13,636 kg (30,000 lbs) gun up that hill. Even with the aid of blocks and tackle, it couldn't have been an easy task. For those wondering, the whole gun assembly weighed approximately 31,800 kg (70,000 lbs). Note that the weight of each piece of the gun assembly is stamped upon it. Ironically the seven-inch guns only had a range of about 16 km (10 miles) and even the military deemed this largely ineffective. Note the graffiti inscribed on the cement 'Battleing (sic) Battery B-276C'.

Matira Point

(2 km)
Best beach on the island.

Camping Ground

(2.2 km)
Not the largest but without a doubt the most beautiful camping ground in French Polynesia. It consists of a small grassy strip of land shaded by coconut trees, adjacent to the beach.

Hotel Marara

(3 km)
This hotel caters mostly for a European and South American clientele. It was built in 1977 by film maker Dino De Laurentiis to house his movie crew during the filming of *Hurricane* (which was a dreadful bomb).

Anau Village

(8 km)
Most typically Polynesian of the villages on Bora Bora. The village has churches, a

school, a general store and rambling, tin-roofed homes with well-kept gardens. Not really a friendly place.

Mt Otemanu & Otemanu Cave
(8.5 km)

At this juncture you are in the shadow of Mt Otemanu, highest point on the island. Near the summit but not easily accessible is the cave, formerly a burial area. On its walls, graffiti proclaims that 'Kilroy was here'. Do not attempt to climb to the cave – the ascent is steep and dangerous.

Marae Aehua-tai
(12 km)

Upon reaching the summit of the island's only hill, do not speed down. The road may be rutted and ultimately unhealthy for downhill racers. Descending from the hill to the beach below is a path to Marae Aehua-tai, an ancient Polynesian temple, and one of several on Bora Bora. The next several km past the temple are virtually uninhabited, sprinkled only with a few houses and several banana groves, coconut palms and taro patches.

Marae Taharuu & Coastal Defence Guns – Tuivahora Point
(12.5 km)

Marae Taharuu, on Tuivahora Point, is a tall, natural obelisk which appears to still be used by non-Christian Tahitians. Note the stones placed before the shrine bearing Polynesian words or names inscribed on them. Tuivahora Point is also the locale for the most spectacular gun emplacement on the island. To get there take the first right at the bottom of the hill (past Marae Aehua-tai) which is a rutted jeep track that follows the beach. Continue along this lonely road until you see a concrete platform that looks to be a foundation for a home. At this point park your bike and back track a few metres. Note a jeep track that goes straight up the hill. Follow it and voilà, you have arrived. Great view here and easy access to the site.

Revatua Club & Chez Christian Restaurant
(12.8 km)

One of Bora's newest hotels, a chartreuse-green colonial-looking structure right on the water and in the middle of nowhere. Great place to stop for a refreshment and by now you will need something to quench your thirst. Chez Christian is one of the better restaurants on the island. Great seafood and French cuisine. Just a few metres past the hotel is a small stand selling souvenirs and the cheapest drinking nuts (coconuts) on the island.

Taimoo Bay
(13.5 km)

Great swimming and clear water for snorkelling. Another km down the road you will note the many holes which land crabs call home. If you have the courage grab them from behind, place in a sack and cook them up for a splendid meal.

Taihi Point
(16 km)

This is the northernmost point of the island and the beginning of a track that will take you to an old radar installation constructed by the US forces on the top of Popotei Ridge. The hike is long and arduous. Better to take a jeep.

Bora Bora Bungalows
(17 km)

The 'bungalows' perched on stilts on the hillside are condos, some of which are owned by Jack Nicholson and Marlon Brando. Don't look too hard though; chances are the stars will be enjoying other tax write-offs than these. Adjacent to the bungalows was the site of a Hyatt Hotel. However, the developer ran out of money and the half completed hotel now slowly deteriorates in the tropical sun.

Ferry Boat Pier & Seaplane Ramp
(18 km)

The pier still used today was another product

of Yankee engineering. Just prior to that is a concrete ramp that slopes gently under the water of the lagoon and was used as a seaplane base.

Marae Fare-Opu & Submarine Slip
(19 km)
This temple is just along the side of the road. Look for turtle petroglyphs on some of the slabs. Turtles were a sacred animal to the ancient Polynesians, and were only consumed by chiefs and priests. Note that adjacent to the marae is a large concrete slip reaching into the lagoon where most likely children will be swimming. This was built to accommodate submarines but has seen more action as a swimming hole. A few metres from the sub slip note the remnants of a pier, which was where the seaplanes would tie up. The pier could accommodate up to 12 OS2U single-engine float seaplanes.

Faanui Bay & Village
(20 km)
This is the section of the island where most of the 6000 American servicemen were stationed during operation Bobcat in WW II. Faanui Bay (see map) was chosen by the US Navy as the most strategic place for a base – protected on all sides by land and directly opposite a motu. Thus, the base could only be seen from the air. The bay had to be extensively dredged to accommodate submarines and other vessels and to this day remains severely environmentally damaged. Visible in the area are pilings from a dock, the water for seaplanes, and several Quonset huts nestled in the bushes along the roadside. Also visible is a massive ammunition bunker on the hillside.

Marae Tianapa
(20.5 km)
This fairly large temple has two small petroglyphs and was associated with Mt Pahia, the 700 metre peak that towers over Vaitape. It is in a field close to the base of the nearby mountain.

Marae Marotetini
(21 km)
A five-minute walk from the road, the marae lies on the shore behind a small coconut grove. According to the old religion, the marae is associated with Mt Otemanu and was the most important temple on Bora Bora. It was restored in 1968 by Dr Y H Sinoto. It was used in the old days by a religious sect entertaining the local population. Near the marae are two tombs built for the Bora Bora royal family during the last century.

Stories of those who purposefully or inadvertently defile the old shrines and suffer the consequences abound in French Polynesia. Supposedly in 1973 a labourer working near Marae Marotetini discovered a rusted biscuit tin containing what were believed to be the charred remnants of the clothing of the last queen of Bora Bora. The tin was accidentally destroyed and not long afterwards (despite the efforts of modern medicine) the worker died of a mysterious malady.

According to author Milas Hinshaw's account of the incident in *Bora Bora E*, after the worker's death his body 'turned black – resembling a corpse that had been consumed by fire'. Hinshaw and his son claim to have been cursed by this same marae when they picked up several human bones there and took them home as souvenirs. Not until five years later, after returning the bones to their resting place, did the author's spate of bad luck stop. Why it took him five years to figure this out, I do not know.

Faanui Power Station
(21 km)
In the village of Faanui, this steam generator is powered by coconut husks. Several hundred metres past the station is a sturdy freight dock built by the US Seabees during the war. It is still used as the major freight unloading facility on Bora Bora. If your map indicates a track across the mountains to Anau and Vairau Bay, this is incorrect. There is a track from Faanui to the water catchment tank near a waterfall. The route to the water-

fall is obscured by deep brush and if you go looking for it, make sure you can get back.

Le Recif
(21.5 km)
The island's only after-hours haunt. Weekends are the best.

Yacht Club
(22 km)
A watering hole and hotel. Very good food at reasonable prices.

Coastal Defence Guns
(23.4 km)
About 50 metres prior to Club Med is a marked path leading up the hill to another battery of Mark II coastal defence guns. They protected Teavanui Pass directly below, which is the island's only access to the ocean. It's a 10 to 15-minute walk up a steep hill.

Club Med
(23.5 km)
The Club Med scene at Bora Bora is much smaller than the one on Moorea. It is one of the few night spots on the island and it is open to the public.

Oa Oa Hotel
(24 km)
This hotel has replaced the Yacht Club as the current 'in' spot.

Denise & Fariua Hostel
(24.5 km)
Opened in 1986, this is one of the best bargain places in Bora Bora. It has a much better reputation than its 'sister' lodging in Tahiti.

Vaitape Village
(25-26 km)
This is Bora Bora's major community. There is a plethora of shops and boutiques including Magasin Roger (a general store); Establissements Loussan (best selection of meat and produce); Chin Lee (largest market on the island) and a gas station. There are also

banks, schools, a gendarmerie, the Air Tahiti bureau (across from the mayor's office), post office (which boasts a new microwave installation for international calls), a commercial centre which has a doctor/ dentist surgery, bank, and Bora Bora Rent A Car. There are also several inexpensive pensions. Several eateries are recommended later in the Places to Eat section.

Near the pier is a granite slab monument to Alan Gerbault, a seaman who sailed his yacht, the *Firecrest* around the world from 1923 to 1929.

Medical Care Those needing medical attention on the island should call Dr Paul-Robert Thomas (tel 67-70-92) who has been recommended by fellow travellers Jay & Robin Simke. His surgery is around the corner from the post office in Vaitape.

Governor's Mansion
(27 km)
The weathered grey building that looks to be a grand turn-of-the-century home is actually a façade. It's part of a movie set built by Di Laurentiis for his bomb, *Hurricane*, and is meant to be a replica of the governor's mansion in American Samoa.

Remnants of Tautu's Museum
(29 km)
The two large hulks of ships on the reef, a collection of anchors, a Mark II coastal defence gun, the carcasses of army vehicles and other objects strewn around make up what was informally known as 'Tatau's Museum'. Tautu is a large Tahitian who likes large things. He used to live in the A-frame behind the collection which made up his front yard. Tautu's aim was to convert the ships into a floating bar/museum some day. To no one's surprise, it didn't quite happen.

TV Tower & Vista Point
(29.7 km)
Keep your eye out for a road that begins next to a double-columned telephone pole and park your bike. Stay to the left and don't

wander into someone's front yard (which will be on your right). A steep five-minute walk up the hill will reward you with one of the best views on the entire island. Don't climb the TV tower, you will get into trouble.

Bloody Mary's

(30 km)

A Bora Bora institution. Outside is a huge carved double-boomed canoe with one boom longer than the other for tacking against the wind. There is also a huge slab of wood where the names of celebrities who have hallowed Bloody Mary's (à la Jimmy Buffet, Ringo Starr, etc) are carved. The fabled bar/restaurant is under fairly new management and the food is still good. Gone are the rooms to stay though. Great place to hang out, sip on a beer, and meet the local American crowd. Very expensive.

Moana Arts

(31.5 km)

A fine shop run by famous Tahiti photographer Erwin Christian. There is a great selection of cards, posters and fashions.

Hotel Bora Bora

(32 km)

The swankiest hotel on the island. The hotel has an excellent restaurant and well maintained, spacious bungalows. It is rated among the best luxury hotels in French Polynesia.

PLACES TO STAY

Bora Bora has changed a lot since the last time I deigned to walk on its shores three years ago and is fast approaching the point of hotel saturation. Any more development would be 'trop' as the French say. There are some excellent places to stay both mid range and top end but still there are far too few good quality budget places for backpackers. One note of caution: campers should take care not to use the facilities at other hotels – even if you are just going in to use the bathroom – management frowns upon it.

Places to Stay – bottom end

Hotel Royal Bora Bora (tel 67-71-54) in the main community of Vaitape has eight bungalows with two single beds or a double bed (including bathroom) and three rooms with two single beds (common bathroom). Although the Royal Bora Bora looked nice enough from the outside, I didn't think much of the rooms which appeared musty, and with meals, were way overpriced. What's more, the owner will not refund advance payments if one decides to leave and stay elsewhere. In a word, this hotel is not recommended. The rates for bungalows are 8000/10,600/16,000 CFP per day for single/double/triple occupancy including breakfast and dinner. Individual rooms including breakfast and dinner are 4500 CFP per day per person and 1200 CFP with breakfast.

*Marama Bungalows** (tel 67-72-97) is a bargain basement special in Vaitape, just behind Snack Bar Marama. There are two *fares* with four furnished studios for two or four people. Each *fare* has one room, a mezzanine and private bath. There is a refrigerator, TV and kettle for the patrons. Food is also available on request. The rates are 5500 CFP for a single or double, 6500 CFP for a triple and 7500 CFP for four people. The tariff includes breakfast. The postal address is PO 11, Vaitape.

*Fare Corail** (tel 67-70-30, 67-70-92) is a house constructed of white coral belonging to the French explorer Emile Victor. On Motu Tane, five minutes by boat from the Bora Bora Airport it is comparatively isolated and has a great white sand beach and excellent swimming conditions. The house consists of a living room, bedroom, dining room, kitchen, terrace and bath. Activities include outrigger canoeing, visits to Vaitape and round trip transfer is provided. There is a three-day minimum stay. There is no phone on the island so one must leave a message at the above numbers. Rates are 7000 CFP for double and 10,000 CFP for four including breakfast.

*Chez Nono Leverd** (tel 67-71-38) on Matira Beach has two houses, one of which is available on a room by room basis and the other house is for groups of up to six people. Food is available on request as are excursions. The first house has three bedrooms, a living room, bathroom and shared kitchen facilities with the owners. Rooms cost 4000/7000 CFP for a single/double. The second home (for up to six) rents for 25,000 CFP per day. The postal address is PO 12, Vaitape.

*Chez Robert & Tina** (tel 67-72-92) is one of the few bargains on the island. Located on Matira near the beach the house has two bedrooms with double beds, living room, kitchen and terrace. Although the house is spartan the place is clean and there is one common bath. The kitchen facilities are furnished but one must purchase sugar, salt and condiments from the store. Round trip transfers from the dock are provided and circle island tours via outrigger or picnics on the beach are available. Robert's lagoon tours are highly recommended. The only downside is that Robert has a tendency to pursue female guests (single or attached) so women should be forewarned. The rates are 3000/5000 CFP for a single/double, and 2500 CFP for an extra person.

*Fare Toopua** (tel 67-70-62) is on Motu Toopua, facing Vaitape and has a white sand beach. There are four *fares* each with a bedroom, mezzanine, bathroom, and kitchen. Rates (which include breakfast) are 8300 CFP double, 9500 CFP triple and 10,700 CFP for four. A small aluminum boat is at the disposal of the guests (with a 20,000 CFP deposit). The minimum stay is three days and confirmed reservations require a 20% deposit. The owners are reportedly reliable people – a quality rare in this part of the world.

Chez Fredo (tel 67-70-31) has two bungalows with one double bed and two single beds plus private bath and kitchen. There is also one bungalow with one bedroom, bath and kitchen. As if that weren't enough there is a house with three bedrooms, each containing two single beds and a communal bath. The bungalow costs 5000 CFP for a double and 1000 CFP per extra person. The room goes for 1200 CFP and 1000 CFP for every following day. Chez Fredo would be recommended except for the reports that it gets a bit noisy with a multitude of children running around the place. The minimum stay is two days. Phone or write to M Alfred Doom, Vaitape.

Chez Rosina (tel 76-70-91) five km from Vaitape, in Poofai Bay, has two rooms with double beds – two with private bathrooms and two with common bathrooms. The rates are 5500/9000 CFP for a single/double. Guests share cooking facilities with the owners. Excursions are available. The postal address is PO Box 51, Nunue.

*Denise & Fariua** (tel 67-72-08) is the newest – and perhaps one of the best – hostels on the island and is directly in front of the lagoon, about a km outside of Vaitape near the Oa Oa Hotel. According to its owners it is built in the 'typical Tahitian style' but basically it is a large shed with a large floor which accommodates up to 30 people. A modern 'lofty' (meaning big) kitchen/dining area is available with utensils. There is also a garden with a BBQ grill and food can be provided on request. The cost is 1000 CFP for the first two nights and 900 CFP for the third. From the fourth consecutive day on, the price is 800 CFP. For a private room (accommodating up to three people) with bathroom and terrace the price is 4500 CFP per night. There is no phone but you can write to the owners at BP 128, Bora Bora. Denise and Fariua also have bikes and boats for rent and excursions. Those who have stayed here like it and it seems to be a good place to meet fellow travellers.

Camping In the Matira Point area, just prior to the Marara Hotel, is Bora Bora's only campground, sometimes called *Chez Pauline* (tel 67-72-16, 67-71-38). The locale is gorgeous, a white sand beach shaded by lovely coconut palms. The only disadvantage is that it's almost 10 km from town so it is a long walk to the corner store for groceries. Still the minor inconvenience is worth it.

Amenities include shower, several picnic tables, a refrigerator, and two gas burners for cooking. Aside from the camping area there are two bungalows priced at 4000/6000 CFP single/double. The bungalows are as good as any other private lodging one will find on the island. Camping 'rates' are 700 CFP per camper. Pauline provides round trip transfer to the boat dock and a great environment for backpackers. The postal address is BP 215, Vaitape, Bora Bora.

Places to Stay – middle

Eight km from the village of Vaitape near the finest beach on the island is *Hotel Matira* (tel 67-70-51). It has 28 bungalows, some with kitchenettes. There is a good, moderately priced Chinese restaurant on the premises. The restaurant prices range from 1000 CFP to 2000 CFP and the menu includes chop suey, seafood, fish and lobster. Room prices begin at 8200/9600 CFP for a single/double without kitchenette and 8600/10,200 CFP for a single/double with kitchenette. The cabins are nice but like many things on this island are way overpriced. The postal address is PO Box 31, Vaitape, Bora Bora. Transfer to Vaitape is not included.

Hotel Oa Oa (tel 67-70-84) is an American-owned establishment with 14 Tahitian-style *fares*, water sport activities, six yacht moorings and a white sand beach. It is considered the 'in' spot for yachties. Generous American-style drinks are served at the bar and Mexican food is served on Friday nights. The hotel is on the Vaitape lagoon one km from the ocean terminal. The rates are 9000/10,400 CFP for a single/double. The postal address is Box 10, Nunue, Bora Bora.

Ten minutes from the airport, *Yacht Club de Bora Bora** (tel 67-70-69, 67-71-34) has one of the best moderately priced restaurants on the island and also has the distinction of having French Polynesia's only floating bungalows. They are equipped with kitchenette, bathroom and solar electricity and accommodate four people. The Yacht Club also has three over-the-water

bungalows, for two, and two garden bungalows with two bedrooms, for four. There are moorings for 17 yachts as well as laundry and bathing facilities for yachties. Other amenities include water sport activities and boat rentals. Prices begin at 8000 CFP per day for a garden bungalow, 10,000 CFP for a floating bungalow and 15,000 CFP for an over-the-water bungalow. The postal address is PO Box 17, Vaitape, Bora Bora.

Bora Bora Bungalows (67-71-33) is in Faanui, near the half completed Hyatt Hotel. There are eight bungalows on the mountain side and three over the water. Each bungalow has two bedrooms, a living room, dining room, bathroom and terrace. I have been told this place is good for long term rentals but frankly the area seems rather spooky and deserted. Prices begin at 10,000 CFP per day for a garden bungalow and 13,000 CFP for an over-the-water bungalow. Monthly rentals begin at 120,000 CFP.

*Revatua Club** (tel 67-71-67) is set far away from the masses on the opposite side of Bora Bora from Vaitape. Where two years ago there was nothing, there is now a chartreuse, colonial-style bar/restaurant with a terrace on the water that belongs in a Bogart movie. The atmosphere is definitely barefoot, local and French, which I found comfortable. Chez Christian the hotel restaurant serves 'Marseille-style' cuisine and is the best on the island. The bar, which serves excellent *tapas*, is amongst the friendliest in French Polynesia and is a good spot to meet locals – sometimes not the easiest thing to do in this country. The only possible fault is that the rooms are a bit spartan for the price. Revatua is ideal for people who want to feel isolated. There is excellent snorkelling close by and I'm sure the only glass-bottom double canoe with stereo. Prices begin at 9500 CFP for a single or double and add an extra 4100 CFP for breakfast and dinner. Tours are also available. The postal address is PO 159, Anau.

*Ibis Bora Bora** (tel 67-71-16) at the

time of writing is under a management change. It is no longer part of the 'Ibis' chain but currently does not have a new name! It is a fairly new hotel, and it is comfortable and modest like all Ibis clones. Located on Matira Beach – the best on the island – it has 36 rooms, restaurant, bar, windsurfing, water-skiing, snorkelling, and excursions. Rates begin at US$80 for a single or double. The postal address is PO Box 252 Nunue, Bora Bora.

Places to Stay – top end

Club Med (tel 67-72-57) – a Club Med village – is 1½ km from Vaitape. It is much smaller, and perhaps more intimate than Club Med on Moorea. It has a bar, restaurant, nightclub, snorkelling, windsurfing, volleyball, outrigger canoe rides, visits to a neighbouring motu, excursions, and all the usual Club Med activities. It is virtually the only 'social scene' on Bora Bora and is open to outsiders for dinner or dancing. There are 41 twin units but they are as bare as bathtubs, and as appealing as army barracks. I was told they would be 'remodelled' in the near future. The price is US$700 per week, all meals and activities included. Though the rooms leave much to be desired, the price is very reasonable as far as French Polynesia goes.

Hotel Bora Bora (tel 67-70-28) has perhaps the best location on the island with terrific views and a good beach. It was recently purchased by a Hong Kong businessman but has retained the same management. Immaculately maintained, Hotel Bora Bora was named by *Andrew Harper's Hideaway Report* as the 'Island Resort of the Year'. It is probably the best resort of its type in French Polynesia.

The feeling at Hotel Bora Bora is 'country club' – quiet, reserved and about as efficient as one can be in French Polynesia. There are 80 bungalows (including 15 over the water), a conference room, a good restaurant, two bars, a boutique, scuba facilities, snorkelling, shark-feeding expeditions, canoes, tennis, a white sand beach and bicycles. In the early evening huge manta rays glide gracefully to the pier under the lights and the fish can be fed off the dock. Car rentals are available at the hotel. Charter cruises are available on American expat Rich Postma's sleek vessel, the *Vehia*. Rich, a veteran skipper, who is savvy to Tahiti's ways, has taken out numerous celebrities but treats everyone like they are someone special. His presence at the Hotel Bora Bora is a huge plus. The hotel is six km from the main village of Vaitape in Nunue, Bora Bora. Prices begin at US$225 for a single or twin and go all the way to US$405 for the top of the line over-the-water bungalow. *Sofitel*

*Hotel Marara** (tel 67-70-46) was *Marara 350* originally constructed by Italian film producer Dino De Laurentiis to house his staff during the production of *Hurricane*. Although the movie bombed, the hotel was a better investment. Located on Matira Beach, it has 64 bungalows, a good restaurant, bar, boutique, an excellent array of water sport activities, tennis, jeep tours, car rentals, windsurfing, deep-sea fishing, a disco, bicycles, glass-bottom boat trips and sunset cruises. One of the hotel staff told me they invented the 'shark feeding' which is now a regular item at most of the resorts. The clientele is about 60% North American and the rest are Europeans or South Americans, thus providing an 'international' flavour.

If the Hotel Bora Bora is a 'country club', then Marara is more of a 'resort'. The atmosphere is more relaxed, the staff are friendly and the prices are much less than the Bora Bora – though they are not 'cheap' by any means. The Marara also has an excellent Tahitian dance review – perhaps the best on the island. It can be seen daily at 8 pm and admission is free. Though I recommend the Marara, mostly because of the ambience, the rooms are in need of refurbishing, something I was told is in the offing. Rates begin at US$155 a single and US$170 a double. The postal address is PO Box 6, Bora Bora.

Bora Bora Moana Beach Hotel is so new, the finishing touches were just being put on when I visited. It is adjacent to the Matira

Hotel, just a few metres down the road from the Hotel Bora Bora, and is considered to be the most 'deluxe' hotel in all of French Polynesia. It is also the most expensive hotel in French Polynesia, so one would expect the Bora Bora Moana to live up to its claim. It is managed by the same organisation that has enjoyed tremendous success with the Beachcomber in Tahiti so one can justifiably expect high standards. The hotel's 30 over-the-water bungalows are the lap of luxury. The touches include woven pandanus mats and tapa cloth on the walls, rattan furniture, and glass coffee tables that enable one to peer directly into the lagoon below. There is also direct international dialling service from each room, room service from 6 am to 9 pm and transportation via a speedboat directly from the airport to the individual bungalow. Activities include the usual water sports, sunset cruises and the like. The food is California *nouvelle*, and the chef is imported from the Bel Air in Los Angeles. There are 10 beach bungalows and 30 over-the-water bungalows. Rates are US$285 (single or double) for the garden bungalow and US$395 for the over-the-water bungalows.

PLACES TO EAT
In addition to the hotels, there are several good restaurants on the island. *Restaurant Matira* near Matira Point serves basic Chinese, no frills, from 1000 CFP to 2000 CFP. About one km down the road from the Matira (towards the campground) is a *Vietnamese* takeaway which consists of a picnic table and cookshack. The food is good and cheap – about 1000 CFP. They are only open during the day.

Going up the scale, the *Yacht Club* in the Club Med area has very good French food and seafood in the 1500 CFP to 3000 CFP range. It's a favourite of many of the locals and it is a 'tourist menu' restaurant. If you want to treat yourself try *Chez Christian* at the Revatua Hotel, on the far side of the island which has first-class 'Marseille-style' seafood and French cooking. If you make a reservation, they will pick you up from any

hotel on the island. Prices are in the 2000 CFP to 4000 CFP range and worth it. There is a good bar scene during the day and nice *tapas*.

Bloody Mary's near the Hotel Bora Bora is an institution on the island. The patron chooses his or her own fish and the chef slaps it on the grill. Fish couldn't be fresher, but it is pricey – 2500 CFP to 4500 CFP for dinner. Lunch is much more reasonable at US$10 to US$15. The ambience is quite nice – sand floor, thatched roof and coconut tree stumps for chairs. It's an American hangout and a favourite of celebs as witnessed by the names of the rich and famous who have dined there such as John Denver, Mac Davis, Judge Rheinhold, Willie Nelson and others.

There are also a few inexpensive eateries in Vaitape the best being *Mama Chou's*, others include *Snack Tiare*, *Bora Bora Burgers*, and the *Marama Snack Bar*. Try the coconut ice cream at *Bernadette's Ice Cream Parlour*.

NIGHTLIFE
Taking into account Bora Bora's small size, it has more hangouts than you might expect. On a Friday evening begin the circuit by hitting Bloody Mary's for a beer or two. More than likely there will be an informal Tahitian combo strumming away on guitars and ukuleles. Next stop is the Club Med variety show, always good for a few chuckles. Following this it is disco time. Assuming your appetite for nightlife is insatiable (as is the case with most Tahitians), next on the agenda is *Le Recif*, Bora Bora's only after-hours club. It is a Tahitian-style disco – crowded, noisy and full of drunks.

After the disco closes it's time to pile into the car, drive around to the other side of the island and (beer in hand) watch the sun come up. By this time you have undoubtedly worked up an appetite, so like your Tahitian hosts, you can breakfast on *poisson cru* (raw fish marinated in lemon juice) which is delicious and will give you the strength to carry on until the following night.

Top: Octagonal Church – the oldest European building in French Polynesia (RK)
Bottom: View of Faaroa Bay from Pension Greenhill, Raiatea (RK)

Top: Tie-dyed pareus, Bora Bora (RK)
Bottom: View from TV tower, Bora Bora (RK)

WATER SPORTS
Diving
There are two dive operators on the island, Erwin Christian, whose headquarters, Moana Adventure Tours (tel 67-70-23), is next to the Hotel Bora Bora, and Claude Sibani who runs a nautical centre called the Calypso Club near the Matira Beach Hotel. Christian, an internationally known photographer, has an exclusive arrangement as a dive operator with the Hotel Bora Bora and can be reached through them. The rates are 6000 CFP for a lagoon dive and 7000 CFP outside the reef. The cost for a resort dive is 6000 CFP. Claude Sibani's shop not only provides services to divers but has waterskiing, parasailing, outrigger tours, jet skis, motorboat rental, hobie cats, windsurfing, glass-bottom boat tours, pedal cars, underwater still cameras and videos, and a snack bar. He takes divers out from all the hotels (except the Bora Bora) and charges 4000 CFP per dive inside the lagoon and 5000 CFP outside. He can be contacted through the various hotels.

Fishing
Sport fishing is quite good just outside Bora Bora's reef where one may hook blue marlin, yellowfin tuna, sailfish, wahoo, mahi mahi as well as bottom fish such as snapper and grouper. There are two charter boats both run by Americans catering to different interests. Both of them are good fishermen but very different people. Leo Wooten, age 50, skipper of *Aquaholics IV*, is both a charter captain and fishes commercially, supplying the daily fresh catch for Bloody Mary's. Leo is an easy going native of Lubbock, Texas fond of Waylon & Willie, and long days at sea. He takes up to four fishermen on five-hour stints for US$350 or US$500 which includes lunch and booze. He can be contacted through Bloody Mary's (tel 67-72-86) or by writing to PO Box 38, Bora Bora. Better yet, if you wish to meet him you are likely to find him perched on his barstool at Bloody Mary's sipping a gin and tonic in the evening.

Keith 'Taaroa' Olson, age 39, strapping native of the San Francisco Bay area who tuned in to the Tahitian way of life while visiting French Polynesia with his parents in the '60s, dropped out of American society to make Bora Bora his home. His vessel, the *Te Aratai II* is a 25-foot Farallon Fishermen and he charges 35,000 CFP for five hours (booze included) or 45,000 CFP for a full day (nine hours). Keith speaks fluent Tahitian and is also well versed in the local culture. After residing here for 20 years, he is a good source of information about French Polynesia and has seen it all. He is amenable to shorter trips for neophytes who don't want to spend five hours at sea. He can be reached at home (tel 67-71-96) or at Bloody Mary's (tel 67-72-86). Write to him at PO 91, Vaitape, Bora Bora.

GETTING THERE & AWAY
There are flights to Bora Bora from Papeete four to six times daily and once daily from Moorea. The flight time is about 50 minutes. There is an air service to Bora Bora from Raiatea, Huahine, Manihi, Maupiti and Rangiroa. See the Getting Around chapter for more details. There is a free shuttle service run by the airport from the small motu where the airport is and the main dock in Vaitape. You can thank Uncle Sam for building the runway during WW II.

Bora Bora is accessible from Papeete via the inter-island vessels *Taporo IV*, the *Temehani II*, and the *Raromatai Ferry*. The island can also be reached from Raiatea with the *Taporo I*. The journey takes a full day.

GETTING AROUND
Car Rental
All major hotels can arrange car rentals; if you are not staying at a large hotel, auto rentals can be made through Bora Bora Car Rentals (tel 67-70-03), south of Vaitape; Rene Chancelades, just south of Club Med (he has scooters and bicycles too); and Alfredo Doom, who rents scooters, bicycles and autos. You will find that most of the larger hotels provide bicycles for their

patrons and that Bora Bora is small enough to make this type of transportation sufficient. Expect to pay around 5000 CFP for a half day and 6000 CFP for full day rental not including gas and insurance.

Tours

Bora Bora Jeep Safari The Jeep Safari operated by a charming Frenchman by the name of Vincent, is a four-wheel-drive circle island tour of Bora Bora, taking in the rugged (and seldom seen) interior of the island. This includes the most scenic WW II gun emplacement on Bora Bora and the radar station atop Popotei Ridge, which is otherwise inaccessible. This tour is one of the best things to happen to Bora Bora and should be put on the 'must-do' list, especially for WW II buffs. The two-hour tour in a sturdy, brand new Land Rover also takes in some of the ancient marae (temples), rusting Quonset huts, ammo dumps, the TV tower and some other great panoramas. Call 67-70-34 and Vincent will pick you up at your hotel or ask at the tour desk. The price is approximately US$30 and well worth it.

Lagoonarium The lagoonarium, on the reef opposite the gun emplacement on Tuivahora Point, is basically a pen with a number of captive fish, turtles and other sea creatures on display. Since it is on the lagoon, one is not exactly able to walk up to the lagoonarium. However, most of the hotels have excursions that visit this watery zoo.

Shark Feeding This is another one of those 'no-miss' activities in Bora Bora. Reportedly originated by the Hotel Marara, feeding the sharks is a common activity run by all the hotels. Someone takes you, snorkel and flippers in hand, to part of the lagoon that is roped off. Your guide stands in the roped of section throwing bait in the water while a dozen or so black tip reef sharks get into their patented feeding frenzy. The audience stands a safe distance away.

Cruises

Dean of the cruise scene is Rich Postma, a long time French Polynesia resident who hails from the San Francisco Bay area. His vessel, the *Vehia* is affiliated with the Hotel Bora Bora but he will naturally take anyone who wishes to come along. Rich has a knack for making everyone feel very special on his cruises and recently took Raquel Welch for a spin around the lagoon. He has a variety of trips including sunset cruises (US$24), deep-sea fishing, or six hour 'BBQ picnics' which includes snorkelling, beachcombing and an isolated motu (US$62). He will charter the *Vehia* for US$300 to US$400 per day.

A young French couple also have a similar day trip which they call the 'Catamaran Lagoon Tour'. The tour includes snorkelling and reef walking, or simply lounging on the beach of a motu. The price is 3600 CFP and the tour lasts for four hours. Their cat is docked at the Hotel Ibis.

A local Tahitian, Johnny Tinorua, also takes people out on his 14-passenger outrigger speed canoe for day trips which include a BBQ on a motu, visit to the lagoonarium and snorkelling. His tours are recommended and leave daily at 9.30 am. The cost is 4000 CFP per person.

Those interested in a luxury yacht would do well to check out the *Epicurien II*, a 19-metre sloop with a teak interior and all the acoutrements of the good life. The vessel, which comes with crew, can be chartered for day trips. For more information contact the Marara Hotel or your tour desk.

Maupiti

Maupiti is the unexploited gem of French Polynesia. It is the smallest (25 square km) and the most isolated of the Leewards. It lies 37 km west of Bora Bora and has a population of about 800. In two hours or less, you can hike the nine km road that circles the island without seeing another human being. A 20-minute walk from the main village is the snow-white, crescent-shaped Tereia Beach on the edge of a turquoise lagoon.

Maupiti is surrounded by small coral islets on the fringing reef called motus and there is one archaeological site on nearby Motu Pae'ao. Maupitans have a disarming friendliness that matches the pristine beauty of their island. They are perhaps the most hospitable islanders in the Society Island group.

You will find that the hotels will provide transport for day trips to some of the nearby motus. The airport is on Motu Tuanai and transport is provided to Farauru village. There is no deluxe accommodation on Maupiti; the visitor must either stay in a pension-style arrangement or lodge with a family. As one travel writer, James Kay (no relation to the author) described Maupiti:

There are no hotels, just a few no-star rated boarding houses, no rental cars, bikes, or motor scooters, no taxis or buses, no bars or restaurants, no bank, no credit cards, and nothing in the way of planned activities. I mean nothing.

Maupitans have adopted a 'no hotel' policy to preserve the island as it is. They have had several offers to build modern hotels, which the village elders have refused – Bora Bora's hotels are just a few km away.

On Maupiti, as in many isolated communities, the residents have the curious habit of burning their lanterns all night. If you ask why, they may or may not tell you that the reason is to keep the *tupa'pau* (ghosts) away. If we are to believe the inhabitants, Maupiti is a haven for every type

of ghost, spirit and supernatural creature imaginable. There is even a semiannual beach party strictly for ghosts; every so often someone from the village passes the beach while these exclusive affairs happen to be going on. Maupitans say that from the empty beach – once the site of a village – the sounds of musical instruments and laughter are quite audible.

PLACES TO STAY

Travellers to Maupiti should note that the hotels in the main village, Vai'ea, have had some serious water shortages. Consequently, water consumption is restricted by the community. This is not so for the hotels on the motus.

Pension Tavaearii, Vai'ea Village, is a four-room house and each room has a double bed. Activities include canoe rides, island tours and long walks. The price is 4000 CFP per person per day including three meals, or 3600 CFP per person per day with breakfast and dinner. The postal address is BP 1, Vai'ea, Maupiti.

Chez Mareta has three rooms with double beds, 'salon', terrace, kitchenette and common bath. Activities include trips to the motus, picnics, and the like. The rates are 4000 CFP per person including all meals, or 2500 CFP per person with breakfast and dinner. The address is Vai'ea, Maupiti.

Hotel Avira*, on isolated Motu Hu'apiti, is the top accommodation on the island. The food is great as is the beach and the owners are very hospitable. There are eight bungalows in all. Three of them are on the beach, two have one room with a double and single bed and a bath; the other is a family unit with one double bed and three singles, plus bath. There are five 'garden bungalows' with communal bath. Four have a double and single bed the other has two single beds. Swimming on the beach is exceptional. There is also a restaurant/bar, washing machine, fishing trips, and tours of Maupiti. Day trips can be easily organised. The rates are about 7000 CFP per person including all meals for the beach bungalows and 6000 CFP per person for the garden bungalows. Write to Mme Edna Terai, PO 2, Vai'ea, Maupiti for reservations.

*Fare Pae'ao** (tel 43-69-32) is another top rated place but the catch is that there must be a group of at least eight people. The food is very good as is the hospitality. This pension is also on a motu with a great beach and swimming, 15 minutes from the airport and the 'big' island. It consists of one home with two bedrooms, each with a double bed and another room with two cots. There is also a kitchen, bathroom and large terrace on the premises. Activities include windsurfing, snorkelling, beachcombing, fishing and other water sports. The cost is 15,000 CFP per day, not including food. Write to Jeannine Tavaearii, Motu Pae'ao, Maupiti or Quartier, Taunoa, Tahiti.

GETTING THERE
Flights are available twice a week from Bora Bora, Raiatea, Papeete and Huahine. The flight time is 30 minutes from Raiatea and 20 minutes from Bora Bora.

Maupiti is regularly served by the *Taporo I* from Raiatea. See the Getting Around chapter for more details.

The Tuamotus &
The Marquesas

The Tuamotus

The Tuamotus, also called Paumotu, meaning 'low or dangerous archipelago', are comprised of one upthrust coral island, a dozen fairly large atolls and countless small atolls and reefs. The coral island, Makatea, is one of the Pacific's three phosphate islands. The 78 islands are scattered over 15° of longitude and 10° of latitude immediately east of the Society Islands. With the exception of Makatea, the islands are extremely low with an elevation not exceeding two to three metres above sea level. The Tuamotus conform to the pattern of the coral atoll. Some are complete, unbroken circles of land, while others are a necklace of islands with intervening spaces of deep channels, shallow water or bare coral rock. Fakareva and Rangiroa are good examples of large atoll islands with navigable passes into their interior lagoons.

Apart from a cultured pearl industry established over the last 20 years on several of the islands, the economy is based on copra. Harvesting copra is tedious, back-breaking work that involves splitting ripe coconuts with a machete, drying them in the sun, plucking the meat out and drying the meat once more in an area protected from land crabs – usually in overhead racks. The atolls are divided into family parcels so that each clan has sufficient land from which to harvest a crop. Thanks to generous subsidies from the Tahitian government, the price of copra is kept artificially high to make certain the islanders will be able to make a worthwhile income. After the copra is harvested, it is placed in burlap bags, weighed and recorded in the Chinese shopkeeper's ledger. The shopkeeper usually acts as a middleman by giving credit at his store in exchange for the crop, which is eventually shipped to Papeete via the copra boats. As in all the islands of French Polynesia, the trading schooners are the most important link with the outside world. When a boat arrives, the entire village flocks to watch copra being loaded and staples from the mainland being unloaded. On board there may be a store run by the supercargo, that sells staples and luxury items such as cigarettes, hard liquor, chocolate and coffee.

If you have a desert island fantasy, the Tuamotus are the place to live it out. Be prepared to live on quantities of fish, rice, corned beef, stale French bread, *ipo* (a Tuamotan dumpling) and perhaps some turtle. The actual settlements consist of little more than a church, Chinese store, pier, water tower or cistern and several rows of clapboard or fired-limestone homes with tin roofs. In the evening the major pastime is playing guitar or, for the older folks, listening to Radio Tahiti, which broadcasts news, music and messages to the outer islands. For the young people, time is spent cooking, fishing, harvesting copra and planning liaisons with girl or boy friends.

The Tuamotus have an eerie ambience not found on other high islands. You notice it several days after arriving. There is something elementally different about an atoll, something you feel but which is hard to articulate. Perhaps it is because you are forced to look inward. There are no caves to hide in, no mountains to climb, no valleys to explore and nowhere to escape. You become aware that you are on an insignificant speck of coral in the middle of an immense ocean. You feel stripped of all the familiar trappings of civilisation, with nothing to fall back on. Despite the monotonous sound of lapping waves on the coral reef, the rustle of ceaseless trade winds through palm fronds and the mercilessly brilliant sun, the primal beauty of an atoll casts an unforgettable spell.

RANGIROA

Rangiroa is the largest atoll in the Tuamotus (the lagoon has an area of about 1020 square km) and is the second largest atoll in the world. Located 322 km north-west of Papeete, it measures 68 km in length and 23 km in width. This huge atoll has miles of empty white sand beaches and silent groves of coconut palms. Rangiroa atoll is so wide that it is impossible when standing on one side of the lagoon to see the opposite shore. A highly recommended activity is to hire a boat and play Robinson Crusoe for a day. Rangiroa's lagoon has an exceptional variety and quantity of marine life. Fish of every size and description – including sharks, manta rays, jack, surgeon fish, mullet, pompano, parrot fish, grouper, puffer fish, butterfly fish, trumpet fish and eels – live in its waters. Some of the local hotels specialise in diving, snorkelling and glass-bottom boat excursions. From the port it is possible to see local divers spear fish and then feed the unfortunate, wriggling creatures to the nearest shark. Rangiroa's major drawback is that, like Bora Bora, it is a prime example of what happens to an island inundated by tourists – the locals can be indifferent to guests. The population is about 1500 and local crafts include making shell hats and necklaces.

Avatoru & Tiputa

There are two main villages on the island, Avatoru (on the same islet as the Kia Ora Hotel) and Tiputa, directly on the other side of the pass. Each village has pension-style accommodation and is one-fifth as expensive as the Kia Ora. Tiputa, the major administrative community, has a Maire (town hall), post office, gendarmerie, infirmary, primary school and boarding school. You'll see many trees, stately walkways and even manicured lawns – a rarity in islands where water and soil are precious commodities. Once a prosperous community with revenues coming from the pearl-shell trade, Tiputa lost its gleam and economic life with the widespread use of plastics. In its glory, soil was actually brought in by those who could afford it.

Avatoru is near the airport and has offices of the civil aviation and fishing departments, schools, a hospital and another post office. Many of the homes in both villages are constructed from solid, limestone-fired material much like concrete in texture and durability. Their whitewash has long since worn away, leaving ancient, weather-beaten surfaces.

Places to Stay – bottom end

Note that prices on many of the pensions are 'approximate' and always subject to change or perhaps the whim of the proprietor.

Chez Iris (tel 324, Rangiroa) in Avatoru rents out a house which has one room with a double and single bed, with the possibility of extra bedding, and room for one person in the 'salon'. There is a complete kitchen, indoor toilet and an outdoor shower. Electricity is available from 5 to 10 pm. Rates are approximately 7000 CFP per day for the house. There is snorkelling gear and bicycles for rent. For reservations call 341 and ask for Iris or 319 during office hours and ask for John.

Accommodation at *Chez Glorinne** (tel 358, Rangiroa) in Avatoru is highly rated as bargain accommodation and has good food and hospitality. It is five km from the airport on the lagoon. There are three bungalows each with two single beds and private bathrooms. There are also two bungalows with double beds and private bath. Rates are approximately 6000 CFP per day including meals. Excursions are available.

Chez Marie (tel 392, Rangiroa) is in Avatoru on the lagoon. There are four bungalows with double beds and private bath, and three bungalows with a double and single bed. The rates are approximately 5500 CFP per day including meals. There is a restaurant/bar and excursions. Electricity is available from 8 am to 1 pm and 6 to 9 pm.

Chez Yves, (tel 334, Rangiroa), has been set up for divers and is in Avatoru near hotel La Bouteille a la Mer. There is one double room and communal bath. Activities are centred around diving. The room plus meals is approximately 4000 CFP per day. Diving

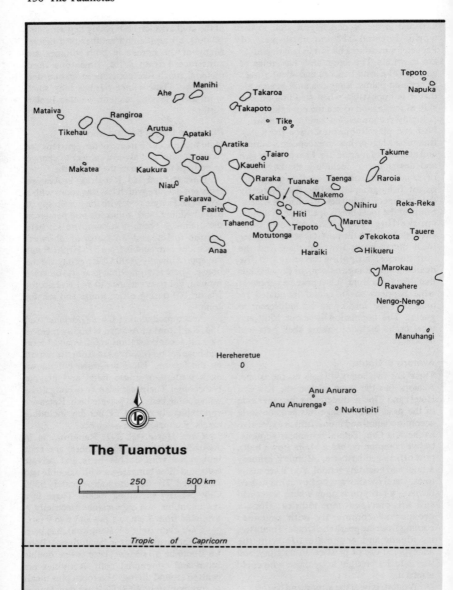

The Tuamotus

0   250   500 km

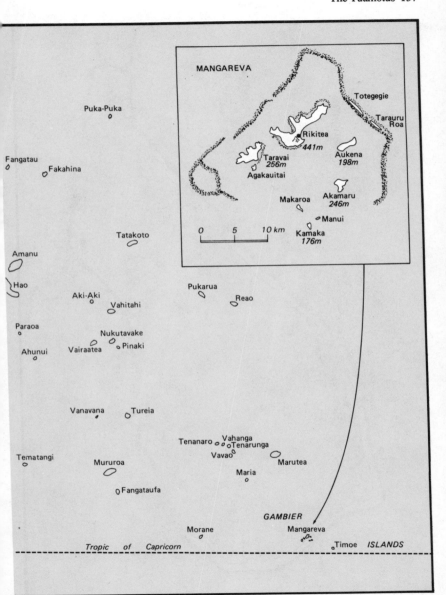

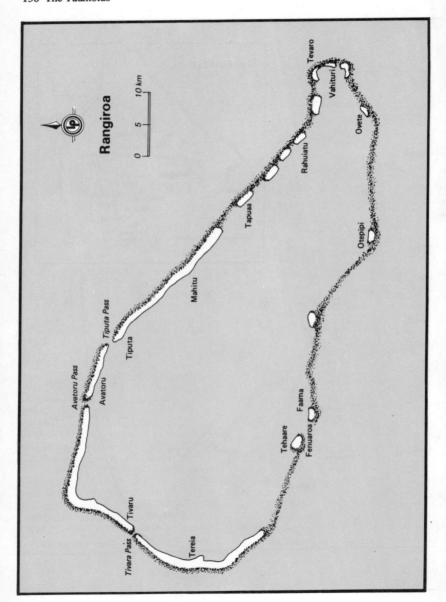

is 3500 CFP per dive and 2000 CFP for resort dives. There are night dives, underwater photography and overnight dive excursions. Write to the Manta Ray Club, PO 55, Avatoru, Rangiroa.

In Tiputa Village, *Chez Jimmy** is two km from the Maire (town hall). Accommodation consists of four bungalows, each with a double and single bed and private bathrooms. The rates are approximately 6000 CFP per person per day including meals. Excursions to the lagoon and picnics are available. Highly recommended.

Chez Jacqueline (tel 356, Rangiroa) in Avatoru has one house with three rooms, each with a double and single bed and private bath. Excursions around the island are available. Rates are approximately 5000 CFP per day with meals and 2500 CFP per day without meals. There is free transfer to the airport.

Chez Tama (tel 326, Rangiroa) in Tiputa is five km from the airport. There are two homes each with three rooms and a communal bath. Rates are approximately 3500 CFP per person per day including meals.

Places to Stay – middle

Village Sans Souci (tel 42-48-33, Papeete) is an hour's boat ride from Avatoru on a tiny islet or motu. Travellers have found this resort to be the best in its class in Rangiroa. There are 15 bungalows, each with a single and double bed, and a seafood restaurant but they don't have electricity. Visitors are provided with sheets but they don't have a maid service. The tariff includes breakfast, lunch, dinner and round trip transportation from the hotel to the airport. Activities include fishing and scuba diving. The rates for three nights are 27,000/43,000 CFP for a single/double. Rates for one week are 48,000/85,000 CFP for a single/double. The address is c/o Greg and Louise Laschelle, Avatoru.

Located one km from the airport, on a beach facing the lagoon, is *La Bouteille a la Mer* (tel 334 in Rangiroa, 43-99-30 in Papeete). It has 10 double/triple bungalows, a bungalow for five people, a restaurant and a bar. Activities include snorkelling, fishing, sailing, diving, windsurfing, water-skiing and excursions to islets. The diving programme at this hotel is associated with the Manta Ray Club. Hotel rates per day are 12,000/20,000/28,000 CFP for a single/double/triple with all meals included. The postal address is PO Box 3564, Papeete.

Rangiroa Village (tel 383) is one km from Avatoru. There are 10 bungalows, restaurant/bar, a great beach, snorkelling, outrigger canoes, bicycles and windsurfing. Rates are approximately 9000/15,000/20,000 CFP for a single/double/triple – all meals included. The postal address is PO Box 8, Avatoru.

Places to Stay – top end

*Kia Ora Rangiroa** (tel 384, Rangiroa) is the nicest hotel on this beautifully forlorn atoll and the best in the Tuamotus. A short drive from the airport, it has 25 bungalows, five suites, a restaurant and a bar. There are excellent facilities for diving which is the main attraction. Complementary activities include snorkelling, windsurfing, sailing and fishing. Diving facilities at the Kia Ora are first class and the equipment is well maintained. Rates begin at US$185/250 for a single/double. The postal address is PO Box 306, Papeete.

Diving

Diving is a main attraction for many of Rangiroa's visitors – sharks are the big attraction in the lagoon. There are two main operators on the island, Eric Jullian at the Hotel Kia Ora and Yves Lefevre of the Manta Ray Club, which is associated with La Bouteille a la Mer. Lefevre's tariffs start at 3500 CFP per dive including transportation and equipment and 2000 CFP for resort dives. He also teaches. Jullian also charges 3500 CFP while resort dives are 2500 CFP. Both will dive the lagoon, the passes and the open sea. Jullian's programme at the Kia Ora is well respected.

Getting There & Away

There are flights every day of the week from Papeete – the flight time is 70 minutes. There are also flights to Bora Bora, Huahine, Manihi, Moorea and Raiatea.

The most comfortable inter-island schooner to Rangiroa is the *Aranui*, but others are available on an irregular basis.

MANIHI

You can find Manihi 520 km north-east of Papeete. I found Manihi's 300 inhabitants to be much friendlier than those of Rangiroa, the only other atoll in the Tuamotus with a hotel. The presence of the hotel (called Kaina Village) and a cultured pearl industry have made the island a comparatively prosperous community. In the Tuamotus, prosperity means owning Mercury outboards, Sony tape decks and clothing without holes. Islanders embrace their improved standard of living as they know what it is like to do without. The old outhouses built on stilts over the water's edge serve as graphic reminders of the way life was not too long ago.

Manihi's villagers take pride in their limestone and clapboard homes, which are lined along two main 'streets' of sand. Most homes have attractive front and back yards arranged with shells, shrubs and flowers. They are either fenced in or surrounded by curbs to discourage the bands of scrawny, marauding dogs that always populate Polynesian villages. There is one main concrete dock, a flagpole and a village square where old people gossip under the shade of a huge tree.

Local Pearl Industry

The island's 15-year-old cultured pearl industry provides the bread and butter for the island. Throughout the lagoon are rows of stakes resembling barbecue spits. From these hang metal rods to which growing oysters are wired. They produce lustrous 'black pearls' with a silver sheen unique to French Polynesia. Every year, Japanese specialists are flown into Manihi to implant tiny spheres

of Mississippi River mussel shell in the black pearl oysters collected from the lagoon by local divers. After three years the oysters are harvested. Out of every 100 oysters, only seven will yield commercially usable pearls.

The Kaina Village gives an excellent tour of the pearl facilities, located in an unobtrusive shack nearby on the village waterfront. The tour includes a boat ride in the lagoon, where a diver is sent to retrieve an oyster. The 'ripe' oyster is opened and the pearl is extracted and passed around the boat for inspection by the guests. There are no free samples; prices for a 'cheap' string of pearls start at around US$750 and go up exponentially from there. A more affordable souvenir is the 'demi-pearl', a sort of pearl on the half-shell. It is actually a hemisphere of plastic that has been glued to the inside of a live oyster and, over the course of a year, is overlaid with mother-of-pearl. These cost about US$15 each.

Places to Stay – bottom end

Chez Marguerite Fareea* is rated as the best budget accommodation on the island. She has one bungalow with a double bed and private bath; and two other bungalows each with one room and two single beds and a communal bath. The pension is located on a motu. Electricity is available from 6 am to noon and 6 to 10 pm. Activities such as picnics on the motus and fishing are extra. Rates are approximately 5000 CFP per person per day, including meals. Airport transfer is provided; please advise as to date of arrival and flight number. Write to Ilot Topiheiri, Manihi, Tuamotu.

Chez Teiva also requests that when making reservations you give arrival date and flight. They offer one house which has three rooms (with single and double beds), private bath, and kitchen. There are also four *fares* each with double and single beds, kitchen and communal bath. Rates are 4500 CFP per person per day including meals. Write to Mme Puahea, Turipaoa, Manihi, Tuamotu.

Chez Faura Pitori (tel 42-95-39, Tahiti)

provides accommodation on a motu with a great beach. There are three bungalows each with two single beds and a common bath. Rates are approximately 5000 CFP per day per person. Call the number in Tahiti for reservations.

Places to Stay – top end

Kaina Village (tel 42-75-53, Tahiti), set on a white sand beach, is a smaller-scale operation than Kia Ora and boasts bungalows constructed over the lagoon's shore that have self-contained waste treatment systems. There are 16 bungalows and two suites, a bar, a restaurant and excellent snorkelling/diving. Although the hotel is isolated from the village, it is more accessible to guests than are the villages in Rangiroa, and visitors are apt to have more contact with locals. A visit to a nearby black pearl 'farm' and the local Paumotu Village are also attractions. Spearfishing is good in the lagoon, and the villagers have an easy time catching dinner in their fish trap. Kaina Village once inspired a popular song on the Tahitian hit parade called, appropriately enough, *Kaina Village in Manihi*. The prices begin at approximately 16,000 CFP for a single and 25,000 CFP for a double. The address is PO Box 2460, Papeete.

Diving

Kaina Village (tel 42-75-53, Tahiti) has a diving operation run by Coco Chaze. Rates are 3500 CFP for dives inside the lagoon and 5000 CFP outside the reef.

Entertainment

Entertainment in Manihi consists of Sunday soccer games, shooting pool, a local version of bocce ball, and catching sharks off the pier. The last one is done at night with a handline attached to a giant hook baited with a chunk of moray eel. When the participants land a shark, they slash its spinal cord with a machete and extract the shark's jaw for a souvenir. Near the pier is a pool filled with harmless nurse sharks with which village boys like to wrestle for the tourists' cameras.

Getting There & Away

There are flights from Papeete four times a week. The flight time (including a stopover in Rangiroa) is two hours and 15 minutes. Flights to Manihi are also available to and from Rangiroa, Huahine, Bora Bora, Moorea and Raiatea.

There are several inter-island vessels sailing to Manihi regularly from Papeete.

AHE

Ahe, the most popular of the Tuamotus with the yachting community, can only be reached by launch from neighbouring Manihi. Ahe does not reap the benefits of any tourist trade or commercial pearl industry; consequently it is isolated and poor. On Manihi, most residents have modern cisterns, sleep on beds and wash their dishes under a freshwater tap. On Ahe, a cistern is apt to be a rusty oil drum, the kids may sleep on a mat on the ground, and the dishes are likely to be done in the waters of the lagoon. Items that some westerners would consider rubbish – tin cans, glass bottles and plastic bags – are all used and re-used. What Ahe lacks in comfort, however, is made up in the kindness of the inhabitants. The axiom about 'the poorer a people, the more generous', certainly holds true on this island. There are no locked doors, and a visitor is always offered what little the family has.

Ahe's inhabitants make their living by harvesting copra and selling fish to a refrigerated storage boat that makes a regular stop on its way to Tahiti. The island was originally settled by people from Manihi and there is a friendly rivalry between the two communities. There is one small but comfortable pension for visitors.

On Ahe, you learn to appreciate life's simple pleasures. I spent a memorable evening there with some locals. Sitting outside the home of a man whose wife was expecting a baby at any moment, we sang, passed around a battered guitar and slugged away at a bottle of Algerian red wine. The expectant father disappeared inside between songs to comfort his wife. The brilliant moon that loomed over us added to the tension in the air. The baby was not born that evening, so our vigil continued through the next night. We traded ghost stories and passed around a bottle of cheap Caribbean rum. Finally, the father announced the birth of a girl and the entire village was invited to the man's one-room shack for a fête. Inside, the single bed where the mother held the newborn child was partitioned off by a blanket. A few jackets and a spearfishing gun hung by nails tacked to the clapboard wall, and several men sat on rough-hewn chairs drinking beer by the light of a kerosene lamp. Throughout the party, three children slept soundly on floor mats in a corner of the shack.

Getting There & Away

There is no air service to Ahe but from Manihi there is a daily skiff.

MURUROA, FANGATAUFA & HAO

Mururoa and Fangataufa are not atolls open to the visitor but are well known as nuclear testing sites. Testing began (above ground) in 1962 but was moved underground in 1974 and restricted only to Mururoa. Total tests exceed 80 to date including neutron weapons, and the publicly acknowledged hydrogen series. The staging area and airfield for the nuclear testing is Hao, another atoll. Hao, while built to provide logistical assistance for the military, is also an airfield used by civilian (Air Tahiti) flights and visitors to some Tuamotu destinations may find themselves landing there.

RAROIA

It was on Raroia's reef that Thor Heyerdahl's raft *Kon Tiki* was wrecked in 1947 and his crew of five other Scandinavians (including author Bengt Danielsson) were washed ashore. They were en route to Mangareva in the Gambier Islands group to test Heyerdahl's theory (based on an Inca legend) that it was possible for men to sail from South America to Polynesia. Instead, the intrepid adventurers had been off course and drifted into Raroia instead.

TAKAPOTO

Located 624 km north-east of Papeete, there are only 150 people living on this forlorn atoll. Most dwell in the community of Fakatopatere. Despite the miniscule size of the settlement there are flights from Papeete twice a week with connections to two other Tuamotu islands, Kaukura and Apataki. Takapoto has beautiful white sand beaches and a cultured pearl facility within its lagoon. There are no hotels but arrangements can be made to stay with a family through OPATTI.

GETTING THERE – THE TUAMOTUS

See the Getting Around chapter for more details of transport to these islands.

The Marquesas

Jutting vertically from the ocean floor, the emerald-green Marquesas Islands form the most spectacular and remote archipelago in French Polynesia. Situated 1250 km north-east of Tahiti, the six major islands were settled over 2000 years ago by Polynesian mariners from Samoa or Tonga. The first European to discover them was the Spanish explorer Alvaro de Mendana, who called them Las Marquesas de Mendoza in honour of his patron, Don Garcia Hurtado de Mendoza, the Viceroy of Peru. Mendana assumed he had discovered these islands en route to establishing a new Jerusalem in the Islands of Solomon.

Called by Marquesans 'Te Henua' – the Land of Men – the islands are divided into two subgroups: the windward group in the south-east comprising Hiva Oa, Tahuata, Fatu Hiva and the smaller islets of Motane, Fatu Uku and Thomasset; and the leeward group 110 km to the north-west comprising Ua Pou, Nuku Hiva and Ua Huka.

The islands, because of their proximity to the doldrums of the equator where the south-east trade winds begin to wane, have always been in a sort of backwater of the Pacific and even in this day of air travel they remain isolated. Volcanic in origin and geologically young, they rise like spires from the sea with their jagged and precipitous profiles, and they lack reefs. There are no coastal plains, and valleys are deep, trench-like and lush. The climate in the Marquesas is on the average hotter and wetter than that of the rest of French Polynesia. The mean temperature is 28°C.

The islands' main product is oranges, which were exported to California, New Zealand and Australia in the 19th century. Marquesans depended more on breadfruit and food cultivated from the land than on food from the sea, which was less accessible to them because of the lack of reefs. They were a warlike lot who practised human sacrifice and, unlike their Tahitian cousins, were cannibals.

After Mendana's discovery (in which he massacred 200 Marquesans) the islands remained undisturbed for almost 200 years until Captain Cook arrived in 1774. This was the beginning of the end for Marquesan culture. After Cook's appearance, the first whalers and slave ships came, leaving behind venereal disease, tuberculosis, influenza and virtually every other malady that white civilisation had to offer. The slavers, needing labourers for guano islands and South American plantations, picked up their unfortunate victims with promises of a better life and sold them to the highest bidder. The sum of these tragic events destroyed the Marquesan people. When Cook first visited the islands, the population numbered about 50,000. Fifty years later it was down to about 5000 and fell to 1200 before the population started to increase again. Today it stands at about 7000.

The first missionaries arrived on the scene in 1798 and in the following half-century different evangelistic sects zealously competed for the souls of the Marquesans. During this period of intense missionary activity the American writer Herman Melville jumped ship from a whaler and eventually wrote *Typee* based on his experiences in the Marquesas. His autobiographical account about the effects of changes made by missionaries on the indigenous population created a storm of controversy in the US and England. In 1842 the French, just beaten to New Zealand by the English, sent Admiral Dupetit-Thouars to colonise the islands and establish a naval base but found relatively little use for them. The late 19th century was a time of darkness and death for the Marquesan race, marked by periods of savagery, killings and, as Greg Denning states in his book *The Marquesas*, 'orgiastic cannibalism'. The French

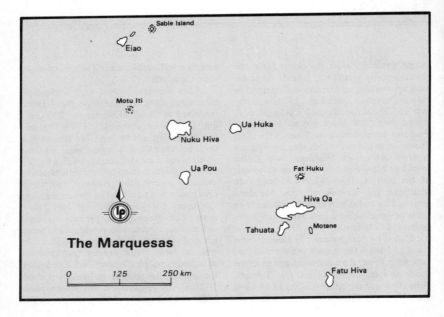

administration could do little more than preside over the death of a people.

The Marquesans were most famous for their skill as tattoo artists and carvers of wood and stone. Local artisans are famous for woodcarvings and hand-crafted ukuleles. Today they still carve statues and bowls but skilled artisans are few. The remains of their temples and imposing stone tikis still stand.

Perhaps the most maddening thing about these islands is a tiny, ubiquitous creature called the 'no-no', a nasty gnat whose bite causes an itching welt.

NUKU HIVA

Nuku Hiva is the most important island in the Marquesas – it is the economic and governmental centre of the archipelago. It is also dramatically beautiful, with three major bays along the southern coast and equally breathtaking inlets on the northern coast. There are numerous remains of pre-European life such as *paepae*, the stone foundations on which the Marquesans constructed their homes; *akua*, fortifications; and *mea'ae*, temples. The ruins testify to the once large population that the island supported. Nuku Hiva is 340 square km in area and supports a population of about 1800. It is 112 km north of Hiva Oa and 37 km west of Ua Huka.

Taiohae

Taiohae, the administrative centre, is located on the shores of Taiohae Bay, the central bay on the southern coast. The town has banks, shops, a post office and other government facilities. General tourism info can be found in the Public Works Building, in front of the pier at Taiohae Bay. Ask for Debora Kimitete (tel 372) or write to PO 38, Taiohae, Nuku Hiva, Marquesas. Maps are for sale for about US$11.

Taiohae long visited by whalers and soldiers (both from the US and France), has remnants of an old fort and jail built for

Top: Marae Aehua-Tai, Bora Bora (RK)
Bottom: Campground, Bora Bora (RK)

political exiles. There is also the Cathedral of Notre Dame which was constructed in 1974, and is the largest church in the Marquesas. The church has magnificently carved sculptures adorning the interior. The Bishop's house contains a small (but still a gem) collection of Marquesan artefacts. The best view of Taiohae is from Muake, 863 metres above the bay.

About 10 km to the west is Hakaui Bay, into which one of the three largest rivers of the Marquesas flows. The gorges above the banks of the river are almost vertical and rise 1000 metres on the western side. Deep in this same valley is the Hakaui Waterfall, which cascades 350 metres down.

Toovi Plateau

The central portion of the island is dominated by the fertile Toovi Plateau. The plateau is rich in flora and fauna and the government has an agricultural station which tests potential crops and tree-planting projects.

The Coast

The west coast is high, rocky and dry; the eastern side of the island is a formidable line of sheer cliffs. Tucked away in the Taipivai Valley, just west of the coast, are many old temples called *paepae* and large tikis. It is perhaps the most beautiful valley in the Marquesas and was where Herman Melville sojourned in 1842 after deserting his whaler.

The northern bays, accessible by boat and in some cases by four-wheel-drive vehicle, are also spectacular and some have beaches. The landscape sloping down from the plateau is volcanic and almost lunar in texture. The village of Hatiheu, on Hatiheu Bay, provides accommodation, horse riding and boating excursions to the area.

Places to Stay

Taiohae *Hotel Moana Nui* (tel 330) is a km from the dock and has four rooms each with one large bed and three more rooms each with two small beds. Bathrooms are common

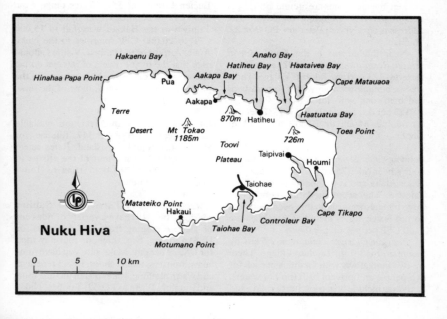

Nuku Hiva

Hakaenu Bay
Hinahaa Papa Point
Pua
Aakapa Bay
Aakapa
Terre
Desert
Mt Tokao
1185m
870m
Hatiheu Bay
Anaho Bay
Hatiheu
Toovi
Plateau
Haataivea Bay
Cape Matauaoa
Haatuatua Bay
726m
Taipivai
Houmi
Toea Point
Taiohae
Matateiko Point
Hakaui
Taiohae Bay
Controleur Bay
Cape Tikapo
Motumano Point

0   5   10 km

and the nightly cost, including breakfast, is US$25 for a single or double. The address is c/o Robert Pelletier, PO Box 9, Taiohae. Lunch or dinner is US$23.

The *Keikahahui Inn* (tel 382) is two km from the wharf and has three Polynesian-style bungalows with a view of the bay. Each bungalow has a large and small bed, shower (hot water), bathroom and verandah. Including breakfast, singles are US$64, doubles US$86, triples US$109. Activities include sunbathing on the nearby beach, diving, snorkelling, hiking, tennis, horse riding, village tours with visits to local wood sculptors, and excursions to other bays. The inn is run by an American couple and is considered to be the premier resort in the Marquesas. The address is c/o Frank Corser, PO Box 21, Taiohae.

Chez Fetu (tel 366) is just 500 metres from the dock and consists of three houses, each with one room with two single beds, a room with one single, shower (with hot water), kitchen with refrigerator, stove and kitchen utensils. Rates are around US$13 per person per day including breakfast. The address is c/o Cyprien Peterano, PO Box 22, Taiohae.

Near the airport is the *Hotel Moetai Village Restaurant/Bar* (tel 491) at La Terre Deserte, 32 km from Taiohae Village. There are six bungalows, five with two twin beds and bath, one with three twins. Rates are US$23 per day for single and US$32 per day for double. Meals are US$18 for lunch or dinner.

Hatiheu *Chez Severin Katupa* is about an hour's boat ride (25 km) from the airport of Nuku Ataha and is two hours by road from Taiohae. The accommodation consists of three bungalows – all double occupancy but no hot water. Rates including breakfast are 1300 CFP per person per day.

Pension Clarisse Omatai is 29 km by mountain road from Taiohae Village. There are two bungalows with facilities in each for two people and private bath (no hot water). Activities include boat trips, horse riding and hikes to visit tikis. Rates are approximately 1000 CFP per person per day.

Places to Eat

Taiohae *Kovivi's Restaurant* is about 500 metres from the Taiohae Bay pier. Lunch is US$9 to US$15 and dinner, around US$20. *Snack Pakiu*, about 500 metres from the market on the waterfront street of Taiohae Bay has meals in the US$8 range.

Getting Around

Airport Transport A few km inland from the northern part of the west coast is the Nuku Ataha Airport – the most important in the Marquesas. To reach the main settlement of Taiohae you must take a 15-minute bus ride to the coast and then catch a boat from the coast almost halfway round the island. The boat ride lasts about an hour and 45 minutes.

Boat Boat tours are available from a number of people including Laurent Falchetto (tel 393), Armand Leau Choy (tel 372) and Lucien Lirzin (tel 351). Rates range from 5000 CFP to 6000 CFP for half hour trips to Taipivai or the Hakaui waterfall to 15,000 CFP to 20,000 CFP for rides to the Nuku Ataha Airport or to Hatiheu. Visitors should note that the major points of interest on the island are accessible, but only with the proper transportation and, most of the time, with the aid of a guide.

Car Rental Cars (with driver) are available from Joseph Puhetini (tel 347, Taiohae) for excursions around the island. Rates range from 1000 CFP for a tour of the village to 15,000 CFP for 2$1/2$-hour trips to Toovi Plateau or to Hatiheu

Horseback Riding Patrick and Sabine Marinthe (tel 410) have a variety of rides out of Taiohae ranging from half day rides for US$16 to one, two, three, or four-day trips for US$29 per day. Make sure you have rain-coats, trousers, tennis shoes, insect repellent and warm clothing. Rates do not include food and lodging. Write to PO 52, Taiohae, Nuku

Hiva for more information. Horses can also be obtained from Louis Teikiteetini (known as 'Coucou') (tel 335), Raymond Gendron and Roo Rootauhine in the village.

From Hatiheu Boat excursions from Hatiheu can be made to various bays and valleys including Aakapa, Anaho, Taiohae and Pua. Fares range from 5000 CFP to 20,000 CFP. Round trip transportation to the airport is also available for 19,000 CFP. Fishing trips cost 8000 CFP and horse rides to ancient temples and tikis are 2000 CFP per person. The address is c/o Yvonne Katupa.

UA HUKA

Ua Huka, is 1448 km north-east of Papeete. It is around 80 square km with a population of about 500. Ua Huka is believed to have the oldest archaeological sites in the Marquesas and scientists postulate it was the dispersal point for settlement of the archipelago. It was never popular with early

Ua Huka

0   5   10 km

traders due to the lack of sandalwood and protected anchorage, but today its tiny airstrip is serviced once a week for connections to other Marquesas Islands and Tahiti. On Ua Huka numerous wild horses and goats run free and sometimes pilots must be wary of horses grazing near the runway.

Main attractions are the ruins in the Hane Valley, the view from the high plateau, and excursions to Vaikivi Valley and bird islands near Invisible Bay on the southern coast. All the villages (Hane, Vaipaee and Haavai) are on the southern coast and have accommodation. The island is famous for its woodcarvers, and offshore lobster and fish are plentiful. The best way to get around on this island is by horse. The highest point is Mt Hitikau at 884 metres.

Places to Stay

Vaipaee Village *Chez Laura Raioha* is a house with four rooms, each with double bed, electricity, communal kitchen and toilet. Daily costs are 3000 CFP per person with meals or 1500 CFP per person without meals.

Chez Joseph Lichtle is a house with three double rooms, common bath and kitchen and electricity. Daily costs are about US$26 per day with meals.

Chez Miriama Fournier also has three rooms available for single or double occupancy. There is a toilet, shower, electricity and common kitchen. Daily rates are 2000 CFP per person including meals.

Hane Village *Chez Jean & Celina Fournier** (tel 43-89-90, Papeete) is seven km from the airport and consists of a duplex home with four rooms, each with double bed. There is a communal bath, a restaurant/bar, and excellent excursions to the valleys and to Bird Island, a bird sanctuary. Rates for room only are 2000/3000 CFP for a single/double and 5500 CFP per person with meals. Recommended accommodation.

Haavai Village *Chez Joseph Lichtle* is close to a nice beach with good swimming, five km from the nearest settlement. He has a small archaeological display with many Marquesan artefacts. The owner is the only person living in the valley and has a farm with fresh vegetables, fruit, cattle, pigs, chickens and ducks. He has three bungalows, each with double bed, private bathroom and electricity. In addition there are two houses, each with three rooms (double beds), common kitchens and bathrooms. Daily cost including meals is 2500 CFP per person. Horse riding is available for 1500 CFP per day and there are excursions to Bird Island which is just offshore.

HIVA OA

Hiva Oa is 1433 km north-east of Papeete and perhaps is best known as the burial place of the painter Paul Gauguin. The island was originally named Sunday Island by Mendana when he discovered it on a Sunday in 1595. Almost 300 years later, Robert Louis Stevenson said of the island, 'I thought it the loveliest, and by far the most ominous spot on earth'. To this day it still retains the paradox of wild beauty and sombre bearing. Very little of the island's 320 square km is flat, but an airport has been labouriously constructed on a ridge above Atuona. The highest point on the island is Mt Temetiu at 1190 metres.

Atuona

The main settlement of Atuona, the second largest town in the Marquesas, has the only safe bay on Hiva Oa, created by the flooding of a tremendous crater. Towering 1190 metres above this is Mt Temtiu, the highest point on the island. The largest building in town is the boarding school for girls, run by the sisters of St Joseph of Cluny. There are three stores, a hospital, two banks, two restaurants and a variety of accommodation possibilities with the locals.

The current population of Atuona is about 1500, only a vestige of the large population the island once had. Many homes are built on the foundations of *paepae*. At one time there were many large tikis on the island but most of those that were within easy reach

of the town have now been scattered to museums all over the world.

Atuona's most famous resident was Paul Gauguin, who came to the island in 1902 from Tahiti and died here in 1903. He is buried on a hill that overlooks the village. On his tomb is a replica of his ceramic work, Oviri, which translates from Marquesan as 'the savage' and symbolises the goddess of death, mourning and destruction. Nothing remains of the home he built, his 'Maison du Jouir' (House of Pleasure), only the well where he drew his water still exists. In Atuona, Gauguin learned from the locals how to carve wood, but found no peace on the island. He was constantly at odds with the local gendarme and priest, who looked on with displeasure at his drinking orgies with the natives. Meanwhile, the humid, sweltering climate intensified the suffering caused by venereal disease which he had contracted in Paris years before. When he died, the villagers wept and the gendarme and priest sighed in relief. For more information on Gauguin see the Facts for the Visitor chapter.

Near Gauguin's grave is the tomb of French singer Jacques Brel, who also spent his last years on Hiva Oa and died in 1978.

Excursions in four-wheel-drive Land Rovers to visit Puamau's stone tikis can be reserved at Atuona Town Hall (Maire). The cost is US$138.

Arts & Crafts

Those interested in purchasing sculptures or precious woods from Marquesan forests such as tou, sandalwood and miro (rosewood) can contact Guy Huhina in Puamau. To purchase woven baskets contact Germaine Timuamoea in Hanapaaoa.

Around the Coast

On the north-east coast near the village of Puamau are the largest stone sculptures in the Marquesas, considered archaeological links to the tikis on Easter Island and those of Necker Island near Hawaii. There is accommodation available in Puamau and excursions can be made to the tikis overland from the main community of Atuona.

Places to Stay

Atuona The *Atuona Town Hall* (tel 332, Atuona) has three small bungalows, each with double bed, shower, bathroom, electricity, refrigerator and hot plate. In addition there are two larger double bungalows, each with two rooms, two double beds, shower, bathroom, gas stove and verandah. The daily rates for the small bungalows are approximately US$14/24 for a single/double and the larger bungalows are US$17/28 for a single/double. Meals are not included in the price. The address is Maire d'Atuona, Village of Atuona, Hiva Oa. From Atuona visits can be made by Land Rover to tiki sites in Puamau. The cost is 10,000 CFP for vehicle and guide.

Saucort's Bungalow (tel 333, Atuona) consists of one large bungalow with double bed, dining room, kitchen, bathroom and electricity. The rates are approximately US$28 per person per day without meals.

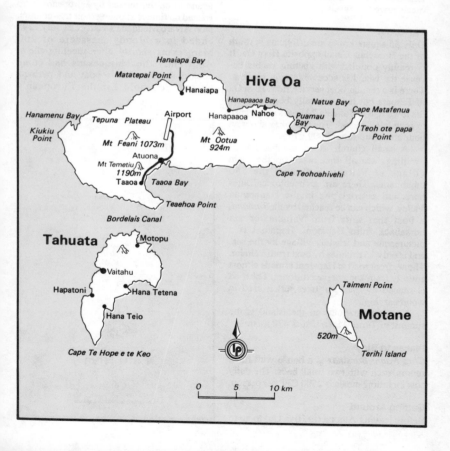

Puamau *Chez Bernard Heitaa* has a house with two rooms with double beds, electricity, common bathroom and kitchen. Daily rates are approximately US$28 per person with meals or US$14 without meals. Lunch or dinner is US$11 per meal. Mr Heitaa also has excursions to visit the famous tikis of Puamau via Land Rover.

Places to Eat

Atuona *Restaurant/Bar Bonna* has 'local' fare, 500 CFP for breakfast and 1800 CFP for lunch or dinner. *Batillard* has full course meals priced between US$6 to US$12.

TAHUATA

Only 55 square km in area, Tahuata is south of the Bordelais Canal opposite Hiva Oa. It is mainly popular with visiting yachts because the island is accessible only by boat. There is a regular boat service from Hiva Oa to Tahuata but it is generally best to notify the town hall in Tahuata 24 hours in advance to schedule a vessel. The trip takes about an hour and costs about 9000 CFP.

A small church, store and handful of dwellings are all that make up the main village of Vaitahu and serve the 550 inhabitants. There are archaeological sites here and petroglyphs in the Hanatahua Valley, which can be reached by the *Tamanu*, a boat that sails from Vaitahu, or via horseback from Hapatoni. Hapatoni is a picturesque and friendly village by the sea, and is only 15 minutes by boat from Vaitahu. The seafront road in Hapatoni is made almost entirely from ancient paved stones. The road is shaded by 'tamanu' trees, often used in wood carving.

The highest point on the island is the summit of Tumu Maea Ufu at 472 metres.

Places to Stay

Chez Naani Barsinas is a house with three rooms, each with two small beds. The daily cost including meals is 2500 CFP per person.

Getting Around

Before leaving Atuona (in Hiva Oa) to go to Tahuata via boat, it is advisable to notify the Mayor of Tahuata of your arrival 24 hours in advance by radio telephone. The communal boat that operates between the two islands holds a maximum of eight passengers and departs the Atuona quay for the one hour voyage. Mr Naho Tiefitu also takes passengers between the two islands and has capacity to take four passengers. Round trip price is 8000 CFP.

FATU HIVA

History records that Fatu Hiva was the first island to be discovered by Europeans, who wasted no time in showing their true colours. Don Alvaro Mendana's visit of 21 July 1595 ended in a bloody massacre of 200 Marquesans shortly after meeting them. Apparently the Marquesans had come aboard the Spaniard's boat and perhaps became too bold for the European's

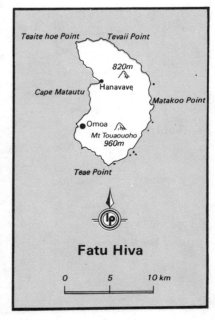

Fatu Hiva

Teaite hoe Point
Tevaii Point
820m
Hanavave
Cape Matautu
Matakoo Point
Omoa
Mt Touaouoho
960m
Teae Point

0   5   10 km

sensibilities. The 'natives' were warned with a few shots and once they fled the Spanish followed by murdering all they could find. As a 'gift' they left behind three large crucifixes and carved the date in a tree. The first meeting was a fitting preamble to the horrors of venereal disease, rum, kidnapping, and all the other delights of civilisation which were to be bestowed on the lucky Marquesans in future years.

Although lacking good anchorages the island was popular with whalers in the mid-19th century. This was due to the fact that it was well away from the authorities' eye and visitors could debauch and raise hell without interference.

The 80-square-km island was famous for its tattoo artists and a man might have his body tattooed completely by the time he died. Unfortunately this great art went with him to the grave. Today Fatu Hiva is the only island in the Marquesas where tapa cloth, produced from the bark of mulberry or breadfruit trees, is regularly made. Local artisans also carve wooden tikis and manufacture *monoi*, a perfumed coconut oil with fragrances derived from tiare blossoms and sandalwood.

Fatu Hiva is famous for its own variety of monoi called *Umu Hei*, blended with seven herbs, sandalwood, Tiare Tahiti (a type of flower), pitate, and ylang ylang flower. The fragrant oil is used as perfume, for massages, to ward off mosquitoes or to seduce a boyfriend.

There are two principal valleys – Hanavave and Omoa – on the western coast and each have several *paepae*. Hanavave Village, located on the Bay of Virgins, is particularly lovely. Nature has blessed Fatu Hiva with more rain than any other island in the Marquesas, giving it a land and seascape that a Tahitian described to me as 'shockingly beautiful'.

The population of the island is about 400. The highest point on Fatu Hiva is Mt Touaouoho at 960 metres. Activities include horse riding, wild pig hunting, and visits to the archaeological sites in Omoa and Hanavave. Contact the Maire (town hall) for further information.

Thor Heyerdahl (of *Kon Tiki* fame) spent most of 1936 on Fatu Hiva and wrote a book of the same name about his time here.

Places to Stay

Omoa Village *Chez Joseph Tetuanui* is a house with two rooms and charges 2000 CFP per person per day with meals. The story is exactly the same at *Chez Kehu Kamia* and *Chez Francois Peters*. *Chez Jean Bouyer* has only one room and the cost is 3000 CFP per person per day.

Hanavave Village *Chez Veronica Kamia* is a house with two rooms at the standard cost of 2000 CFP per person per day with meals. *Chez Jacques Tevenino* has just one room at a cost of 1500 CFP per person per day. Nearby are orange, grapefruit and banana trees and coffee plants. Tapa cloth and sandalwood oil processing can be observed by visitors.

Both *Chez Lionel Cantois* and *Chez Ahutoui Tevenino* have one room in the family home with shared facilities. Room and board are 2000 CFP per person per day. *Chez Tutai Koheinui* has a room in the family home for 1000 CFP per day without meals. Likewise, *Chez Daniel Pvavouau* provides a room in a family home, sharing facilities for 1500 CFP per person per day without food.

Getting Around

Boat The island is accessible by regular boat service from Hiva Oa, but there is no airstrip. The 3½-hour boat trip costs 2500 CFP per person. Travel from Omoa to Hanavave villages is 300 CFP. A complete tour of the island via boat costs 10,000 CFP.

Horseback Riding Horses are available in Omoa Village for 500 CFP per hour or for all day at 5500 CFP.

UA POU

Ua Pou is 110 square km with 1800 residents. It has a jagged, scarp-like relief and six main

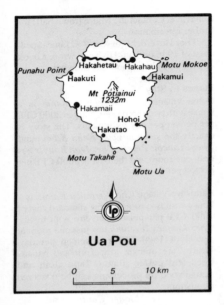

Ua Pou

0   5   10 km

(tel 333) appear to be the transportation moguls of the island. They have one house with three bedrooms, kitchen and bath. Car, boat and horse rentals are available as well as tours of the archaeological sites and beaches. The price is approximately US$15 per day per person – no meals.

Chez Marguerite (tel 376, Hakahau) consists of a three bedroom home with double beds in each room, large living room and communal bath. Rates are 1700 CFP per person per day. Meals range in price from 700 CFP to 1500 CFP extra.

Chez Julienne Pahuaivevau (tel 380, Hakahau) has one room in the family home, sharing kitchen and bath. Price is US$14 per person per day and meals are extra.

Chez Rene (tel 315, Hakahau) is 100 metres from the quay. There is one bungalow with two bedrooms, each with a double bed and two singles, kitchen and private bath. There is also a house with three bedrooms – two with a double bed, the third with two single beds, kitchen and private bath. Rates are 1500 CFP single and 2500 CFP double. Please write or call the owner, Mr Dordillon,

valleys. Mt Oave (1232 metres) is the highest point in the Marquesas. There are seven organised places to stay and the administrative area near the airport, Hakahau, has six shops. Every other settlement (Hakatao, Hohoi, Haakati Hakamaii) is lucky to have one shop, except for Hakahetau and Hakahato which have four. The islanders fashion stone and wood carvings and weave hats and mats for a small income. Best way to spend time on Ua Pou, says the intrepid David Harcombe, author of Lonely Planet's *Solomon Islands – a travel survival kit*, is 'horseback riding along the track that circles the island'.

Places to Stay

Chez Juliette Bruno (tel 391, Hakahau) has one house with two bedrooms each with a double bed. There is also a living room, kitchen and bath. Meals are not available and the daily cost is 1500 CFP per person.

Chez Yvonne & Jules Hituputoka

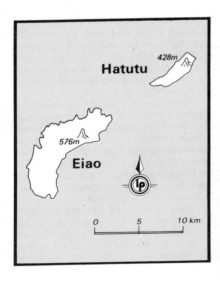

Hakahau, Ua Pou, Marquesas, prior to your transfer from the airport to pension.

Chez Rosalie Tata (tel 311, Hakahau) is just a few blocks from the waterfront. Rosalie has one room with twin beds in a large family home which the visitor shares. She also has a restaurant in her home. Rates are US$14 per person per day. Meals are extra and they range from US$3 for breakfast to US$14 for lunch or dinner.

Chez Samuel & Marie Jeanne (tel 316, Hakahau) is one house with two bedrooms, each with double bed, kitchen, and communal bath. Car and boat rentals are available. Rates with meals are 4000 CFP per person per day.

Places to Eat

Hakahau There are four inexpensive eateries – *Chez Pahuaivevau, Chez Rosalie Tata, Chez Marguerite* and *Snack Vehine.* Prices range from US$3 to US$5 for breakfast and US$15 to US$20 for lunch or dinner.

Getting Around

Hakahau has the island's only car rental agency (tel 333) run by Jules and Yvonne Hituputoka. Road conditions necessitate a local driver and prices (which include driver and fuel) range from US$15 for a half day to US$41 for longer journeys. The Hituputokas are also in the boat rental business (which includes skipper) and will shuttle visitors on throughout the region for US$15 to US$50 depending on the destination. One can also saddle up a horse in Hakahau for US$18 per half day or US$28 for a full day by calling (you guessed it) the Hituputokas.

GETTING THERE – THE MARQUESAS

Visitors to these islands need to be independent travellers, patient (as in all the islands) and able to rough it a bit. Travel is often by four-wheel-drive vehicle, boat and even horseback. Not many tourists except those on yachts see the Marquesas because the air services are limited and flights are booked up to six months in advance. The flight takes seven hours; the journey by copra boat takes seven days. Getting to the Marquesas from Papeete is not cheap either; round trip air fare costs just under US$500 and travel by inter-island steamer, although sometimes less expensive, is very time consuming. For this reason, the islands are among the least physically adulterated in French Polynesia. This will undoubtedly change in the near future. Tourist authorities are already planning to expand airport facilities to accommodate jet planes.

The *Aranui*, a modern inter-island freighter which has been converted to take on passengers, is the most comfortable (and probably the best) way to see the Marquesas. It also stops in several of the Tuamotu Islands (Manihi and Takapoto). Cruises last for 16 days and take in Ua Pou / Nuku Hiva / Hiva Oa / Tahuata / Fatu Hiva / Ua Huka in the Marquesas. The cabins on the 264-foot vessel have been completely refurbished for 'tourists' and even a small dining room and bar have been installed. Despite the upgrading for 'tourists' and the excellent food, this vessel has no pretensions of being a luxury cruise boat. It is a working freighter and stops at every island, loading and unloading cargo like clockwork. Prices which include food and land tours start at US$1130 for deck passage and range from US$1920 to US$3160 for cabins. For those with the means and enjoy travelling on inter-island vessels the *Aranui* is the ticket.

The alternative to the *Aranui* are the irregularly scheduled boats which may not be as 'user friendly' and may entail trips of up to 25 days at sea. Over the years the most consistent visitors to the Marquesas have been American yachts which often make the Marquesas part of their itinerary because the islands are the first landfall en route to Tahiti from the west coast of the United States. For further information in the US call (415) 5410674.

Aside from inter-island vessels such as the *Taporo V*, the *Tamarii Tuamotu* and the newly refitted *Aranui*, Air Tahiti has a regularly scheduled service two days a week from Papeete to Nuku Hiva for a fare of

36,700 CFP. From Nuku Hiva, which is in effect a hub for the other islands in the archipelago, there are flights to Hiva Oa, Ua Huka and Ua Pou. Air fares within the Marquesas range from 4500 CFP to 7800 CFP. The other islands are only accessible by boat.

The Australs &
The Gambiers

The Australs & The Gambiers

These archipelagoes are the outermost and least visited islands in French Polynesia. Lying near the Tropic of Capricorn, they are also the most temperate.

The Austral Islands

The Austral Islands lie about 600 km south of Tahiti and consist of five high islands (Tubuai, Rimatara, Rurutu, Raivavae and Rapa) and two atolls (Hull and Bass). The islands are of volcanic origin, and are not very high (100 to 200 metres) except for Rapa, whose highest point is 1460 metres. Rapa, the farthest south, is sometimes called Rapa Iti (Little Rapa) to differentiate it from Rapa Nui, the Polynesian name for Easter

Island. Tubuai (accessible by air) is the administrative centre of the Australs and offers accommodation with local families. Rurutu (also accessible by air) has the only modern hotel in the entire region.

TUBUAI

Discovered by Cook in 1777, Tubuai is the largest of the Austral Islands, and lies 670 km south of Papeete with a population of about 1400. The climate is temperate and it has a windswept, desolate beauty. The white sand beaches, fishing and horse riding provide the main diversions.

In 1789 it was the first settlement of the HMS *Bounty*'s mutinous crew, who called their outpost Fort George. After six months of considerable bloodshed between the natives and mutineers, the Englishmen

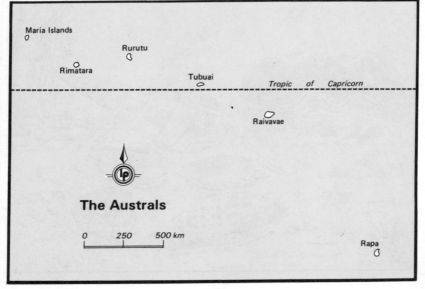

Maria Islands

Rurutu

Rimatara

Tubuai

Tropic of Capricorn

Raivavae

The Australs

0   250   500 km

Rapa

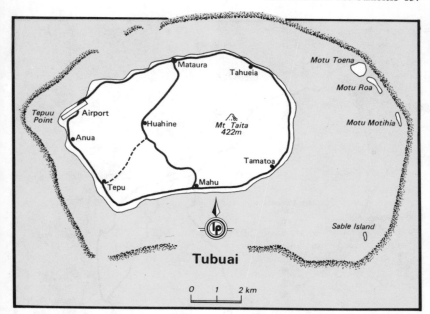

Tubuai

0   1   2 km

decided to leave and eventually settled on Pitcairn Island. All that remains of Fort George today is a rectangular ditch where the walls of the stockade used to be.

Since the *Bounty* episode, Tubuai has had a predilection for attracting expatriates. The best known on the island is Noel Illari, a proud Frenchman and former president of the French Polynesian Territorial Assembly. In 1947, Illari sided with Pouvanaa and a group of Tahitian veterans protesting the hiring of several civil servants sent from France to fill jobs the veterans felt they were entitled to. Illari was sentenced to five months in prison by the government he had served faithfully as an artillery officer in WWI and as an administrator in French Indochina. Illari never forgave France. He became a self-imposed exile on Tubuai and established the Ermitage St Helene, named after Napoleon's place of asylum. Illari took a Tubuaian wife, invested in real estate, spent his time writing anti-government newspaper articles, and helped the local population fight the monopolistic business practises of local merchants. In the early 1970s he developed lip cancer, and feeling that he was close to death, decided to construct his own tomb. He built a 10-foot-tall granite monument that sits conspicuously on his front lawn opposite the main road. The inscription reads:

In memory of Noel Illari
Born in Rennese, France
11 September, 1897
died faithful to his God
to family and to his ideals
to his grateful country
after long years of moral suffering
within isolation and solitude at this place
Passersby, think and pray for him.

Next to the empty tomb is a sign that says:

Interdite aux Chien et aux Gaullists

Illari never succumbed to cancer and remains alive and well in Tubuai. He also rents out the best accommodation on the island.

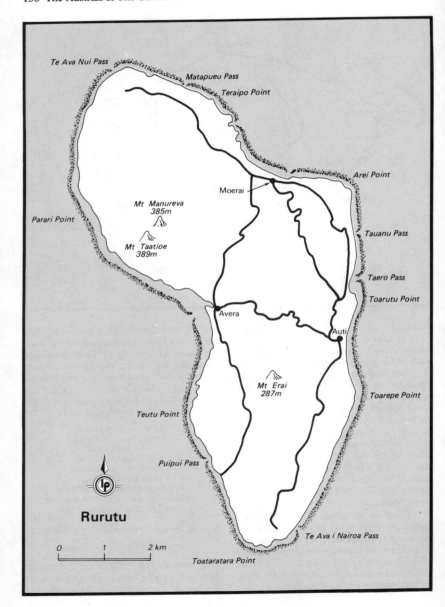

Te Ava Nui Pass

Matapueu Pass

Teraipo Point

Arei Point

Moerai

Parari Point

Tauanu Pass

Mt Manureva
385m

Taero Pass

Mt Taatioe
389m

Toarutu Point

Avera

Auti

Mt Erai
287m

Toarepe Point

Teutu Point

Puipui Pass

Rurutu

Te Ava i Nairoa Pass

0   1   2 km

Toataratara Point

Places to Stay

Ermitage Sainte Helene (tel 479) on Tubuai has three houses, each with two bedrooms, a kitchen and a bathroom. The Ermitage is owned by the colourful Noel Illari, a minor player in French Polynesian history who chose seclusion after disillusionment with the colonial government many years ago. The rates are 2000 CFP per person per day. The address is PO Box 79, Tubuai (Mahu Village).

In Mataura Village on Tubuai, *Chez Caroline* (tel 346) has two homes with three double rooms, private bathrooms and a common kitchen. The cost is 2500 CFP per person per day.

Chez Taro Tanepau (tel 382 in Tubuai, 43-87-32 in Tahiti) is also in Mataura Village on Tubuai. Accommodation is two homes, two double rooms, a common bathroom and a kitchen. The rates are 2500 CFP per person per day.

Chez Turina Victor (tel 327) is in Taahuaia Village. It is a chalet-style home with kitchen and bathroom. The cost is 2000 CFP per person per day and activities include bicycling and boating.

RURUTU

Rurutu is 572 km south of Papeete. It has a dry and temperate climate, especially in the months of June, July and August. The population of this seldom visited island is 1500. The outstanding physical surroundings feature white sand beaches which nearly lay at the foot of mountains thick with vegetation.

Rurutu was discovered in 1769 by Captain Cook and the navigator Eric de Bishop spent the last years of his life here. Rurutu is renowned for its fine woven hats and mats.

Archaeological finds on Rurutu suggest that the island was settled from the Society Islands group about 1100 AD. Though each island developed its own cultural distinctions, there was trade and contact between the Australs and the Society Islands, the Tuamotus and the Cooks. Today, much of the fine plaitwork available in Tahiti is done by natives of Rurutu living in Tahiti.

Places to Stay

In Moerai Village there is *Chez Patrice* (tel 42-88-50 in Tahiti, 443 in Rurutu). There is a house with two rooms, a common bathroom and a kitchenette (for couples or families only). One room is available in another house, single or double. The rate is 2000 CFP per person per day, including meals.

Chez Atai Aapae (tel 455), also in Moerai Village, has four rooms, each with a double bed, a common bathroom and a kitchen. The cost is 1000 CFP per person per day.

Chez Metu Teinaore (tel 434) has four rooms, shared bathroom and kitchen. It costs 2000 CFP per person per day.

Chez Maurice, (tel 43-60-19 in Tahiti, 448, 426 Rurutu), is a house with one large room capable of boarding 13 people, shared bathroom and fully equipped kitchen. The cost ranges from 1600 CFP to 2500 CFP per person per day depending on the length of stay.

Rurutu Village (tel 42-93-85 in Tahiti, 392 in Rurutu) is undoubtedly one of the most isolated hotels in the South Pacific. It has 16 bungalows, a restaurant, bar, pool, tennis court, reef excursions and library (which comes in handy in this backwater setting). The rate is 8000 CFP for a single. The address is PO Box 605, Papeete, Tahiti.

Chez Catherine (tel 377) in Moerai Village has 10 rooms – five with double beds and five with two singles – all have private bathrooms. There is a restaurant on the premises. The rates are 10,000 CFP per person per day including meals.

RAPA

Perhaps the most isolated of all French Polynesia, Rapa lies 1100 km south-south-east of Tahiti. The island's terrain is rugged and barren, with grey cliffs of up to 300 metres towering over the sparsely covered landscape which is home to about 400 people and plenty of goats. The island has many deep caves and cleft valleys some of which open to the sea. Once the island had a volcano, which has since collapsed at its centre, and now makes up a large bay. During the days of the mail boats between Australia, New Zealand and Panama, this bay served as a coaling station.

Discovered (but not claimed for Britain) by the great explorer Vancouver in 1791, Rapa is sometimes called Rapa Iti to distinguish it from Rapa Nui, otherwise known as Easter Island. France established it as a protectorate in 1867 and annexed the island in 1881. Long negotiations with Britain were inconclusive in resolving the ownership though New Zealand hoped that France would cede Rapa to Britain so that it could become an entrepôt between New Zealand and Panama.

The island has fortifications constructed by its former Polynesian residents – dozens of terraces on steep cliffs supported by walls built with basalt blocks piled on top of one another. Carbon-14 dating indicates that there were approximately 2000 to 3000 inhabitants in the 18th century. Subsequent epidemics from the first ships quickly decimated the local population.

Boats visit Rapa infrequently and accommodation depends on whoever happens to open their home up. Thanks to government largesse there is electricity. The main staple on the island is that South Pacific favourite – taro. The climate is chilly by Polynesian standards and the soil is comparatively poor.

GETTING THERE & AWAY

An airline service operates on Mondays and Fridays to Tubuai and Rurutu from Papeete, Raiatea and Moorea. The flight time is just under two hours. Rapa does not have an air service. The fare is 17,900 CFP one-way to Tubuai and 16,000 CFP one-way to Rurutu.

The Australs are served by the *Tuhaa Pae II*, (tel 42-93-67), PO Box 2082, Motu Uta, Papeete. The itinerary is Tubai / Rurutu / Raivavae /Rimatara / on occasion Rapa / Maria – twice monthly.

The Gambier Islands

The Gambier Islands group, comprising four high islands and a few atolls, was once an independent entity within French Polynesia. It had its own flag, and inhabitants were not required to serve in the military. This independent status no longer exists and none of the Gambier Islands are inhabited except Mangareva, which has a population of about 500. The population of the Gambiers once numbered about 5000 but most of the inhabitants have migrated to Tahiti.

In recent years, an exciting plan for the Gambiers was fomented by a young man of American and royal Tahitian blood. He inherited an uninhabited island near Mangareva and planned to settle there with his wife and child. He wanted to live a self-contained existence, free to do as he pleased, unencumbered by society's conventions. He had gone so far as to pack most of the family's belongings and to contact a writer from *National Geographic* magazine to do a story. Unfortunately, his plans fell apart when he was arrested for growing several hundred marijuana plants amidst a taro patch on a Tahitian hillside. Several years later, his dream came true and he now lives happily with his family on his secluded island home.

MANGAREVA

Mangareva is 1650 km south-east of Tahiti and is surrounded by small mountainous islands. On one of these is the airport of Totegie. The coming of the missionaries to the Gambier Islands was anticipated in a vision by the prophetess Taopere. In 1883, the Picpus fathers of France settled on the chief island, Mangareva, and by 1836 the entire archipelago had been converted to Catholicism. Under the tyrannical leadership of Father Laval, a Belgian priest, the converts built on Mangareva the largest cathedral in French Polynesia (St Michel of Rikitea), using fired limestone and mother-of-pearl for its interior. The strange saga of this fanatical missionary inspired one of

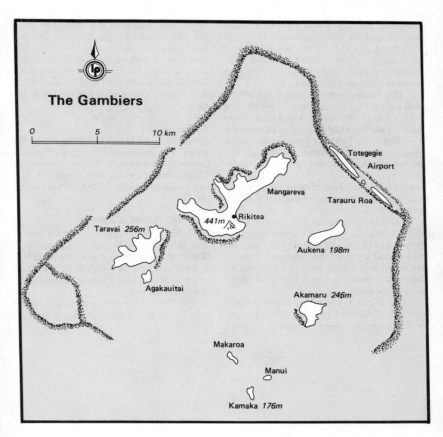

Michener's stories in *Return to Paradise*. Although the cathedral is in need of repair, it is still in use and open to visitors. Across the path from the church is the 140-year-old rectory, occupied by the parish priest. A mile down the road is a tumble-down abbey surrounded by a well-tended vegetable garden. The garden is farmed by an industrious Mangarevan under the supervision of the priest, who sells the produce to islanders and to residents of the nearby nuclear testing site on Muroroa.

Of interest there are also the ruins of a convent, a triumphal arch, watchtowers, prisons, a court and dominating the village, the tomb of Gregorio Maputea, the last king of Mangareva, who died in 1868, after having requested status as a French Protectorate for Mangareva.

Mangareva's main industry is jewellery-making, which involves cutting and grinding items out of mother-of-pearl. Aesthetically, the island is very pleasing with its rolling brown hills reminiscent of California's coastal mountains. It is the home of French Polynesia's former vice president and venerated politico Francis Sanford, and also the home of the former president of French Polynesia, Gaston Flosse. Because of its proximity to the nuclear testing site, permission to travel to Mangareva must be secured from the government.

The Mangarevans preserve a tradition that a chief 'Tupa' once came to Mangareva with a fleet of rafts from a 'vast and populous land'. Thor Heyerdahl used this as evidence that Peruvians (perhaps Incas or an earlier people) came to Polynesia and brought the sweet potato, a native plant of South America, with them. The Mangarevan legend holds that Tupa cleared the coral reef that surround the island through a passage still called Teava-o-Tupa.

There is also a legend that Tupa Inca, the second emperor of the Inca world (ruling between 1471 and 1493) heard that seaborne traders had arrived from westward islands. He sailed with a large fleet of balsa rafts to the Pacific returning a year later with black people and gold.

The lagoon until the last century routinely sheltered large rafts which carried on trade and commerce to faraway islands.

Heyerdahl postulated that Mangareva was the destination of the Spanish explorer Sarmiento who sailed with Mendana 1567. However, a premature course correction caused them to discover the Solomons instead! Sarmiento had heard the story of the Inca journey and perhaps intended to do the same.

Places to Stay
Chez Francois Labbeyi in Rikitea is near the wharf. For reservations write to Francois Labbeyi, Mangareva, French Polynesia. There is one house and two bungalows. The rate is approximately 2000 CFP per person per day.

GETTING THERE & AWAY
Air Tahiti visits Mangareva once a month from Tahiti. The flight time is four hours and 40 minutes with a stop at Hao. Upon arrival in the Gambiers, sea-shuttle is provided between Totegie and Rikitea. The crossing time is 30 minutes.

The *Maire II* has a twice monthly service to the Tuamotu and Gambier Group. It takes 12 days.

Glossary

Aito Ironwood.

Archipelago A group or chain of islands.

Ari'i High chiefs, the nobility of pre-European Tahitian society.

Arioi Travelling minstrels and entertainers of pre-European time, making up a religious society.

Atoll A low-lying island built up from successive deposits of coral. The classic atoll is ring-shaped, enclosing a shallow lagoon.

Atua God.

Bark Cloth See 'tapa'.

Barrier Reef An offshore reef sheltering a coast or an island from the open sea but separated from the land by a lagoon or expanse of sea. See 'fringing reef'.

Breadfruit The staple food of the South Pacific, sought after by the *Bounty* expedition to transplant in the West Indies.

Coral Members of the animal group known as *coelenterates* which also include jellyfish and anemones. Corals live together in colonies and can produce a fibrous or calcified skeleton. As they die new colonies form upon the skeletons of the old and eventually a reef can be built up. Coral requires clear, warm water of an ideal depth in order to flourish.

Cyclone A powerful tropical storm which rotates around a central low pressure 'eye'. In the Caribbean a cyclone is known as a hurricane; in the Pacific it is known as a typhoon.

Embayed A coastline created by land subsidence when flooded valleys become bays.

Emergence Geological activity which raises a land mass above the ocean surface to become an island.

Fare Tupa'pau 'Ghost house', where dead bodies were laid in pre-European Tahitian funeral ceremonies.

Fringing Reef A reef found around the shore of an island or along a coast which does not contain a lagoon – see 'barrier reef'.

High Island Islands either volcanic in origin or the result of an upheaval from the ocean floor.

Kava Beverage derived from the root of the pepper plant *piper methysticum*.

Lagoon An area of water enclosed by a reef.

Lee Downwind side; to be in the lee of something is to be sheltered by it.

Leeward The side of an island sheltered from the prevailing winds – see 'windward'.

Le Truck Local form of public transport; hybrid bus or jitney.

Makatea 'Middle island', atoll islands raised up by some geological disturbance.

Mana Sacred essence, prestige, power.

Manahune The common people of pre-European Tahitian society.

Manava Soul of a god.

Marae Ancient Polynesian open temple.

Maru'ura Feathered girdle, highest symbol of real and spiritual power.

Melanesian People of the far west of the Pacific characterised by their dark skins. They include the people of Papua New Guinea, the Solomons, Vanuatu, New Caledonia and Fiji.

Micronesian People of the north-west Pacific, believed to be of Malay-Polynesian origin. They include the people of Guam, the Marianas, the Federated States of Micronesia, the Marshalls, the northern Palau Islands and the islands of the Gilbert-Phoenix-Northern Line Islands region.

Noa Non-sacred.

Ora Life.

'Oro God of war and son of Ta'aroa, red feathers are his special symbol.

Oromatua Ghosts.

Pahi Traditional fighting canoe with raised platform above the twin hull on which the warriors would stand.

Pareu Woman's sarong like a wrap-around skirt.

Pirogue Traditional outrigger canoe.

Pohe Death.

Polynesian People who colonised the central and southern Pacific islands – including Hawaii, Tahiti, the Cook Islands and New Zealand – through great sea voyages.

Ra'atira The 'middle class' of pre-European Tahitian society.

Reef Structure formed by the skeletons of coral colonies, grown over by successive generations which include the most recent, living group.

Ro'o Important pre-European Tahitian god.

Seamount A volcanic mountain that does actually rise above the surface of the sea.

Seaward Side of an island facing the open sea, in contrast to a side facing a sheltered lagoon.

Sennit Woven coconut fibre string.

Ta'aroa Important pre-European Tahitian god.

Tahu'a Craftsman priest.

Tamanu Ebony-like wood.

Tamure Modern, hip-shaking version of a traditional dance.

Tane Important pre-European Tahitian god; also a word for 'man'.

Tapa Bark-cloth, the everyday clothing in pre-European Tahiti. Made by beating the inner bark of mulberry or breadfruit trees.

Tapu Taboo; the English word is derived from this Tahitian word.

Taro Staple root vegetable.

Tatau Traditional tattoos, from which the English word is derived. Both males and females were tattooed, particularly on the buttocks. Joseph Banks was one of the members of Cook's party who came back with a tattoo.

Ti'i or Tiki Human-like wood icon, generally representing family ancestors. Particularly found on traditional canoes.

Tiputa Bark-cloth poncho.

To'o Symbols of Tahitian gods.

Tu Important pre-European Tahitian god.

Tupa'pau Ghost or spirit; may be benevolent or malevolent.

Vahine Woman.

Windward The side of an island facing the prevailing winds – see 'leeward'.

Index

MAPS

Temperature

To convert °C to °F multipy by 1.8 and add 32

To convert °F to °C subtract 32 and multipy by · 55

Length, Distance & Area

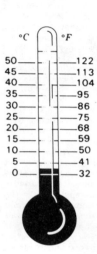

	multipy by
inches to centimetres	2.54
centimetres to inches	0.39
feet to metres	0.30
metres to feet	3.28
yards to metres	0.91
metres to yards	1.09
miles to kilometres	1.61
kilometres to miles	0.62
acres to hectares	0.40
hectares to acres	2.47

Weight

	multipy by
ounces to grams	28.35
grams to ounces	0.035
pounds to kilograms	0.45
kilograms to pounds	2.21
British tons to kilograms	1016
US tons to kilograms	907

A British ton is 2240 lbs, a US ton is 2000 lbs

Volume

	multipy by
Imperial gallons to litres	4.55
litres to imperial gallons	0.22
US gallons to litres	3.79
litres to US gallons	0.26

5 imperial gallons equals 6 US gallons
a litre is slightly more than a US quart, slightly less
than a British one

Lonely Planet

Lonely Planet published its first book in 1973. Tony and Maureen Wheeler had made a lengthy overland trip from England to Australia and, in response to numerous 'how do you do it?' questions, Tony wrote and they published *Across Asia on the Cheap*. It became an instant local best-seller and inspired thoughts of a second travel guide. A year and a half in South-East Asia resulted in their second book, *South-East Asia on a Shoestring*, which they put together in a backstreet Chinese hotel in Singapore in 1975. The 'yellow book', as it quickly became known, soon became *the* guide to the region and has gone through five editions, always with its familiar yellow cover.

Soon other writers started to come to them with ideas for similar books – books that went off the beaten track and took an adventurous approach to travel, books that 'assumed you knew how to get your luggage off the carousel,' as one reviewer described them. Lonely Planet grew from a kitchen table operation to a spare room and then to its own office. It also started to develop an international reputation as the Lonely Planet logo began to appear in more and more countries. In 1982 *India – a travel survival kit* won the Thomas Cook award for the best guidebook of the year.

These days there are over 60 Lonely Planet titles. Nearly 30 people work at our office in Melbourne, Australia and another half dozen at our US office in Oakland, California.

At first Lonely Planet specialised exclusively in the Asia region but these days we are also developing major ranges of guidebooks to the Pacific region, to South America and to Africa. The list of walking guides is growing and Lonely Planet is producing a unique series of phrasebooks to 'unusual' languages. The emphasis continues to be on travel for travellers and Tony and Maureen still manage to fit in a number of trips each year and play a very active part in the writing and updating of Lonely Planet's guides.

Keeping guidebooks up to date is a constant battle which requires an ear to the ground and lots of walking, but technology also plays its part. All Lonely Planet guidebooks are now stored and updated on computer, and some authors even take lap-top computers into the field. Lonely Planet is also using computers to draw maps and eventually many of the maps will be stored on disk.

. The people at Lonely Planet strongly feel that travellers can make a positive contribution to the countries they visit both by better appreciation of cultures and by the money they spend. In addition the company tries to make a direct contribution to the countries and regions it covers. Since 1986 a percentage of the income from each book has gone to aid groups and associations. This has included donations to famine relief in Africa, to aid projects in India, to agricultural projects in Nicaragua and other Central American countries and to Greenpeace's efforts to halt French nuclear testing in the Pacific. In 1988 over $40,000 was donated by Lonely Planet to these projects.

Lonely Planet Distributors

Australia & Papua New Guinea Lonely Planet Publications, PO Box 88, South Yarra, Victoria 3141.
Canada Raincoast Books, 112 East 3rd Avenue, Vancouver, British Columbia V5T 1C8.
Denmark, Finland & Norway Scanvik Books aps, Store Kongensgade 59 A, DK-1264 Copenhagen K.
Hong Kong The Book Society, GPO Box 7804.
India & Nepal UBS Distributors, 5 Ansari Rd, New Delhi – 110002
Israel Geographical Tours Ltd, 8 Tverya St, Tel Aviv 63144.
Japan Intercontinental Marketing Corp, IPO Box 5056, Tokyo 100-31.
Netherlands Nilsson & Lamm bv, Postbus 195, Pampuslaan 212, 1380 AD Weesp.
Singapore & Malaysia MPH Distributors, 601 Sims Drive, #03-21, Singapore 1438.
Spain Altair, Balmes 69, 08007 Barcelona.
Sweden Esselte Kartcentrum AB, Vasagatan 16, S-111 20 Stockholm.
Thailand Chalermnit, 108 Sukhumvit 53, Bangkok 10110.
UK Roger Lascelles, 47 York Rd, Brentford, Middlesex, TW8 0QP
USA Lonely Planet Publications, PO Box 2001A, Berkeley, CA 94702.
West Germany Buchvertrieb Gerda Schettler, Postfach 64, D3415 Hattorf a H.
All Other Countries refer to Australia address.

Lonely Planet guides to the Region

Micronesia – a travel survival kit
Amongst these 2100 islands are beaches, lagoons and reefs that will dazzle the most jaded traveller. This guide is packed with all you need to know about island hopping across the north Pacific.

Rarotonga & the Cook Is – a travel survival kit
Rarotonga has history, beauty and magic to rival Hawaii, Tahiti or Bora Bora. Unlike those better known islands, however, the world has virtually passed it by. The Cook Islands range from mountainous islands to remote and untouched coral atolls.

Fiji – a travel survival kit
This is a comprehensive guide to the Fijian archipelago. On a number of these beautiful islands accommodation ranges from camping grounds to international hotels – whichever you prefer this book will help you to enjoy the South Seas.

Papua New Guinea – a travel survival kit
Papua New Guinea is truly 'the last unknown' – the last inhabited place on earth to be explored by Europeans. This guide has the latest information for travellers who want to find just how rewarding a trip to this remote and amazing country can be.

Solomon Islands – a travel survival kit
The Solomon Islands are the Pacific's best kept secret. If you want to discover remote tropical islands, jungle-covered volcanoes and traditional Melanesian villages, this book will show you how.

New Zealand – a travel survival kit
Visitors to New Zealand find a land of fairytale beauty and scenic contrasts – a natural wonderland. This book has information about the places you won't want to miss, including ski-resorts and famous walks.

Australia – a travel survival kit
Australia is Lonely Planet's home territory so this guide gives you the complete low-down on Down Under, from the red centre to the coast, from cosmopolitan cities to country towns.

Ecuador & the Galapagos Islands – a travel survival kit
Ecuador is the smallest of the Andean countries, and in many ways it is the easiest and most pleasant to travel in. The Galapagos Islands and their amazing inhabitants continue to cast a spell over every visitor.

Chile & Easter Island – a travel survival kit
Chile has one of the most varied geographies in the world, including deserts, tranquil lakes, snow-covered volcanoes and windswept fjords. Easter Island is covered, in detail.

Lonely Planet Guidebooks

Lonely Planet guidebooks cover virtually every accessible part of Asia as well as Australia, the Pacific, Central and South America, Africa, the Middle East and parts of North America. There are four main series: 'travel survival kits', covering a single country for a range of budgets; 'shoestring' guides with compact information for low-budget travel in a major region; trekking guides; and 'phrasebooks'.

Mail Order

Lonely Planet guidebooks are distributed worldwide and are sold by good bookshops everywhere. They are also available by mail order from Lonely Planet, so if you have difficulty finding a title please write to us. US and Canadian residents should write to Embarcadero West, 112 Linden St, Oakland CA 94607, USA and residents of other countries to PO Box 88, South Yarra, Victoria 3141, Australia.

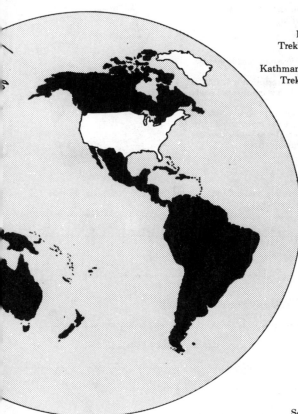

Indian Subcontinent
India
Hindi/Urdu phrasebook
Kashmir, Ladakh & Zanskar
Trekking in the Indian Himalaya
Pakistan
Kathmandu & the Kingdom of Nepal
Trekking in the Nepal Himalaya
Nepal phrasebook
Sri Lanka
Sri Lanka phrasebook
Bangladesh

Africa
Africa on a shoestring
East Africa
Swahili phrasebook
West Africa

Middle East
Egypt & the Sudan
Jordan & Syria
Yemen

North America
Canada
Alaska

Mexico
Mexico
Baja California

South America
South America on a shoestring
Ecuador & the Galapagos Islands
Chile & Easter Island
Peru

Lonely Planet Update

We collect an enormous amount of information here at Lonely Planet. Apart from our research there's a steady stream of travellers' letters full of the latest news. For over 5 years much of this information went into a quarterly newsletter (and helped to update the guidebooks). The new paperback *Update* includes this up-to-date news and aims to supplement the information available in our guidebooks. There will be four editions a year (Feb, May, Aug and Nov) available either by subscription or through bookshops. Subscribe now and you'll save nearly 25% off the retail price.

Each edition has extracts from the most interesting letters we have received, covering such diverse topics as:
- how to take a boat trip on the Yalu River
- living in a typical Thai village
- getting a Nepalese trekking permit

Subscription Details

All subscriptions cover four editions and include postage. Prices quoted are subject to change.

USA & Canada – One year's subscription is US$12; a single copy is US$3.95. Please send your order to Lonely Planet's California office.

Other Countries – One year's subscription is Australian $15; a single copy is A$4.95. Please pay in Australian $, or the US$ or £ Sterling equivalent. Please send your order form to Lonely Planet's Australian office.

Order Form

Please send me

☐ One year's subscription – starting next edition.   ☐ One copy of the next edition.

Name (please print) ....

Address (please print) ....

....

....

Tick One

☐ Payment enclosed (payable to Lonely Planet Publications)

Charge my   ☐ Visa   ☐ Bankcard   ☐ MasterCard   for the amount of $ ....

Card No .... Expiry Date ....

Cardholder's Name (print) ....

Signature .... Date..

US & Canadian residents
Lonely Planet, Embarcadero West, 112 Linden St,
Oakland, CA 94607, USA
Other countries
Lonely Planet, PO Box 88, South Yarra, Victoria 3141, Australia